Pirates Through the Ages

Almanac

Pirates Through the Ages

Almanac

Sonia G. Benson
Jennifer Stock, Project Editor

GALE
CENGAGE Learning™

Detroit • New York • San Francisco • New Haven, Conn • Waterville, Maine • London

GALE
CENGAGE Learning™

Pirates Through the Ages: Almanac
Sonia G. Benson

Project Editor: Jennifer Stock

Rights Acquisition and Management:
Robyn Young

Composition: Evi Abou-El-Seoud

Manufacturing: Wendy Blurton

Imaging: John Watkins

Product Design: Kristine Julien

For product information and technology assistance, contact us at
Gale Customer Support, 1-800-877-4253.
For permission to use material from this text or product,
submit all requests online at **www.cengage.com/permissions.**
Further permissions questions can be emailed to
permissionrequest@cengage.com

Cover photographs reproduced by permission of Howard Pyle/The Bridgeman Art Library/Getty Images (painting of pirates forcing a captive to walk the plank) and Mass Communications Specialist 1st Class Cassandra Thompson/U.S. Navy via Getty Images (U.S. Navy investigates a suspected Somali pirate skiff).

Library of Congress Cataloging-in-Publication Data

Benson, Sonia.
  Pirates through the ages reference library / Sonia G. Benson, Elizabeth Shostak, Laurie Edwards.
     3 v. cm.
  Includes bibliographical references and index.
     ISBN 978-1-4144-8662-8 (set) -- ISBN 978-1-4144-8663-5 (almanac) -- ISBN 978-1-4144-8664-2 (biographies) -- ISBN 978-1-4144-8665-9 (primary sources)
     1. Pirates--History--Handbooks, manuals, etc. I. Shostak, Elizabeth, 1951- II. Edwards, Laurie, 1954- III. Title.

G535.B38 2011
910.4'5--dc22   2010051978

Gale
27500 Drake Rd.
Farmington Hills, MI, 48331-3535

ISBN-13: 978-1-4144-8662-8 (set)
ISBN-13: 978-1-4144-8663-5 (Almanac)
ISBN-13: 978-1-4144-8664-2 (Biographies)
ISBN-13: 978-1-4144-8665-9 (Primary Sources)
ISBN-13: 978-1-4144-8666-6 (Cumulative Index)

ISBN-10: 1-4144-8662-6 (set)
ISBN-10: 1-4144-8663-4 (Almanac)
ISBN-10: 1-4144-8664-2 (Biographies)
ISBN-10: 1-4144-8665-0 (Primary Sources)
ISBN-10: 1-4144-8666-9 (Cumulative Index)

This title is also available as an e-book.
ISBN-13: 978-1-4144-8667-3 ISBN-10: 1-4144-8667-7
Contact your Gale, a part of Cengage Learning sales representative for ordering information.

Printed in Singapore
1 2 3 4 5 6 7 15 14 13 12 11

Table of Contents

On April 8, 2009, in waters about 350 miles (563 kilometers) off the coast of Somalia, four pirates boarded the Maersk Alabama in a botched attempt to seize the cargo ship. After a stand-off with the ship's crew, the Somali pirates took the captain, Richard Phillips (1963–), hostage and sped off in a life boat. They were soon surrounded by military warships and helicopters from several nations, and for five days the pirates held the captain at gunpoint on the small boat. Footage of the hostage situation was broadcast to millions of television viewers throughout the world. In the end, U.S. Navy snipers killed the pirates and rescued Phillips. But piracy experts noted that the rescue of Phillips was the exception; at the time of his rescue, pirates held hundreds of other hostages in Somalia. The Maersk Alabama incident, only one among hundreds of pirate attacks in the waters off Somalia over the period of a few years, brought international attention to the rise in piracy in the twenty-first century, after many twentieth-century history books had pronounced piracy a thing of the past.

For most of us, it is difficult to connect the Somali pirates—young men and boys in t-shirts and jeans using modern technology and carrying automatic weapons—with the familiar image of pirates we have known since childhood: the swarthy seafarers with peg-legs or eye patches wearing tri-cornered hats and bearing parrots on their shoulders, who are known for phrases like "avast, me hearties," "shiver me timbers," and "aarr." The familiar image, a product of both fact and fantasy, is based on the historical era known as the golden age of piracy, a brief period during the late eighteenth and early nineteenth century when famous pirates like Blackbeard (Edward Teach; c. 1680–1718), William Kidd (c. 1645–1701), and Bartholomew Roberts (1682–1722) ruled large areas of the

Caribbean Sea. But Somali piracy and golden age piracy both take their place in a long, global history of similar pirate eras, periods when seas in certain regions became infested with pirates who managed to resist law enforcement agents for extended periods of time.

Who were these pirates? Pirates through the ages have been as diverse as the rest of the human population. Pirate leaders have ranged from poor English sailors to highly successful Chinese businessmen and ferocious Scandinavian warriors. Like most criminal paths, piracy has drawn courageous adventurers, sadistic psychopaths, and many who fall somewhere in between. Most were drawn to piracy as a rare means to lift themselves out of poverty, but not all pirates chose their trade. Many sailors were forced into it by pirates who raided their ships. Others, on the other hand, traveled long distances and some even converted to new religions for the opportunity to get rich by raiding ships at sea. Pirates have come from all nationalities and races. The Chinese pirates included women among their ranks, and there were also several notorious European women pirates, but overall, the overwhelming majority of pirates have been men.

On land and at sea, pirates have always sought places where they could carry out their plundering (robbing of goods by force) while living outside the law. They spent much of their lives on the high seas, the open waters of the ocean that are outside the limits of any country's territorial authority. At sea, most pirates have established their own codes of conduct and social structures. Pirates also need land to carry out large-scale operations. In pirate havens, usually remote sea ports or islands without any strong governmental presence, pirates have been able to establish rough societies of their own where they live and carry out their business under their own rules. In pirate havens, as at sea, pirates defied law enforcement authorities—but only for a time. After every major pirate era, law and order has been restored, pirate havens have been destroyed, and many notorious pirates have faced prison or the hangman s noose.

Pirates have fascinated people from ancient times to the present day. Studying them provides insight into history and human nature in all its complexity. Historians study pirates in a surprisingly wide variety of contexts, such as the wars they fought in, their contribution to the settlement of new lands, the social institutions they have established at sea, and the social classes from which they arose. Lawmakers and international diplomats ponder the unique challenges of trying to stop piracy by establishing law and order on the high seas. Fiction writers, poets, playwrights, and filmmakers have all been drawn to the romantic aspects of piracy, such as the courage and ingenuity of the raiders, their thrilling adventures, the freedom of the seas, and the brotherhood of pirates.

The abundance of legends and writings about pirates has led to a strangely comfortable image of piracy in modern times. Children dress as pirates for Halloween, watch pirate cartoons on TV, and play pirate video games. In studying real piracy, though, it quickly becomes apparent that pirates are dangerous, and often violent, criminals. Pirates have murdered, raped, tortured, and enslaved their victims. They have disrupted trade and made sea travel a terrifying experience. Though they may fascinate us with their adventures at sea, they are predators who do a great deal of harm in the world.

Pirates v. privateers

Many of history's major pirate eras began with governmental policies that encouraged the licensing of privateers, private ships or ship owners commissioned by their government to raid enemy ships during war-time. The actual work that pirates and privateers do is the same. They attack ships, usually merchant vessels, or coastal communities, and they use violence or the threat of violence to rob their victims of valuables, sometimes taking the ship itself as a prize. The main difference between pirates and privateers is that pirates work solely for their own profit, while privateers, at least in theory, work for their country. While piracy is illegal, privateering is considered legal, at least by the nation that licenses the privateers.

The history of pirates cannot be separated from the history of privateers. Since ancient times, warring nations have frequently enlisted privateers to destroy their enemies' trade and harass military shipping. Ancient Greece, the Ottoman Empire, late eighteenth-century Vietnam, and the European nations of Spain, England, the Netherlands, and France, to name a few, all relied heavily on privateers in war-time. Privateers often greatly aided their countries. Some privateers, such as Englishman Francis Drake (1540–1596), were considered heroes and went on to prestigious careers in their countries. Other privateers, however, took a very different path. When wars ended, they found themselves armed, equipped with sea vessels, and highly skilled at raiding enemy ships, but suddenly unemployed. Many simply continued to raid ships as pirates. The nations that had originally enlisted the privateers' services soon found they had no control over their activities, and often had to muster new naval forces to pursue them.

The many names for sea raiders—corsairs, buccaneers, filibusters, freebooters, picaroons, sea rovers, sea dogs—all signify people who raid at or from the sea, but whether they mean "pirate," "privateer," or a little of both may differ in context.

Coverage and features

Pirates Through the Ages: Almanac presents a comprehensive history of the major pirate eras throughout history and around the globe. The volume's twelve chapters cover ancient and medieval pirates, the Barbary corsairs, the privateers of Spanish Main and the United States, the buccaneers of the Caribbean, the golden age of piracy, piracy in Asia, modern piracy, and pirates in popular culture. Each chapter features informative sidebar boxes highlighting glossary terms and issues discussed in the text. Also included are nearly sixty photographs and illustrations, a timeline, a glossary, a list of research and activity ideas, sources for further reading, and an index providing easy access to subjects discussed throughout the volume.

U·X·L Pirates Through the Ages
Reference Library

Pirates Through the Ages: Biographies profiles twenty-six pirates and privateers. Included are some of the most famous pirates of the golden age, such as Blackbeard, William Kidd, and Bartholomew Roberts; fierce corsairs of the Barbary Coast, including Barbarossa and Dragut Reis; and English and American privateers such as Francis Drake, John Paul Jones, and Jean Lafitte. Also featured are buccaneers such as Henry Morgan and William Dampier; female pirates Cheng I Sao, Anne Bonny and Mary Read, and Grace O'Malley; and pirate hunter Woodes Rogers. The volume includes more than fifty photographs and illustrations, a timeline, sources for further reading, and an index.

Pirates Through the Ages: Primary Sources presents eighteen full or excerpted written works, poems, interviews, or other documents that were influential throughout the history of piracy. Included are the tale of the kidnapping of Julius Caesar by pirates, a letter from a captive of the Barbary corsairs, a pirate trial transcript, and an example of ship's articles. Also featured are literary works such as *Treasure Island* and *The Corsair*, and interviews with Somali and Strait of Malacca pirates. More than fifty photographs and illustrations, a timeline, sources for further reading, and an index supplement the volume

A cumulative index of all three volumes in the U•X•L Pirates Through the Ages Reference Library is also available.

Comments and suggestions

We welcome your comments on *Pirates Through the Ages: Almanac* and suggestions for other topics to consider. Please write: Editors, *Pirates Through the Ages: Almanac*, Gale Cengage Learning, 27500 Drake Road, Farmington Hills, Michigan 48331-3535; call toll free: 1-800-877-4253; fax to 248-699-8097; or send e-mail via http://www.gale.cengage.com.

Timeline of Events

2000 BCE: The Phoenicians begin maritime trading in regions of the Mediterranean; as trade expands, piracy emerges.

1220–1186 BCE: The Sea People, a band of sea raiders, dominate the Mediterranean Sea, attacking merchant ships and coastal towns.

c. 750 BCE: Greek poet Homer writes the *Odyssey;* the epic poem is the first known written description of piracy.

421–339 BCE: Greek city-states engage pirates to attack their enemies in the Peloponnesian Wars in a system similar to what will later become known as privateering.

74 or 75 BCE: Roman statesman Julius Caesar is captured by Cilician pirates and held for ransom.

June 8, 793: Vikings attack the religious center at Lindisfarne, England.

1100s: A group of Germanic towns form the Hanseatic League to secure trade routes in the Baltic Sea and fight piracy.

1200s: The Wokou, a group of pirates that originated in Japan, attack the coasts of Korea and China.

1243: England's Cinque Ports, a league of sea towns, begins to license private merchant ships to raid enemy ships and ports. This is considered the origin of the privateer system that Europe would use for centuries to come.

1392: A powerful band of pirates known as the Victual Brothers attacks Norway's major city, Bergen, and sets up headquarters in Visby, Sweden.

1492: Spain captures Granada from the Moors and begins to expel the Moors from Spain. Tens of thousands of Spanish Muslims migrate to the Barbary Coast in northern Africa.

1492: Explorer Christopher Columbus, serving Spain, arrives on a Caribbean island, beginning an era of Spanish exploration and colonization in the Americas.

1494: The Catholic pope issues the Treaty of Tordesillas. Under the treaty, Portugal receives authority to control the non-Christian lands in the designated eastern half of the world, and Spain is awarded the lands in the west.

1516: Barbary corsair Aruj leads a large force of corsairs in an attack on the city-state of Algiers. The corsairs gain control of the city and the surrounding region.

1523: French privateer Jean Fleury captures two Spanish ships returning to Spain from Mexico. They are loaded with Aztec treasure that conquistador Hernán Cortéz was sending to the Spanish king.

1530: The Spanish king leases the island of Malta to the Knights of Malta under the condition that they fight "enemies of the Holy Faith." The Knights begin raiding Muslim ships and enslaving Muslim captives.

1550s: Wealthy Chinese businessman Wang Zhi commands a large force of Wokou pirate fleets, comprised of hundreds of junks and, by some estimates, about twenty thousand pirates.

1562: To protect its ships from piracy, Spain requires all ships carrying goods from the Spanish Main to Spain to join one of the two treasure fleets formed annually.

1567: In the Battle of San Juan de Ulúa, John Hawkins and his fleet of illegal traders are badly defeated by Spanish naval forces in Mexico.

1577–60: English privateer Francis Drake circumnavigates (sails around) the globe, raiding Spanish ships in the Pacific and bringing home an enormous booty.

1628: Dutch privateer Pieter Pieterszoon Heyn, commanding an enormous fleet, captures a Spanish treasure fleet.

1600–40: A group of French hunters, called buccaneers, establish a rough lifestyle in the Caribbean, living part-time on the island of Tortuga and hunting feral animals on the northwest coast of Hispaniola.

1606–8: English pirate John Ward and Dutch pirate Simon de Danser join the Barbary corsairs. They are among the first in a long line of "renegades," or Europeans who converted from Christianity to Islam and raided Christian ships and ports with the Barbary corsairs.

Late 1620s: Hoping to expel the buccaneers, Spanish colonial officials exterminate feral animals in the northwestern region of Hispaniola. The buccaneers, no longer able to hunt, become full-time sea raiders.

1655: English ruler Oliver Cromwell sends naval forces to attack Santo Domingo, Hispaniola. The English forces fail to take over Santo Domingo, but take control of Jamaica. Under the English, Port Royal, Jamaica, becomes a pirate haven.

1661: Chinese pirate commander Kho Hsing Yeh attacks the Dutch colony at Formosa (present-day Taiwan) with a fleet of nine hundred junks and twenty-five thousand troops, pushing the Dutch military off the island. Under Kho Hsing Yeh and his sons, Formosa will remain a pirate kingdom for twenty years.

1668: Privateer Henry Morgan, chief of the buccaneers in Port Royal, leads a raid on the well-defended port city of Portobelo, Panama, where treasure from Peru is held for shipping to Spain on the annual treasure fleets.

1678: Alexander O. Exquemelin's *The Buccaneers of America* is first published in Dutch.

1690: The golden age of piracy begins.

1690s: The African island of Madagascar in the Indian Ocean becomes a pirate base in the Pirate Round, a course in which pirates raid African slave traders and merchant ships transporting valuable Asian goods from the shores of India and the Middle East back to Europe.

June 7, 1692: A major earthquake strikes Port Royal, Jamaica, killing thousands, toppling part of the city into the sea, and forcing pirates to look for another base of operations.

August 1695: Pirate captain Henry Every raids the well-armed *Ganj-i-sawii*, the Indian emperor's richly laden treasure ship, making every man in his crew wealthy. The raid inspires many heroic legends in England.

1701: After a lengthy trial in England, William Kidd is hung for piracy, though he claims to have been fulfilling his obligations as a privateer. His body is hung over the Thames River as a warning to all pirates.

1710: In India, Maratha navy commander Kanhoji Angria captures the British East India Company's island headquarters off Bombay and sets up a well-fortified pirate base there.

1714: Pirates of the Caribbean, led by Benjamin Hornigold, Blackbeard, and Charles Vane, establish a base in Nassau, a port in the Bahamas; other pirates soon join them there.

February 1717: Samuel Bellamy and his crew seize an English slave ship, the *Whydah*, near Cuba, and refit it for piracy.

May 1718: With a fleet of heavily armed pirate vessels, Blackbeard blockades the harbor of Charleston, North Carolina.

September 5, 1718: By this date, Bahamas governor Woodes Rogers has granted pardons to more than six hundred pirates on the condition that they stop raiding.

November 1718: English troops commanded by Lieutenant Robert Maynard battle with Blackbeard's fleet; Blackbeard is killed in hand-to-hand combat.

1721: England passes the Piracy Act, which punishes people who trade with or aid pirates.

March 1722: In the largest pirate trial of the golden age, 268 pirates who had sailed under the command of Bartholomew Roberts are tried at Cape Coast Castle, a slave-trading center in West Africa.

1724: *A General History of the Robberies and Murders of the Most Notorious Pirates* is published by Captain Charles Johnson.

1730: The golden age of piracy ends.

April 19, 1775: The Battles of Concord and Lexington begin the American Revolution.

March 1776: The Continental Congress passes legislation allowing American privateers to raid British warships and merchant ships.

September 23, 1779: Continental Navy commander John Paul Jones defeats a Royal Navy warship and utters his famous line, "I have not yet begun to fight."

1788: With the aid of Chinese pirates, the Vietnamese Tay Son rebels defeat Vietnam's military and take control of the country.

1804: The United States sends its recently established naval forces to Tripoli in an attempt to force the Barbary corsairs to stop demanding tribute payments from U.S. merchant ships in the Mediterranean.

1807: Chinese pirate chief Cheng I dies, having organized and led the largest pirate confederation ever known to history, comprised of an estimated 40,000 to 70,000 pirates. His wife Cheng I Sao takes command of the pirate empire.

1810: Cheng I Sao accepts a general pardon for the pirates in her confederation, ending the huge and powerful Chinese pirate empire.

1812: As the United States prepares for war with Britain in the War of 1812, it once again enlists the aid of American privateers.

1814: Lord Byron publishes *The Corsair*, a long poem in which the pirate captain Conrad is portrayed as a brooding, romantic hero. The poem is an instant success.

January 1815: In the Battle of New Orleans, the last battle of the War of 1812, privateer Jean Lafitte aids U.S. forces in defeating the British invasion of the city.

1830s: A combined force of British Royal Navy and English East India Company ships set up an antipiracy base in Singapore. After a long series of fierce battles with the pirates of the Strait of Malacca and surrounding areas over the next thirty years, the antipiracy forces destroy the pirates.

1856: The leading powers of Europe sign the Declaration of Paris, which prohibits privateering. The United States does not sign.

1861: In the first year of the American Civil War, Southern privateers raid scores of Union ships.

1883: Robert Louis Stevenson publishes his children's adventure story *Treasure Island*. His pirate character, Long John Silver, becomes the best-known pirate in popular culture.

1982: The United Nations Convention on the Law of the Sea, which authorizes official ships of all states to seize known pirate ships on the high seas, is signed by 158 nations.

1984: Underwater explorer Barry Clifford discovers the pirate ship *Whydah* off Cape Cod. Relics recovered from the sunken ship and can be viewed today at the Whydah Museum in Provincetown, Massachusetts.

1992: The International Maritime Bureau (IMB), a division of the International Chamber of Commerce (ICC), establishes the IMB Piracy Reporting Centre, based in Kuala Lumpur, Malaysia, to track pirate attacks around the world.

1998: Political unrest in Indonesia leads to a surge in pirate activity in the Strait of Malacca.

1998: Chinese pirates posing as customs officials hijack a Hong Kong cargo ship, the *Cheung Son*, killing the entire twenty-three-member crew. China captures and prosecutes the pirates, executing thirteen of them.

2000: Piracy peaks worldwide, with a reported 469 attacks during the year; 65 percent of the attacks occur in Southeast Asia.

2003: *Pirates of the Caribbean: The Curse of the Black Pearl,* the first in a series of Disney pirate movies featuring Captain Jack Sparrow, is a huge box-office success.

2004: Under the Regional Cooperation Agreement on Combating Piracy and Armed Robbery against Ships in Asia (ReCAAP), Malaysian, Indonesian, and Singapore naval forces begin to work together to combat piracy.

June 2, 2008: The UN Security Council passes Resolution 1816, which authorizes foreign warships to enter Somali waters to stop piracy by any means necessary.

April 8, 2009: The world watches the aftermath of the botched hijacking of the U.S. cargo ship *Maersk Alabama,* after four Somali pirates take the ship's captain, Richard Phillips, hostage.

2009: Two hundred seventy-one pirate attacks were attributed to Somali pirates—more than half of the worldwide total.

July 2010: A new court near Mombasa, Kenya, built with international donations through the United Nations, is established as a place to try pirates from the region for their crimes.

Words to Know

act of reprisal: A document granting permission to individuals to raid the vessels of an enemy in response to some harm that enemy had done.

admiralty court: A court that administers laws and regulations pertaining to the sea.

antihero: A leading character or notable figure who does not have the typical hero traits.

artillery: Large weapons, such as cannons, that discharge missiles.

asylum: Refuge or protection in a foreign country, granted to someone who might be in danger if returned to his or her own country.

barbarians: People who are not considered civilized.

barge: A large, flat-bottomed boat used to transport cargo, usually over inland waterways.

barnacle: A shell-like marine animal that attaches itself to the underwater portion of a ship's hull.

barque: A simple vessel with one mast and triangular sails.

bey: The word for a local ruler in Tripoli and Tunis.

bireme: A swift galley ship with two banks of oars, and sometimes a square sail.

blunderbuss: A short musket with a flared muzzle.

bond: A type of insurance in which one party gives money to another party as a guarantee that certain requirements will be followed. If these requirements are not followed, the party that issued the bond keeps the money permanently.

booty: Goods stolen from ships or coastal villages during pirate raids or attacks on enemies in time of war.

buccaneer: A seventeenth-century sea raider based in the Caribbean Sea.

C

caravel: A small, highly maneuverable sailing ship.

careening: A regular process of cleaning the bottom of a ship.

cat-o'-nine-tails: A whip with nine knotted cords.

cleric: A member of the clergy, or church order.

clinker-built: Construction for boats using overlapping wooden planks.

city-state: An independent, self-governing city and its surrounding territory.

coast guard: A government agency responsible for enforcing laws on the seas and navigable waters.

commerce raiding: Also *guerre de course;* a naval strategy in which a weaker naval power attacks its stronger opponent's commercial shipping.

convoy: A collection of merchant ships traveling together for protection, often escorted by warships.

copyright laws: Laws that grant the creator the exclusive right to distribute, copy, use, or sell his or her product.

corsair: A pirate of the Barbary Coast.

cutlass: A short, heavy, single-edged sword.

D

dey: The word for a local ruler in Algiers.

digital technology: A data technology system that converts sound or signals into numbers, in the form of a binary format of ones and zeros.

duel: A prearranged fight with deadly weapons to settle a quarrel under specific rules.

dynasty: A succession of rulers from the same family line.

E

Execution Dock: The place in London where pirates were hanged; their bodies were often displayed to discourage others from turning to piracy.

extortion: The use of authority to unlawfully take money.

F

failed state: A state without a functioning government above the local level.

flintlock pistol: A small and comparatively lightweight gun that loads through the front of the barrel.

flota: A Spanish treasure fleet that transported goods and riches from the New World to Spain every year.

frigate: A three-masted, medium-sized warship.

G

galiot: A small, fast galley using both sails and oars.

galleon: A large, square-rigged sailing ship with three or more masts that was used for commerce and war.

galley: A long, low ship used for war and trading that was mainly powered by oarsmen, but might also use a sail.

grapeshot: A cluster of small iron balls usually shot from a cannon.

grenado: An early form of hand grenade comprised of hollow balls made of iron, glass, or wood and filled with gunpowder.

guild: An association for people or towns with a similar trade or interest.

H

harem: The area of a Muslim household historically reserved for wives, concubines, and female relatives.

high seas: The open waters of the ocean that are outside the limits of any country's territorial authority.

hijack: To take over by force.

hypocrisy: Pretending to have qualities or beliefs one does not really have.

I

impalement: A process of torture and execution by inserting a long stake through the length of the body and then leaving the person to die a slow and painful death.

impressment: The practice of forcibly recruiting sailors to serve in the navy.

indentured servant: A person working under a contract that commits him or her to an employer for a fixed period of time, typically three to seven years.

intellectual property: A product of someone's intellect and creativity that has commercial value.

J

junk: A Chinese form of sailboat.

jurisdiction: The sole right and power to interpret and apply the law in a certain area.

K

keel: A strong beam that extends along the entire length of the bottom of a ship and supports its frame.

knight: A man granted a rank of honor by the monarch for his personal merit or service to the country.

L

letter of marque: A document licensing a private ship owner to the seize ships or goods of an enemy nation.

M

mangrove: A tropical tree or shrub characterized by an extensive, impenetrable system of roots.

maritime: Relating to the sea.

maritime law: The set of regulations that govern navigation and trade on the seas.

maroon: To strand an individual on a deserted island or shore with few provisions.

matchlock: A musket in which gun powder is ignited by lighting it with a match.

melodrama: A drama, such as a play, film, or television program, characterized by exaggerated emotions, stereotypical characters, and an extravagant plot.

mercenary: A seaman or soldier hired by a government to fight its battles.

militia: A volunteer military force made up of ordinary citizens.

monopoly: Exclusive control or possession of something.

musket: A muzzle-loading shoulder gun with a long barrel.

mutiny: An open rebellion by seamen against their ship's officers.

myth: A traditional story that is partly based on a historical event and serves to explain something about a culture.

N

nautical mile: A unit of distance used for sea navigation. One nautical mile equals 6,080 feet (1.9 kilometers). One mile across land equals 5,280 feet (1.6 kilometers).

navigator: A person who charts the routes of ships at sea.

nostalgia: A bittersweet longing for something from the past.

O

organized crime syndicate: A group of enterprises run by criminals to carry out illegal activities.

P

pagan: A person who does not accept the Christian religion.

parody: A spoof, or a work that mocks something else.

patent: A government grant that gives the creator of an invention the sole right to make, use, and sell that invention for a set period of time.

piragua: A dugout canoe.

pirate base: A place where pirates lived under their own rule and maintained their own defense system.

pirate haven: A safe place for pirates to harbor and repair their ships, resupply, and organize raiding parties.

plunder: To rob of goods by force, in a raid or in wartime.

prahu: A swift, light, seagoing vessel propelled by oars and used by the pirates of Southeast Asia.

privateer: A private ship or ship owner commissioned by a state or government to attack the merchant ships of an enemy nation.

prize: The goods, human captives, and ships captured in pirate raids.

R

rack: A piece of equipment used for torture; a person tied on a rack is slowly stretched by the wrists and ankles, causing extreme pain.

ransom: A sum of money demanded for the release of someone being held captive.

reprisal: An act of revenge against an enemy in wartime.

rigging: The system of ropes, chains, and other gear used to support and control the masts and sails of a sailing vessel.

rudder: A vertical, flat piece of wood or metal attached with hinges to a ship's stern (rear) that is used to steer the ship.

S

sack: To plunder a captured city.

scurvy: A disease caused by a lack of vitamin C, characterized by spongy and bleeding gums, bruising, and extreme weakness.

sea shanty: A sailor's work song.

ship's articles: The written sets of rules and conditions under which pirates operated on any given expedition.

ship of the line: A large, heavy warship designed for line of battle combat.

siege: A military blockade that isolates a city while an attack is underway.

sloop: A fast vessel with a single fore-and-aft rigged mast, meaning that the mast was positioned for sails set lengthwise along the ship.

smuggling: Illegally importing and exporting goods.

swashbuckler: A daring adventurer; also a drama about a swashbuckler.

T

tanker: A ship constructed to carry a large load of liquids, such as oil.

territorial waters: Waters surrounding a nation over which that nation exercises sole authority.

terrorism: The systematic use of violence against civilians in order to attain goals that are political, religious, or ideological.

timbers: The frames or ribs of a ship that are connected to the keel and give the hull its shape and strength.

trawler: A fishing boat that uses open-mouthed fishing nets drawn along the sea bottom.

tribute: Payment from one ruler of a state to another, usually for protection or to acknowledge submission.

Tower of London: A fortress in London, England, that was famously used as a prison.

V

vigilante: Someone who takes the law into his or her own hands without the authority to do so.

W

walk the plank: A form of punishment in which a person is forced to walk off the end of a wooden board extended over the side of a ship and into the sea.

war of attrition: A conflict in which a nation tries to wear down its opponent in small ways, hoping to gradually weaken the enemy's forces.

Research and Activity Ideas

Activity: Design a Jolly Roger

Research the Jolly Roger, the pirate flag. Then design your own pirate flag, choosing from among the symbols (such as skulls or crossed swords) that were used on the Jolly Rogers of golden-age pirates such as Blackbeard (Edward Teach; c. 1680–1718), Bartholomew Roberts (1682–1722), Stede Bonnet (c. 1688–1718), and John "Calico Jack" Rackham (c. 1682–1720). Write a brief paragraph describing the flag and indicate what its symbols are meant to signal to other ships.

Research: Pirates and History

Read up on the following two pirate eras: piracy in the ancient world and the golden age of piracy. Write a short essay discussing how we know about the pirates of those two eras. Take particular note of the primary sources for each era. A primary source is a document that was created during the time under study. Examples of primary sources are autobiographies, diaries, interviews, contemporary newspaper or magazine articles, letters, trial transcripts, photographs, news footage, official records, and contemporary literature.

In your essay, indicate a few writers and historians who wrote about each era. Did they live during the era or write about it at a later time? Did the writers present solid facts, or was their view prejudiced, romanticized, or influenced by other factors? How much do you think we really know about the actual pirates? What kinds of things are not known?

Group Activity: Stage a Pirate Play

Write and stage a short play that dramatizes one aspect of the lives of real historical pirates (rather than fictional ones). Use your knowledge of pirate history and your imagination to create a setting and costumes. Be sure to set the play in a historic era (Barbary corsairs, a seventeenth-century Chinese pirate empire, or the American privateers, for example). Some potential plots are: raiding a ship; a pirate's meal-time; or the marooning of a pirate who has broken the ship's articles, or code of conduct.

Group Activity: Test your friends' pirate knowledge

Some of the things we associate with pirates (like buried treasure) are mainly fictional creations that come from stories, movies, folklore, and the arts. But other things we associate with pirates (like the Jolly Roger), come from real pirate history. Make up a quiz by creating a list of ten things that are commonly associated with pirates, some of which come from history, and others that do not. Make a corresponding column in which the person you're testing can indicate whether that aspect of piracy is "real" or "fiction."

Group Activity: Watch a Pirate Movie

With your class or a group of friends, watch one of the following pirate movies:

Captain Blood (1935)

Treasure Island (1950; rated G)

Blackbeard the Pirate (1952)

Pirates of Penzance (1983; rated G)

Pirates of the Caribbean: Curse of the Black Pearl (2003; rated PG-13)

Before you watch the movie, everyone should choose one of the four aspects of the movie from the list that follows. As you watch the movie, take notes about the aspect you have chosen. After watching the movie, discuss it in terms of these four aspects.

Aspects to observe:

Ships, boats, sea scenes. What did the ships and other sea vessels look like? How big were they? How many people were on deck? How many sails? How many mounted guns did you see? Did the scenes at sea seem realistic? How did the movie depict life at sea?

Sword fights, combat, and other violent behavior. Did the violence in this movie seem real or fake? What kinds of fighting occurred in the film? What kinds of weapons were used? Did the leading characters fight to save themselves or others, or were they doing it out of greed or cruelty? Did you feel fear or suspense, or was it meant to be funny?

Historical setting. Where and when is the movie supposed to be happening? If these things are not stated outright, what are the clues (such as clothing, technology, etc)? Do the historical references in the movie correspond to what you know about the pirates of the era?

Heroes, heroines, and anti-heroes. Who was the movie's hero/heroine? Was there more than one? What made this character a hero or heroine? Was there an anti-hero (someone who is viewed as a leading character and who draws us into his or her character, but who does not have the usual noble traits we associate with heroes)? Which of the lead characters was the most likable?

Research: pirate ships

Research some of the ships used by three of the following pirate groups: (1) pirates of ancient Greece; (2) Vikings; (3) Chinese pirates of the eighteenth century; (4) Barbary corsairs; (5) golden-age pirates; (6) modern Somali pirates. Write a brief essay describing these pirate ships. How were the ships powered? What features did these pirates seek in a ship? How were their ships suited to them? What kinds of problems did these ships present? Compare and contrast the ships of the three groups.

Classroom Activity: A Pirate Trial

It is 1718 and Blackbeard has recently blockaded the Charleston, South Carolina, harbor with his fleet of pirate ships. Imagine that instead of getting away with it, as he did in real life, Blackbeard was captured by the authorities and brought to trial for piracy, a hanging offense. Your class is given the task of conducting Blackbeard's trial. Divide into two groups. Half the class will be his defense team, and argue for leniency. The other half will be the prosecution team, who will seek his conviction and execution. Before the debate, both sides should prepare by reading several sources about Blackbeard and the golden age of piracy. The defense should present aspects of his life and exploits that will make a jury sympathize with him and pardon him for his life of piracy. The prosecution should present evidence that Blackbeard's crimes merit the hangman's noose.

Classroom Activity Talk Like a Pirate

In the late 1990s, John Baur and Mark Summers, two friends from Albany, Oregon, were playing racquetball, when they spontaneously broke into pirate talk. According to their web site, this was the origin of a new holiday:

> Whoever let out the first "Arrr!" started something. One thing led to another. "That be a fine cannonade," one said, to be followed by "Now watch as I fire a broadside straight into your yardarm!" and other such helpful phrases.... By the time our hour on the court was over, we realized that lapsing into pirate lingo had made the game more fun and the time pass more quickly. We decided then and there that what the world really needed was a new national holiday, Talk Like A Pirate Day.

For seven years Baur and Summers celebrated the holiday only with close friends (and forgot it altogether a couple of times). Then in 2002, after stumbling upon the e-mail address of humor columnist Dave Barry (1947–), they wrote to ask him to be spokesperson for the new holiday. Barry liked the idea and wrote a column, and the idea took off. September 19, 2002, was the first International Talk Like a Pirate (TLAP) Day. Since then, there have been annual TLAP celebrations throughout the United States and in countries as far away as Australia. On September 19, people dress in their favorite version of a pirate and use words like "Arrrgh!" "Me hearty,"and "Shiver me timbers."

Have a "Talk Like a Pirate" classroom session. Prepare by studying up on your pirate vocabulary (there are dozens of pirate vocabulary lists available on the Internet) and creating a pirate costume. In class, use as many pirate words and phrases as you can. They do not have to be historically accurate.

1

Piracy in the Ancient Mediterranean

Piracy, defined simply as an act of robbery on the sea, has been going on since human beings first used boats. It is not difficult to imagine an act of piracy in its earliest and most simple form. A fisherman comes to shore, his vessel full with the day's catch. Three people from a different village have been watching him from a ridge overlooking the sea. Jumping into their boat, which is hidden in a nearby cove, they row out and attack the fisherman. They steal his catch and perhaps even take his boat. In some cases the thieves might even kill the poor man and throw him in the sea.

People of the ancient world probably would have seen this act of robbery at sea differently than people of modern times. Suppose, for example, that the thieves came from a village that was in conflict with the fisherman's village. The thieves' fellow villagers would probably honor them for weakening their enemy. The villagers' self-interest would also shape their opinion, particularly if, after ambushing the fisherman, the thieves brought home their booty (the goods they stole) to share with the village. In such cases the thieves would probably not be considered criminals. Without a central government to provide laws for both villages, the thieves did not actually break any laws, and the fisherman has no authorities to whom he could report the theft. In fact, the fisherman's village may later decide to steal from the thieves' village as an act of reprisal, or revenge, starting a cycle of piracy between the two communities.

The world's first-known reports of pirates appeared more than three thousand years ago. Over the years, people of the ancient world came to distinguish between sea raiders. There were those who acted on behalf of a state in times of war and those who were considered criminals, because they acted for themselves, seeking profit. In ancient Rome, sea raiders who acted for themselves became known as *hostis humani generis*, meaning the "enemy of humankind."

WORDS TO KNOW

act of reprisal: A document granting permission to individuals to raid the vessels of an enemy in response to some harm that enemy had done.

barbarians: People who are not considered civilized.

bireme: A swift galley ship with two banks of oars, and sometimes a square sail.

booty: Goods stolen from ships or coastal villages during pirate raids or attacks on enemies in time of war.

city-state: An independent, self-governing city and its surrounding territory.

galley: A long, low ship used for war and trading that was mainly powered by oarsmen, but might also use a sail.

pirate haven: A safe place for pirates to harbor and repair their ships, resupply, and organize raiding parties.

plunder: To rob of goods by force, in a raid or in wartime.

privateer: A private ship or ship owner commissioned by a state or government to attack the merchant ships of an enemy nation.

ransom: A sum of money demanded for the release of someone being held captive.

The Mediterranean Sea and the rise of maritime trade

The Mediterranean Sea, the location of the earliest large-scale maritime (sea) trade, was also one of the earliest recorded sites of widespread and organized piracy. This huge sea is surrounded by three continents: Europe to the north, Asia to the east, and Africa to the south. The Mediterranean coastline is rocky, and the soil is poor. Because farming was difficult, many ancient coastal communities took up trade. Mountains near the coastline, though, made land travel difficult. For the early civilizations, traveling to distant markets by sea was much easier.

In around 2000 BCE, the Phoenicians, a group of people who lived in a region that now includes the countries of Lebanon, Syria, and Israel, began trading at ports in regions of present-day Greece and the Middle East, navigating along the sea's rocky shorelines to transport their wares. Phoenician merchants sailed in galleys, long low ships used for war and trading that had five to ten oars on each side of the ship. The galleys were mainly powered by men working the oars, but most also had a square sail that aided travel on windy days. The Phoenician traders loaded their galleys with trade products, such as dyes, wood, textiles (cloth), and glass.

Phoenician traders at a Mediterranean seaport. The Phoenicians began trading at ports along the Mediterranean coast around 2000 BCE. © NORTH WIND PICTURE ARCHIVES/ALAMY.

In foreign ports they exchanged these goods for metals and other valuables. As their trade grew, the Phoenicians expanded their routes to distant ports, including many in Egypt.

The Mediterranean civilization flourished in these early days of maritime trade. But as Mediterranean trade expanded, piracy emerged and began to threaten the trade and the lives of seamen and coastal villagers. Accounts of sea raiders known as the Lukkas and the Lycians appeared as early as the fourteenth century BCE. Equipped with swift galleys and armed with spears and shields, the early pirates hid in coves and islands, ready to ambush the richly loaded merchant ships that passed their way.

The Sea People

Around 1220 BCE, groups of sea raiders called Sea People began to attack and plunder (rob of goods by force) ships in the Mediterranean. They also attacked coastal villages, stealing food and valuables and capturing men, women, and children to be sold as slaves. The Sea People traveled in galleys that had between ten and fifteen oars on each side of the galley. Armed, fierce, and skilled in the ways of the sea, the Sea People destroyed several major Mediterranean cultures and threatened others.

What is known of the Sea People has been found in inscriptions on monuments in Egypt, Anatolia (present-day Turkey), and Syria. An inscription on the wall of the tomb of the Egyptian pharaoh Ramses III (1187–1156 BCE) in Medinat Habu, near present-day Luxor, Egypt, depicts an attack by the Sea People, providing a visual record of their ships and weapons. Another inscription found at Thebes, an ancient city of Egypt, records an attack on Egypt by its neighbor Libya. In this attack, Libya was joined by migrating northern tribes that many historians believe were the Sea People. The tribes listed are the Shardana, Lukka, Meshwesh, Teresh, Ekwesh, and Shekelesh.

Despite the information that exists about the Sea People, mysteries still surround them. Why they attacked Mediterranean civilizations is unknown. They could have attacked to obtain new territory, or they may have been paid by one of the Mediterranean civilizations to raid its enemies. The Sea People could also have been a group of pirates, working only for their own profit. Like many sea raiders that came after them, the Sea People may have frequently crossed the line between warrior and pirate, sometimes acting on behalf of a state, but at other times robbing ships at sea and people in coastal towns for their own profit.

The Sea People are thought to have dominated the Mediterranean from 1220 to 1186 BCE, when the Egyptians defeated them. During these years, trade in the region was severely reduced. Cultural exchanges were limited, written languages were lost, and many people lived in poverty.

Rise of the ancient Greek civilization

Despite the chaos caused by the sea raiders, Mediterranean civilization rebounded. In time, trade revived, bringing prosperity to Greek market communities. The ancient Greek civilization, which would flourish from about 800 to 146 BCE, began to take shape. Ancient Greece did not have a single, central government as present-day Greece does. Instead, ancient Greece was made up of a collection of political entities that eventually became city-states, or areas that consisted of a single city and the surrounding territory. Thus, there were many centers of power.

An Egyptian relief depicting the Sea People. Little is known about these mysterious raiders who attacked ships in the ancient Mediterranean. © RICHARD T. NOWITZ/ CORBIS.

Records from the early years of ancient Greek culture, from 800 to 450 BCE, show that there was piracy in the Mediterranean throughout the era. Ancient writings do not provide specific information about pirates. However, they do provide an idea of how people of the time viewed them.

Homer's *Odyssey*

Many historians consider the *Odyssey* and the *Iliad*, epic tales by Greek poet Homer, to be the first written records of piracy. Homer's birth and death dates are not known, but historians think he wrote his famous works sometime between 800 and 700 BCE.

The *Odyssey* chronicles the sea adventures of its hero and narrator, Odysseus, as he returns home to his kingdom ten years after the Trojan War (c. 1200 BCE; a war between Greece and Troy). This work provides some insight into how ancient Greeks viewed pirates. For example, when Odysseus and his shipmates arrive in a strange port, they are asked, "Strangers, who are you? From where do you come sailing over the watery ways? Is it on some business, or are you recklessly roving as pirates do, when they sail on the salt sea and venture their lives as they wander, bringing evil to alien people?" These lines show that the ancient Greeks feared pirates as reckless wanderers whose attacks brought suffering. When strangers such as Odysseus and his crew arrive in a sea port, the local people worried that they were pirates who would steal from them or even kill them.

Throughout the *Odyssey*, Odysseus is presented as a hero, but during his adventures he also conducts what appears to be a pirate raid. When his ship is blown ashore at Ismaros, land of the Kikonians, Odysseus reports that he and his crew "sacked their city and killed their people, / and out of their city taking their wives and many possessions / we shared them out, so none might go cheated of his proper / portion." As a war hero, Odysseus thinks he deserves the booty and that it is his fate to come home from war rich. The people of the city he raided, however, no doubt viewed him and his crew as pirates.

In a fifth-century BCE discussion of the *Odyssey*, Greek historian Thucydides (c. 460–c. 395 BCE) notes that most early Greeks did not view raiding and stealing as crimes as long as one did not steal from one's own tribe or community. In fact, everyone outside one's own tribe was an enemy, and therefore stealing from them was a lawful act of war. It was considered the duty of stronger tribe members to raid others and bring home goods for those in need within their tribe. Thucydides describes this view in *The First Book of the History of Thucydides*:

The Ancient Greek and Roman Concept of "Pirate"

The stories of pirates of ancient times come to us from Greek and Roman texts that were written thousands of years ago. What the ancient writers meant by "pirate" is not always clear and has been a source of intensive study in modern times.

A pirate is someone who robs at sea. The ancient Greeks and Romans did not have a word that specifically meant "pirate." Homer, the first known ancient Greek writer to refer to pirates, used the word *leistes*, which comes from the word for booty or plunder and can be translated as "plunderer." A second word, *peirates*, appeared in mid–third-century BCE writings to describe sea raiders. Its root is in the noun *peira*, which means "attempt." Thus, a pirate was someone who made an attempt at something.

Roman words for pirates were similar to the Greek words. *Praedo* and *latro* were both words for "bandit" or "pirate." In later writings, the Romans used the word *pirata*, taken from the Greek *peirates*. All of these terms could be translated as "plunderer" or "bandit" and none of them specified whether the pillaging was done on land or by sea.

Greeks and Romans also did not have words that distinguished between pirates and privateers, or seamen authorized by their state or government to attack the ships of an enemy nation.

Greeks and Romans frequently referred to entire cultures, nations, or tribes as pirates. (In modern times the term *pirate* is used to refer to individuals or groups of individuals, not entire nations.) Experts in ancient languages point out that ancient Greeks and Romans may have used the word *pirate* to describe enemies that raided their ships and shores. At the same time, however, they may have used words such as *warrior* or even *hero* to describe their own raiders, who were carrying out the same activities on enemy ships.

Around 44 BCE the Roman orator and writer Cicero (106–43 BCE) added a new twist to the definition of *pirate*, or *pirata*. In the essay *On Obligations* he describes the obligations owed to enemies in warfare, but argues that no such obligations were owed to a pirate. As quoted by Daniel Heller-Roazen in *The Enemy of All: Piracy and the Law of Nations*, Cicero writes, "For a pirate is not included in the number of lawful enemies, but is the common enemy of all." Over the years, this concept has changed only slightly. Pirates are considered individuals or groups who act outside of any political connections or state affiliations, and as such, they are the enemy of humankind.

For the Grecians in old time, and such barbarians [people not considered civilized] as in the continent lived near unto the sea, or else inhabited the islands, after once they began to cross over one to another in ships, became thieves, and went abroad under the conduct of their most puissant [powerful] men, both to enrich themselves and to fetch in maintenance for the weak; and falling upon towns unfortified and scatteringly inhabited, rifled [plundered] them, and made this the best means of their living; being a matter at that time nowhere in disgrace, but rather carrying with it something of glory.

It is important to note that the acts of piracy described by Homer and Thucydides actually occurred on land, even though they were carried out by sea-faring raiders. This was common in ancient Greece and Rome.

Greek warfare and piracy: 421–339 BCE

There are fewer mentions of piracy in the writings of the classical age of ancient Greece, which began around 500 BCE. At this time, the city-states of Sparta and Athens became strong, expanding their territory and strengthening their alliances with other city-states. Athens formed a strong navy, and Sparta maintained a fierce military force on the ground. Some historians attribute the reduction in piracy to the control these powerful city-states held over wide ranges of the Mediterranean.

In the late fifth century BCE, rivalry among the Greek city-states, particularly Athens and Sparta, over control of various regions led to a series of violent conflicts known as the Peloponnesian Wars. The wars persisted from about 421 to 404 BCE, when Sparta defeated Athens. Even with this war over, fighting continued among the various Greek city-states. With all the warfare, Greek power weakened in the southern city-states. Meanwhile, the kingdom of Macedon in the northern part of the Greek peninsula was gathering strength. In 339 BCE all of the Greek city-states were united under the rule of the Macedonian king Philip II (382–336 BCE).

Privateering and acts of reprisal During the century of war from 421 to 339 BCE, governments of the Greek city-states frequently enlisted the aid of pirates to target their enemies. (Seamen who were authorized by a state or government to raid enemy ships later came to be called privateers.) Pirates were particularly useful to the warring city-states, because the pirates were already equipped with their own ships and had the skills and weapons necessary to conduct raids. Rulers of city-states authorized groups of pirates to attack their enemy's warships, merchant ships, and even coastal villages under the assumption that all such attacks would weaken the enemy. The city-states did not pay the pirates for their work, but instead promised them a portion of the booty they took during their raids. The rest of the booty was to be delivered to the governing authorities of the city-state. In some cases, rulers of the city-states actually provided pirates with ships and supplies.

City-states often issued acts of reprisal, which granted permission to individuals or to the general public to plunder vessels of an enemy in response to some harm that enemy had done. The acts allowed the plunder of any ship flying under the flag of the city-state or a league of city-states from which reprisal was sought. If Sparta issued a general act of reprisal against Athens, for example, the act authorized any Spartan seaman, and even non-Spartan seamen, to attack an Athenian trade merchant ship and steal its cargo. It did not matter that the merchant had never taken part in political or military activities. Acts of reprisal could be issued even when the two hostile states were not at war. The rulers of city-states who issued the acts usually received the booty and then gave the raiders a portion, keeping the rest for the state. Ancient writers note that rulers of the ancient states issued more acts of reprisal when they needed extra cash.

Pirate havens Although privateering and reprisal made plundering ships at sea legitimate in the eyes of the public, Greek rulers came to regret hiring pirates to join their warfare. It was not unusual for pirates, who were motivated by profit rather than loyalty, to attack the ships of the city-states that had hired them. And, once the wars ended, the Mediterranean had become home to thousands of unemployed sea raiders. These raiders had the ships and skills necessary to disrupt sea trade, and no other opportunities could compare to the profits of piracy.

Throughout the Mediterranean, groups of pirates took over suitable coastal coves and villages. They established pirate havens, or safe places for pirates to harbor and repair their ships, resupply, and organize raiding parties. According to ancient writers, the pirates formed their own societies in these havens, with some form of government and an economy based largely on piracy. More and more pirate havens lined the shores along trade routes. Some areas of the Mediterranean Sea became too hazardous for traders to navigate.

During the fourth century BCE, merchants and aristocrats complained to their governments about the growing threat of piracy. A few city-states with strong sea forces initiated antipiracy campaigns. The strongest of these were Athens and the Greek island of Rhodes, which lies in the Aegean Sea near present-day Turkey. Rhodes was considered a protector of the seas. It was the first government to enact antipiracy laws, and its naval forces fought in several wars against a pirate haven on the nearby island of Crete. But there were far too many pirates for the Rhodians to have a meaningful impact on the problem.

St. Augustine on Governments and Pirates

In his work, *De civitate dei* (*City of God*; c. 416), St. Augustine (354–430) makes an eloquent argument that rulers and governments engage in the same kinds of plundering as individual pirates, but on a much larger scale. He writes, as quoted by Daniel Heller-Roazen in *The Enemy of All: Piracy and the Law of Nations*:

> What are great kingdoms but great robberies? And what are robberies themselves, but little kingdoms? The band itself is made up of men; it is ruled by the authority of a prince, it is knit together by the pact of the confederacy; the booty is divided by the law agreed on. . . . Indeed, that was an apt and true reply which was given to Alexander the Great by a pirate who had been seized. For when that king had asked the man what he meant by keeping hostile possession of the sea, he answered with bold pride, "What thou meanest by seizing the whole earth; but because I do it with a petty ship, I am called a robber, whilst thou who dost it with a great fleet art styled Emperor."

Piracy in ancient Rome

By the second century BCE Greek city-states were losing power. The various regions had been united for a time under the leadership of the Macedonian conqueror Alexander the Great (356–323 BCE), but after his death, that unity crumbled. At the same time, the Roman Republic was expanding. By about 200 BCE, most of present-day Italy was ruled by the Republic. Between 150 and 100 BCE, Rome conquered Carthage (near present-day Tunis, Tunisia), a great Mediterranean power, and went on to conquer Greece, Macedonia, Anatolia, and other Mediterranean regions. While Rome was busy conquering new territory, piracy increased in the Mediterranean.

By the first century BCE pirate havens in the Mediterranean had multiplied and grown extremely strong. Crete had been a thriving pirate haven and slave market for centuries. In central Greece a confederation of city-states known as the Aetolian League had created a pirate culture that disrupted trade and travel on the Aegean Sea. There were major pirate havens in the Lipari Islands north of Sicily, the Balearic Islands near present-day Spain, along the Liguria coast in present-day Italy, and in many other locations.

Illyrian pirates face the Romans

The eastern shores of the Adriatic Sea, which separates Italy and the Balkan Peninsula, provided a major base for pirates and was the target of one of Rome's early antipiracy campaigns. Around 230 BCE the king of the region of Illyria, located in present-day Albania, Serbia, and Montenegro, died. According to some sources, when his wife, Queen Teuta, succeeded him, she decided to use the Illyrian kingdom's navy for piracy. Illyrian ships began to attack trade vessels throughout the Adriatic Sea and along the coast of present-day Italy.

The Illyrian queen Teuta orders her attendants to kill the Roman ambassadors who asked for an end to Illyrian piracy. © MARY EVANS PICTURE LIBRARY/ALAMY.

Illyrian piracy grew, and it greatly disrupted trade. Merchants pleaded with Rome to stop these pirate attacks. Roman ambassadors were dispatched to Illyria to seek repayment for the attacked ships and to ask Queen Teuta to end Illyrian piracy. The queen, however, reportedly told the ambassadors that since piracy was a legal enterprise, she would not consider forbidding it. One of the ambassadors responded in anger to the queen, and her attendants killed him. This may have been the reason that the Romans declared war on Illyria in 229 BCE. Sending twenty thousand soldiers on foot, two thousand soldiers on horseback, and two hundred ships, the Romans forced the queen to surrender. In the peace agreement that followed, Illyrians were forbidden to sail armed ships.

Cilician pirates

Meanwhile, Cilician pirates had become some of the most powerful offenders at sea. In the second century BCE a series of pirate communities with tightly run governments emerged along the southern coast of Asia Minor (present-day Turkey). The Cilician pirates had become very wealthy through a profitable slave trade and from the booty of their successful sea raids. By one estimate, there were more than one thousand Cilician pirate ships in the Mediterranean in the first century BCE. Their sea forces were highly effective. The pirates fought in squadrons directed by admirals and were considered as well organized as any navy. Cilician pirates sailed in biremes, fast galleys with two banks of oars that were extravagantly adorned from the wealth of their plunder. These vessels were built to outrun warships, and they had large storage areas for the anticipated booty. Not content to raid ships and coastal villages, the Cilicians plundered towns and even cities along the coast.

Cilician pirates spread fear throughout large segments of the Mediterranean. Investors in overseas trading feared losing their investments to the Cilician pirates. Merchants and travelers lived in fear of being captured and sold into slavery or held for ransom. Villagers near the coast were so haunted by the constant possibility of attack that entire villages moved inland and put up defensive walls. At times Cilician raiding in the Mediterranean was so widespread it stopped trade altogether. Around 88 BCE the Cilician pirates further infuriated the Romans when they joined forces with King Mithridates of Pontus, a kingdom on the coast of the Black Sea in present-day Turkey, who was at the time involved in a fierce war with Rome.

A story about Cilician piracy appears in *Plutarch's Lives*, a collection of biographies of famous Romans that was written in about 100 CE. In 74 or 75 BCE a youthful Julius Caesar (100–44 BCE), who would later become emperor of Rome, was traveling to Rhodes when he was captured by Cilician pirates. The pirates took him to their haven on the tiny Greek island of Pharmacusa and set a ransom. The arrogant young man informed his captors that they did not know who they were dealing with, insisting that they more than double his ransom. Caesar's companions were sent back to raise the ransom money, and Caesar remained with the pirates for more than a month. He entertained them with speeches and took part in their games.

A statue of Julius Caesar, who was kidnapped by Cilician pirates. © PRISMA ARCHIVO/ ALAMY.

When his friends returned with the ransom money, Caesar paid off the pirates and sailed away. He quickly hired a small fleet and returned to Pharmacusa, where he took his former captors prisoner. He took them to Pergamon, a Greek city in Asia Minor, and demanded that Roman officials there execute the pirates according to law. The officials hesitated, thinking there might be a bribe or other advantage to keeping the pirates alive. In fact, by this time in history, many local governments and authorities in ancient Greece and Rome welcomed pirates at their ports. For better or worse, piracy had become so successful that economies in areas with heavy pirate traffic came to depend upon it. The pirates brought in new goods, stimulated the local economy, and often offered bribes to friendly officials. Caesar, though, was determined to see his captors dead and swiftly ordered their crucifixion, a slow and painful death by nailing the hands and feet to a cross.

Rome campaigns to rid the Mediterranean of pirates

By the time Julius Caesar was kidnapped by pirates, the Roman Republic's leaders had resolved to rid the Mediterranean of its powerful thieves. Though piracy may have helped some local economies, it brought lawlessness to Rome, caused people to live in fear, severely damaged trade, and detracted from the authority and the tax revenue of the Republic. The Republic passed a strong new antipiracy law and resolved to attack the pirates in their homes at the numerous pirate havens of the Mediterranean. Crete, the oldest of the havens, was the target of one of the first in a series of large Roman antipiracy campaigns. In 72 BCE military leader Marc Antony (83–30 BCE) led a large campaign to rid Crete of its pirate population. However, the pirates were too strong for his forces. The Romans then launched a second and much larger assault on Crete in 69 BCE, laying siege to the island. After a ferocious struggle, the pirates were defeated. The Romans then went after the Cilicians and the other remaining pirates of the Mediterranean.

In 67 BCE Rome appointed top military commander Gnaeus Pompeius Magnus, or Pompey the Great (106–47 BCE), to a lead a mission against piracy. He was given 270 ships for his campaign and almost unlimited authority over the seas of the Roman Empire. Members of the Roman Senate had initially resisted this measure. They understood that in giving Pompey this great power they would virtually lose their democracy, or government by the people. With Pompey in control of most of the Mediterranean, Rome would basically become a monarchy, a government led by one all-powerful person. But the Roman people were desperate for an end to piracy. The decision to put Pompey in charge went forward.

Pompey's antipiracy campaign was swift, and it surpassed all expectations. By dividing the Mediterranean into thirteen sections and sending fleets to assault the pirates in their own regions, the Roman forces were at last able to eliminate most of the Cilician pirate threat. Pompey's success may have been due in large part to his offer to pardon all pirates who surrendered and give them land and titles in their regions. Many surrendered.

Though Pompey's campaign reduced the number of pirates, Mediterranean piracy continued. In the end it was the rapid expansion of the Roman Empire that cleared the vast region of the last of its pirates. By 27 BCE the Republic (which was ruled by the common people) had given way to the Roman Empire (which was ruled by an emperor). All of the Mediterranean Sea and its coastal regions came under the rule of the Empire. The Empire enacted and enforced new laws. There were no longer any lands where pirate havens were permitted, since all land was ruled by Rome. Pirates were no longer able to raid a ship or town in one region and then disappear into another territory where there were no laws or authorities to stop them. Without safe havens, pirates could not function. For the duration of the Roman Empire, from 27 BCE to 476 CE, when the empire collapsed, ships sailed the Mediterranean Sea freely, without fear of piracy.

For More Information

BOOKS

De Souza, Philip. *Piracy in the Graeco-Roman World*. United Kingdom: Cambridge University Press, 1999.

Heller-Roazen, Daniel. *The Enemy of All: Piracy and the Law of Nations*. New York: Zone Books, 2009.

Homer. *The Odyssey of Homer*. Translated by Richard Lattimore. New York: Harper & Row, 1965, 1967, Book III, lines 71–74, p 53; Book IX, lines 39–43, p. 138.

Konstam, Angus, with Roger Michael Kean. *Pirates: Predators of the Sea*. New York: Skyhorse, 2007.

Ormerod, Henry A. *Piracy in the Ancient World: An Essay in Mediterranean History*. Chicago: Argonaut, 1967.

Travers, Tim. *Pirates: A History*. Stroud, Gloucestershire, UK: Tempus, 2007.

PERIODICALS

Eberhard, Zangger. "Who Were the Sea People?" *Saudi/Aramco World* (May–June 1995). Available online at www.saudiaramcoworld.com/issue/199503/who.were.the.sea.people.htm (accessed on January 3, 2011).

WEB SITES

Thucydides. "The First Book of the History of Thucydides.—Thucydides, *The English Works, vol. VIII (The Peloponnesian War Part I)*." Translated by Thomas Hobbes, 1839. *The Online Library of Liberty*. http://oll.libertyfund.org/?option=com_staticxt&staticfile=show.php%3Ftitle=771&chapter=90126&layout=html&Itemid=27 (accessed on January 3, 2011).

2

Piracy in Medieval Europe

During the Middle Ages (also called the medieval era, which began in the late fifth century and continued through the end of the fifteenth century), northern Europe became one of the world's foremost arenas of sea raiding. In the eighth century sea-going raiders from Scandinavia (present-day Norway, Sweden, and Denmark) called Vikings became the most-feared pirates of the time. As the threat of Viking raids subsided in northern Europe in the tenth and eleventh centuries, an increase in overseas trade, near-constant warfare, and some unfortunate decisions of European rulers led to an increase in piracy in the waters surrounding the Germanic kingdoms, the British isles, and France. The troubles in the North and Baltic Seas and the English Channel—and the popularity of these early pirates in the common imagination—foreshadowed things to come in later eras of piracy.

Europe before the Vikings

During the centuries immediately preceding the Middle Ages, the Roman Empire had established a relatively peaceful rule throughout a vast area. At its height in the second century, the empire's borders went well beyond the Mediterranean coastal regions of Africa, Asia, and Europe, extending throughout western Europe and across the North Sea to include England. However, the stability achieved in this enormous area under one rule would not outlast the empire.

In the beginning of the fifth century, groups of Germanic tribes such as the Vandals, Goths, and Franks began to move from Northern Europe into regions of the vast Roman Empire. As wave after wave of these migrating tribes pushed across the borders of the empire, long, violent, and extremely destructive battles erupted. Rome's power weakened in the constant fighting, and the Germanic tribes were able to establish

WORDS TO KNOW

act of reprisal: A document granting permission to individuals to raid the vessels of an enemy in response to some harm that enemy had done.

booty: Goods stolen from ships or coastal villages during pirate raids or attacks on enemies in time of war.

cleric: A member of the clergy, or church order.

clinker-built: Construction for boats using overlapping wooden planks.

guild: An association for people or towns with a similar trade or interest.

keel: A strong beam that extends along the entire length of the bottom of a ship and supports its frame.

letter of marque: A document licensing a private ship owner to the seize ships or goods of an enemy nation.

maritime law: The set of regulations that govern navigation and trade on the seas.

mercenary: A seaman or soldier hired by a government to fight its battles.

navigator: A person who charts the routes of ships at sea.

pagan: A person who does not accept the Christian religion.

plunder: To rob of goods by force, in a raid or in wartime.

pirate base: A place where pirates lived under their own rule and maintained their own defense system.

pirate haven: A safe place for pirates to harbor and repair their ships, resupply, and organize raiding parties.

privateer: A private ship or ship owner commissioned by a state or government to attack the merchant ships of an enemy nation.

reprisal: An act of revenge against an enemy in wartime.

rudder: A vertical, flat piece of wood or metal attached with hinges to a ship's stern (rear) that is used to steer the ship.

sack: To plunder a captured city.

siege: A military blockade that isolates a city while an attack is underway.

timbers: The frames or ribs of a ship that are connected to the keel and give the hull its shape and strength.

Tower of London: A fortress in London, England, that was famously used as a prison.

---

kingdoms in Spain and Northern Africa. From their new kingdoms, they sacked (captured and plundered) cities in Italy, including Rome. The sacking of Rome in 476 marks the collapse of the western Roman Empire and the dawn of the Middle Ages.

The eastern part of the Roman Empire, which would soon become known as the Byzantine Empire, remained strong. Its capital was Constantinople (present-day Istanbul, Turkey). In the early centuries of the Middle

Ages, the Byzantine Empire struggled against the many varieties of pirates in the Mediterranean region. Its powerful navy was able to keep the trade routes more or less secure, although it never completely stopped the piracy. Later in the Middle Ages, the rise of the Islamic religion and warfare between the Christians and the Muslims (followers of Islam) led to a fierce new age of piracy in the Mediterranean called the age of the Barbary corsairs. (For more information, see **The Barbary Corsairs**.)

In northern Europe, the collapse of the Roman Empire led to an era often called the Dark Ages. With the lack of a strong central rule, small, isolated kingdoms arose. The Catholic Church linked these kingdoms with a common religion, but they had few other economic or political connections. Kings and queens of these states were less powerful than the local lords, who were the primary rulers of the people in the countryside surrounding their estates. Few of the monarchs had significant military or naval forces. Without laws or regulations to provide security in the seas and with little means to enforce laws even if they had existed, trade diminished in the early Middle Ages, coming to a standstill in some places. The lack of strong sea trade might have discouraged most pirates, but at the end of the eighth century, the Vikings stepped in and took advantage of the times.

The Vikings strike

On June 8, 793, on a small island off the coast of northeast England, monks at the religious center known as Lindisfarne rose up in alarm when a group of longboats suddenly appeared off their shores. As the boats arrived on the island's sandy beaches, foreigners armed with swords and axes poured out and swarmed into the unprotected monastery. The raiders stabbed and hacked at anyone in their path as they proceeded to loot the church's abundant treasures. They killed many of the clerics (members of the clergy, or church order), took others as slaves, and terrorized the rest. Simeon of Durham, a twelfth-century historian, describes the brutal scene, as quoted by Philip Pulsiano and Kirsten Wolf in *Medieval Scandinavia: An Encyclopedia*:

> The pagans [people who did not believe in the Christian religion] from the northern regions came with a naval force to Britain like stinging hornets and spread on all sides like fearful wolves, robbed, tore and slaughtered not only beasts of burden, sheep and oxen, but even priests and deacons, and companies of monks and nuns. And they came to the church of Lindisfarne, laid everything waste with grievous plundering [robbing by force], trampled the holy places with polluted steps, dug

The Vikings raided Lindisfarne, a religious center in northeast England, in 793. This attack marked the start of annual pirate raids along the coasts of England, Scotland, and Ireland. HULTON ARCHIVE/GETTY IMAGES.

up the altars and seized all the treasures of the holy church. They killed some of the brothers, took some away with them in fetters [chains or shackles for the ankles or feet], many they drove out, naked and loaded with insults, some they drowned in the sea.

For several decades after the pillaging of Lindisfarne, the Vikings launched many annual pirate raids along the coasts of England, Scotland, and Ireland. They usually arrived in small expeditions of about one dozen ships, and their targets were frequently churches and other sacred sites,

The Narentines of the Adriatic Sea

The medieval Narentine people of southern Dalmatia (present-day Croatia) are best remembered for their piracy. During the eighth and ninth centuries, around the same time the Vikings were raiding ports in northern Europe, the Narentines were raiding coastal towns and merchant ships in the Adriatic Sea, an arm of the Mediterranean Sea that separates the Italian and Balkan Peninsulas. The Narentines' home base was called Pagania by the nations that surrounded it, because the Narentines were pagans, or people who chose not to accept Christianity.

The Narentines raided for profit. Like the Vikings they used hit-and-run tactics, raiding and then fleeing before their targets could defend themselves. They were especially skilled at the slave trade and took many human prisoners to be sold as slaves. By the ninth century, their tactics were so successful that the Adriatic was considered a very dangerous place to sail.

The Narentines were extremely good seamen. Their primary type of ship was a sagena, which resembled the Vikings' *drekar*. Sagenas were long, narrow, shallow vessels with sharp bows (fronts) built for speed. They were propelled by as many as forty rowers. Like Viking crews, the Narentine rowers were also skilled warriors, ready to fight once they reached their target.

The Narentines' favorite targets were the coasts of southern Italy and the Venetian trading ships that passed in the Adriatic. During the ninth century, the powerful republic of Venice dominated the Adriatic Sea. The Narentines, who had no desire to fight the Venetians, waited until the Venetian navy was occupied in a distant conflict and then raided in the Adriatic at will until its return. In 846, while the Venetian naval forces were away, the Narentines managed to sack a port city within the republic. Fourteen years later they kidnapped two important officials of the Catholic Church. At that point, the Byzantine Empire took military action, not only stopping the pirate raids, but also forcing the Narentines to accept Christianity. Although their piracy was greatly reduced, the Narentines remained proud of their pirate tradition and were known to go out on occasional raiding expeditions for the next two centuries.

although they attacked villages and towns as well. They used the tactic of surprise as often as possible, sneaking up on unprepared and poorly defended targets. Their raids were notoriously bloody and vicious. Some Viking fighters, called *berserkers* (or *berserks*), fought in such a furious and unstoppable manner that people described them as mad wolves or raging bulls. Throughout Europe, people believed that berserkers possessed magical powers, and that no lance, knife, or club could kill them.

Terror of Vikings became a fact of life in the British isles. The prayer *A furore Normanorarum libera nos* (From the fury of the Northmen [Vikings] deliver us) was to be heard throughout the land. The Vikings were well pleased with their monstrous reputation. People's fear was so great that they often surrendered without a fight.

The Vikings as pirates

The word *Viking* applies to raiders from present-day Norway, Denmark, and Sweden. The term probably comes from the Norse word *Vik*, which means inlet or creek, perhaps because many of the Vikings surprise attacks were launched from the small rivers they followed inland from the sea in their longboats. The Norse word for a man who went out raiding was *vikingr*. The Viking raiders were, at least in the early years, people who plundered for their own profit, not for political or religious reasons.

When Vikings of the ninth and tenth centuries went to sea on raiding expeditions, they pillaged and looted a region, and then returned to their homes or other bases with their booty. (Booty is the goods stolen from ships or coastal villages during pirate raids or attacks on enemies in time of war.) This type of activity is piracy. In the later part of the Viking age, though, the Vikings began to invade foreign territory, attacking with military strength and then remaining, often as rulers. They assimilated, or blended in, with the rest of the people of the region, marrying into local families and adopting the Christian religion. While the invasions were frequently very brutal, as most wars were in that age, the Vikings would go on to contribute greatly to their new cultures. These invasions and the later Viking migrations and explorations, do not necessarily fall under the definition of piracy. Viking history is full of illegal raiding intermixed with acts of war.

Masters of the sea

Most Scandinavians were farmers, fishermen, artisans, or traders, and did not go out on pirating expeditions. For reasons not entirely clear to historians, in the late eighth century pirating became an attractive means of getting ahead for many Scandinavian men (and perhaps a woman or two). This was partly because Scandinavia had become overpopulated and there was not enough farmland to sustain everyone.

An important factor in the sudden surge in Viking piracy in the eighth century was the Vikings' mastery at sea. Their well-designed boats gave them supreme power and range. Viking vessels were clinker-built, meaning that they were constructed with overlapping oak planks. Skilled Viking shipbuilders began with a strong oak keel, the beam that extends along the entire length of the bottom of the ship and supports the frame. They fixed a few shaped timbers to the keel, using clinch bolts to fasten them. (Timbers are the frames or ribs of a ship that are connected to the keel and give the hull its shape and strength.) The rest of the framework was added on to this structure, with rows of oak planks, each overlapping the one below.

An eighth-century Viking ship. The Vikings' success as pirates was due in large part to their vessels, which could easily navigate inlets and rivers and were easy to pull ashore. © BETTMANN/CORBIS.

Waterproofing was then applied between planks. Viking vessels were long, narrow, and shallow, making them navigable in inlets and rivers, and they were easy to pull ashore. This gave Vikings the capacity to raid towns and religious centers that were far inland.

The smaller Viking longboats that were used in the early years of raiding generally had from ten to thirteen oars on each side. The larger Viking ships, called *drekar*, or dragon ships, might have had as many as sixty oars, and they were also equipped with large square sails to be raised when the winds were favorable. These ships could travel swiftly across the open sea using their sails, and the crews could then switch to their oars for coastal attacks. Viking ships were far more efficient than other northern European ships, making the Vikings' hit-and-run attacks along the coastline very difficult to stop.

Historians say that Vikings were the most skillful navigators (people who chart the route of their ships) in Europe at the time. They were able to cross open seas using acute visual observation of distant shores. They also used their knowledge of tides, winds, and currents to orient themselves at sea. They frequently relied on island hopping, or crossing from island to island, until a distant destination was reached.

The motley crew

Each member of the crew on a Viking ship had many skills; seamanship was only one part of the mission. The rowers were also trained warriors, ready to jump ship and plunge into their raids. They were armed for this purpose with swords, axes, clubs, spears, and bows and arrows. The sides of the ship bore their shields, each with its owner's emblem (an image that represented him), and most Vikings were protected by a helmet and coat of armor.

Nearly invincible at sea, the Vikings undoubtedly found pirating a great deal more profitable than trading. They apparently had little remorse about attacking Europe's cathedrals and abbeys, with their storehouses of sacred treasures and their lack of organized defense. The coastal villages and towns were equally defenseless. With easier targets, the Vikings were able to attack more communities.

The Vikings expand their raids

The trip from Scandinavia to the British isles was too difficult for the Vikings to attempt during winter weather, so the Vikings set up bases on nearby islands. This allowed them to raid the British shores year-round. They also began to take their longboats up rivers, sailing farther inland for their raids. Over decades of raids, they caused such great destruction to England, Scotland, and Ireland that eventually there was little left for them to take. At that point, they turned to the European continent.

Vikings began their attacks on the continent by raiding the large Frankish kingdoms, which covered much of present-day France, Belgium, the Netherlands, and Germany. Beginning around 799, Vikings sailed up the Seine River to raid the region along the North Sea coast known as Frisia (later Dorestad), an important trading city in what is now the Netherlands, and Rouen, in present-day France. In 843 the Vikings raided Nantes, on the Loire River, and set up a permanent base near the mouth of that river. A similar base appeared a few years later on the island of Oissel, in the Seine River in France, and in 845 the Vikings attacked Paris. The Frankish rulers paid the Vikings tribute money to stay away, but the Vikings took the money and continued raiding. Terrified Franks moved inland and monks carted off church treasures to protected cities.

At the same time, Vikings from Sweden, called the Rus, crossed the Baltic Sea and began to sail inland on the river systems of Russia. They raided these lands, but soon settled in them. (In fact, Russia got its name from the Rus.) Other Viking pirates sailed to the Mediterranean, where they attacked Spain and Italy and then crossed to the Black Sea and Constantinople.

By the early tenth century, Viking raids decreased as Vikings settled in the lands they had previously raided. Viking communities appeared throughout Ireland, England, Scotland, Normandy (in present-day France), Russia, and many other regions.

Mercenary piracy in northern Europe

In the eleventh century, as the Viking age ended, a new surge of piracy struck northern Europe. An improving economy had brought about prosperous trading among the English, Irish, Scots, French, Flemish, and Germanic states. Merchants began to transport their goods in well-traveled trade routes across the Baltic Sea, the North Sea, and the English Channel. But conflicts between the various states in the region prevented the cooperation among them that was needed to keep the sea routes safe.

In the late twelfth century, France fought a series of wars against the English, Flemish, and Germanic states. During this time, the warring nations adopted what would prove to be a dangerous and yet very popular practice: they hired private ship owners to raid enemy ships. At first this entailed hiring mercenaries. (A mercenary is a seaman or soldier hired by a government to fight its battles.) To countries without established navies, these hired seamen allowed them to wage war at sea. But when their services were no longer needed, these mercenaries turned to piracy.

Eustace the Monk One such mercenary was the French adventurer Eustace the Monk (also known as the Black Monk; c. 1170–1217). As his name suggests, Eustace began his career training in a monastery, an unusual start for a pirate. He also apparently had some training as a sailor. Eustace worked for a time in a nobleman's service, but in 1205 his employer accused him of stealing from the estate. Eustace fled and took to the seas as a pirate, somehow managing to get his hands on a ship and crew. From 1205 to 1212, he worked as a mercenary in the service of King John of England (1167–1216). For England, Eustace and his pirate fleet raided the coast of Normandy, and established a pirate base in the Channel Islands. (A pirate base is a place where pirates lived under their own rule and maintained their own defense system.) His large community of sea raiders grew extremely powerful.

Eustace ceased to be a mercenary and became a full-fledged pirate when he began raiding and pillaging the ships and coastal towns of England while he was in that country's service. King John threatened him with arrest for his piracy but then pardoned him when he once again needed Eustace's fleets to fight France. Nevertheless, troubles between the English king and the pirate captain increased. In 1212 Eustace switched sides and began fighting for the French. Five years later, in 1217, the English captured him. The English sailors, who detested Eustace for his arrogance and his many crimes against England, immediately beheaded him. Eustace had caused terror throughout England during his lifetime, but after his death, he became the subject of many colorful legends that depict him as a rebel, trickster, and hero.

Hanseatic League

In medieval times, the region of present-day Germany was comprised of many individual kingdoms. The kingdoms had few economic connections with one another, making trade difficult. In the twelfth and thirteenth centuries, a group of Germanic towns began to form guilds to promote profitable trading with each other and with foreign cities and to secure the trade routes through the Baltic Sea. (Guilds are associations for people or towns with a similar trade or interest.) The guilds were called Hansa. Starting in the Germanic towns of Lübeck and Hamburg, the Hanseatic guilds spread to northern Germanic towns and port cities, eventually reaching out as far as England and Scandinavia. One of the primary goals of the Hanseatic League, as it came to be called, was to fight against piracy in the Baltic and North Seas.

By the twelfth century, pirates from regions including present-day Germany, France, Ireland, and England lurked in coves at entrances to the region's rivers. Their attacks on merchant ships disrupted trade and cost merchants dearly. Because there was no single power strong enough to thwart this ever-increasing problem at sea, the Hanseatic League required member port cities to use their own fleets to fight piracy. Although most members in the Hanseatic League did not have full navies, most had fleets that could be used in the antipiracy campaigns. Their highly efficient ships, called *cogs*, were built from oak. They had a single rudder, high sides, and single square sails. (A rudder is a vertical, flat piece of wood or metal attached with hinges to the ship's stern [rear] that is used to steer the ship.)

The Victual Brothers

In the late fourteenth century, Sweden and Denmark fought each other in a war over who would control Scandinavia. The Hanseatic League sided with

Klaus Störtebeker: The Headless Pirate?

Klaus Störtebeker (c. 1360–1401) was a leader of the Victual Brothers, a confederacy of pirates in the Baltic Sea. Little is known about the life of this commander of pirates, but his legend remains strong six hundred years after his death. Historians believe that Störtebeker was a nobleman who had lost his fortune and was known for his drunkenness. The name Störtebeker, in fact, is a nickname that means "to drink a whole beaker (of beer) in one gulp." Störtebeker took to the seas around 1398. As leader of the Victual Brothers, he started out as a privateer in the service of Sweden and the Hanseatic League, but soon began raiding independently. He was responsible for countless incidents of theft, brutal murder, and even the destruction of entire towns. He and his fellow pirates, though, convinced some people that they were helping the poor and fighting the rich and powerful. However, many historians doubt that the Victual Brothers' raids served much purpose beyond enriching the pirates themselves.

In 1402 a fleet from the German port of Hamburg captured Störtebeker and his shipmates. They were taken to Hamburg where they would be executed by beheading. Legend has it that just before his execution Störtebeker made a deal with his executioners. If he could get up and walk after they had beheaded him, the executioners would spare any of the seventy convicted pirates from his ship that he managed to walk past. As promised, after his execution, the headless pirate commander got up and walked past eleven of his crew members. The executioner, however, stuck out a foot and tripped the corpse before he could save the entire crew.

The people of Hamburg, Germany, are still proud of their pirate traditions. A statue of Störtebeker graces a city park and his severed skull has been preserved in a museum. In 2010 the skull was stolen from the museum. Investigators attribute the theft to the popularity of old-time pirates in modern culture.

Sweden. During the war, the Swedish capital of Stockholm was under siege, or cut off by a military blockade that isolated the city while Danish forces attacked. The Hanseatic League and the Swedish government decided to assemble a group of private ships to break the blockade in order to provide food and other supplies to the city. This group was called the *Vitalienbruder* (the Brotherhood of Suppliers, or more commonly, the Victual Brothers). The group did its job well. By the time Sweden defeated Denmark and the war ended, the Victual Brothers had grown strong, but the Hanseatic League and the Swedish government no longer had any use for them. It was not long before the Victual Brothers began raiding ships in the Baltic that were not enemies of the Hanseatic League. The brotherhood became a major force against the very guild that had formed it.

The Victual Brothers quickly attracted thousands of able-bodied seamen from all over Europe. The new recruits sought either easy profit or adventure, and some were lured by the romantic concept of a brotherhood that stole from the strong and gave to the weak. In fact, the brotherhood did establish charitable foundations and exercised a principle of equality. All of the booty it took from its raids was said to be divided equally among its crews. Yet the Victual Brothers terrorized the populations of the northern European coasts. They pillaged towns, murdering and kidnapping people, stealing religious treasures, and sometimes destroying whole communities. They also raided many ships.

At the height of their success, the Victual Brothers virtually stopped trade in the Baltic. In 1392 they sacked Bergen, Norway's leading city at that time, and set up a base in Visby, Sweden. Alarmed by the pirate confederation's strength, the Hanseatic League strengthened its antipiracy forces and allied itself with the Scandinavian countries. The Victual Brothers were initially too strong for them, but by the early fifteenth century the Hanseatic League had wiped out the rebel group. Piracy in northern Europe, however, would continue to flourish.

Piracy in English waters

Across the sea, England had developed a successful sea trade by the thirteenth century. The increase in trade, though, was accompanied by great turmoil in the fourteenth century, as the Black Death, a severe epidemic of bubonic plague, killed about 30 percent of England's population from 1348 to 1350 and forever changed its social and political structures. War was a constant factor in the fourteenth century as well. Prosperous trade and tumultuous times were key ingredients for a new wave of sea raiding. By the early fourteenth century the English Channel and the North Sea were so crowded with pirates, most merchant ships no longer dared to sail there.

In the thirteenth century, the king of England decided to commission traders and merchants from several English port towns to form a confederacy like the Hanseatic League that would protect the English coast. Cinque Ports (meaning five ports) was originally an alliance of the five southeastern English sea towns that were closest to the French coast: Hastings, Romney, Hythe, Sandwich, and Dover. (Rye and Winchelsea joined the confederation later.) These towns established schools of seamanship and became centers of ship-building in an effort to establish defenses along the coast.

One of the rewards the Cinque Ports members received from the king for their efforts was the right to plunder foreign ships in the English Channel. Like the Victual Brothers, these private ship owners became a primitive form of privateer. (A privateer is a private ship or ship owner commissioned by a state or government to attack the merchant ships of an enemy nation.)

Captains of the Cinque Port ships who became privateers found that raiding ships in the English Channel was extremely profitable. Many soon stopped distinguishing between foreign ships and English ships, raiding solely for profit. Local officials of the member port cities got a hefty share of the booty and often supported the thievery, even when it had turned into unauthorized piracy. A few towns along England's southeastern coast willingly became pirate havens, or safe places where pirates could harbor and repair their ships, resupply, and organize raiding parties.

Privateers, acts of reprisal, and piracy

Licenses, such as the one granted to Cinque Ports members allowing private ships to become privateers, are thought to have originated with English king Henry III (1207–1272) in 1243 as a way for him to harass and annoy England's long-time enemy, France. A form of privateer license, known as the act of reprisal, was established in England during the reign of king Edward I (1239–1307) in 1295. Under this arrangement, when a merchant ship or other private vessel was attacked and plundered by a foreigner at sea, the ship owner could apply to the king for a license to obtain repayment for his loss. The license authorized the ship owner to seize the property of the party that had stolen from him or to take the same amount of property from any ship of the same nation as that wrongdoer. Later, European governments began to issue letters of marque, or documents licensing a private ship owner to the seize ships or goods of an enemy nation. Letters of marque were not restricted to those seeking repayment for losses in enemy raids, as acts of reprisal were.

From 1337 to 1453 England and France fought a series of wars known as the Hundred Years' War, in which they vied for the throne of France. Because both countries lacked royal navies, they frequently licensed privateers to attack their enemies at sea. The kings permitted privateers to plunder enemy ships legally. In return, the privateers had to bring their booty back to the king. The king would then take a percentage of the booty and divide the rest among the ship owners and the captains, who then paid their crews. Attacking ships without authorization was considered piracy and was illegal.

During the Hundred Years' War many privateers turned pirate by plundering ships without making a record of it, thereby depriving the

King Edward I. The act of reprisal was a privateer license established in England during the reign of this king.
© LEBRECHT MUSIC ARTS PHOTO LIBRARY/ALMAY.

king of his share of the booty. Others turned pirate by attacking neutral ships and even ships from their own country. Although they frequently committed brutal acts, including kidnapping and murder, in their raids, the privateers and pirates at this time were usually well respected at home, and they were the best seamen in their lands.

Early privateers of England

The Cinque Ports privateers and pirates were not alone in their raids in the English Channel, Dover Straits, and North Sea. Pirates from other English ports, particularly from the western counties of Devon, Cornwall, and Dorset were competing with them.

One such privateer was John Hawley (c. 1340–1402) of Dartmouth, a port town in the county of Devon. Hawley, an accomplished trader and the long-time mayor of Dartmouth, was granted his first privateer license in 1379. With his fleet of trade ships and well-trained crews, he was immediately successful in his raids on French ships, coming home with an abundance of riches taken from the French. In 1399, for example, he captured 34 French ships. The people of Dartmouth viewed Hawley as a hero and enjoyed the economic boost in their town. Still, along with his legitimate endeavors, Hawley was known for sending his ships on "private" raids that had nothing to do with war and were not licensed. For decades his ongoing pirate business did not hurt his reputation or other endeavors. This changed in the early 1400s when King Henry IV (1366–1413) began to crack down on pirates. Hawley spent some time in the Tower of London and was forced to repay Spanish merchants from whom he had stolen. (The Tower of London was a fortress in London, England, that was famously used as a prison.)

An even more colorful pirate was Harry Pay (known as "Arripay" to the Spanish; c. 1360–1419) of Poole, in the county of Dorset. With authority as a privateer to plunder foreign ships and a fleet at his command, Pay was relentless. He raided French and Spanish ships off the coast of Normandy, in the waters of the Bay of Biscay between France and Spain, and off the coast of Castile, a kingdom in what is now Spain. In his hometown of Poole, his adventures, daring escapes, and capture of hundreds of French and Spanish vessels became legendary. To his French and Spanish victims, though, Harry Pay was a monster. In 1398 he burned the Spanish coastal city of Gijón to the ground and stole the Holy Crucifix from the Church of Santa Maria at Finisterre, an island to which Spaniards made religious pilgrimages, or journeys to a sacred place. The Spanish retaliated by sacking the town of Poole. In 1406 Pay is said to have captured 120 French

Scottish privateer Andrew Barton was defeated and captured by the English in 1511. HULTON ARCHIVE/ GETTY IMAGES.

merchant ships with only 15 ships in his command. Apparently he was not very particular about which ships he attacked, because that same year King Henry IV ordered him to return a ship he had captured to its owner, a London merchant.

Far to the north, Scottish merchant and pirate Andrew Barton (c. 1466–1511) convinced the Scottish king that his father had been robbed and murdered by men on a Portuguese ship many years earlier. The king issued him a letter of reprisal. With the letter in hand, Barton sailed with two ships to Flanders (the region inhabited by the Flemish, in present-day Belgium), where he proceeded to raid and plunder ships of all nations. The king of England finally sent his own ships to stop Barton. Barton's ships were captured in 1511 and added to the English navy.

Many coastal towns had their own famous pirates and proud traditions to go along with them. Port city economies prospered with the incoming booty, and the careers and fortunes of many local officials were given a boost by the illegal plunder of pirates. Thus, when the central government of England tried to enforce antipiracy policies, the locals usually managed to evade these measures.

Despite the pirates' popular acclaim, by the thirteenth and fourteenth centuries the English government began efforts to stop piracy. The seas had become infested with raiders from all countries and trade suffered. Because local communities gave safe harbor to privateers, many did not obey the national laws designed to keep piracy under control. Fearing complete lawlessness at sea, some of the English kings recognized a need for an established system of maritime law that could control piracy on the seas. (Maritime law is the set of regulations that govern navigation and trade on the seas.) This is a tricky area of law, because the seas are not owned or governed by any one nation. Regulating them requires that nations agree about the many different activities upon the seas, including privateering and piracy. For most of the Middle Ages, the few agreements that were reached between nations about rules of the sea were based mainly on customs, not on law.

At the end of the Middle Ages, piracy was on the increase in European waters. Some of Europe's leaders had learned that engaging mercenaries and privateers could wind up doing more damage than good. But the temptation of gaining naval strength and harming one's enemies with very little initial investment was strong. In the centuries to come, the use of privateers would grow rapidly and create overwhelming problems in the world's seas.

For More Information

BOOKS

Anderson, Alan Orr. *Scottish Annals from English Chroniclers: AD 500–1286*. London: D. Nutt, 1908.

Gosse, Philip. *The History of Piracy*. New York: Tudor, 1932, 1995.

Konstam, Angus, with Roger Michael Kean. *Pirates: Predators of the Sea.* New York: Skyhorse Publishing, 2007.

Pulsiano, Philip, and Kirsten Wolf. *Medieval Scandinavia: An Encyclopedia.* NY: Garland Publishing, 1993, p. 166.

Travers, Tim. *Pirates: A History.* Stroud, Gloucestershire, UK: Tempus, 2007.

WEB SITES

"History of the Vikings." *History World.net.* www.historyworld.net/wrldhis/PlainTextHistories.asp?historyid=ab86 (accessed on January 3, 2011).

Rukhadze, Okropir. "The Pirates of Hamburg: From Medieval Romanticism to 21st-Century Reality." *Radio Free Europe Radio Liberty.* www.rferl.org/content/Pirates_Hamburg_Medieval_Romanticism_21st_Century_Reality/2086110.html (accessed on Janueary 3, 2011).

The Barbary Corsairs

The Barbary corsairs were sea-going raiders based in large port cities along the Mediterranean Sea's Barbary Coast, an area roughly encompassing the present-day countries of Morocco, Algeria, Tunisia, and northwest Libya. Barbary Coast piracy was in its heyday from the early sixteenth century to 1820, but during that time it went through three distinct phases. In the first phase, which lasted throughout most of the sixteenth century, the Barbary corsairs were involved in the ongoing war for control of the Mediterranean between Christian forces on the western part of the sea and the Muslim forces on the eastern side. Pirates in the Barbary states usually maintained independence from any government, but during these wars they worked closely with the leaders of the Ottoman Empire, and their fleets were often used against the Christian forces.

The second phase began in the last quarter of the sixteenth century. At that time, the Ottoman Empire ceased fighting in the Mediterranean, but the Barbary corsairs continued to raid ships and coastline communities. By this time, their pirate bases in the port cities of Algiers (present-day Algeria), Tunis (present-day Tunisia), Tripoli (present-day Libya), and later, Sallee (present-day Morocco), were thriving communities. Adventurers were arriving there from all corners of the world to make their fortunes in piracy. Barbary corsairs had acquired new types of sailing vessels and navigation that allowed them to strike out on the open seas far beyond the Mediterranean.

In the last phase, which spanned most of the eighteenth century, the Barbary corsairs were less active. They had persuaded countries that wished to trade in the regions around them to pay for the privilege of not being attacked. In fact, the corsairs had become so powerful that European nations and the United States were forced to appoint ambassadors to deal with them. By the early nineteenth century the Barbary corsairs had pushed Europe and the United States too far, and this proved to be their downfall.

Barbary Coast in the 16th Century
- - - - - 16th century boundary
● Corsair base

FRANCE

ALPS

ATLANTIC OCEAN

PORTUGAL   SPAIN

PYRENEES

Corsica

Sardinia

Balearic Is.

Algiers

Sallee

ATLAS MOUNTAINS   ALGIERS

MOROCCO

Tunis

Sicily

Malta

Mediterranean Sea

Tripoli

TUNIS

N

OTTOMAN EMPIRE

TRIPOLI

0   200   400 mi
0   200   400 km

A map of the Barbary Coast in the sixteenth century. MAP BY XNR INFORMATION SERVICES, INC./CENGAGE LEARNING.

Before Barbary piracy

In ancient times, piracy had been rampant in the Mediterranean Sea, but it was virtually eliminated by the Roman Empire, which maintained control of the region from 27 BCE to 476 CE. (For more information, see **Piracy in the Ancient Mediterranean**.) The western Roman Empire collapsed in 476 after its capital, Rome, was captured by invading Germanic tribes. However, the eastern portion of the empire, which quickly came to be known as the Byzantine Empire, remained strong. The Byzantime Empire, with its capital at Constantinople (present-day Istanbul, Turkey), would thrive for one thousand years.

In the seventh and eighth centuries, trade in the Mediterranean continued to flourish and expand. Great centers of commerce, such as the city-states of Venice, Genoa, and Pisa (all in present-day Italy), traded extensively throughout the coasts of the Mediterranean. (A city-state is an independent, self-governing city and its surrounding territory.) Piracy expanded with the increased trade, but for many centuries, Byzantine naval powers kept it within reasonable limits.

During this period of relative calm, the religion of Islam arose in the Arabian peninsula. Its founder was the prophet Muhammad (c. 570–632).

WORDS TO KNOW

artillery: Large weapons, such as cannons, that discharge missiles.

bey: The word for a local ruler in Tripoli and Tunis.

booty: Goods stolen from ships or coastal villages during pirate raids or attacks on enemies in time of war.

city-state: An independent, self-governing city and its surrounding territory.

corsair: A pirate of the Barbary Coast.

dey: The word for a local ruler in Algiers.

galiot: A small, fast galley using both sails and oars.

galley: A long, low ship used for war and trading that was mainly powered by oarsmen, but might also use a sail.

pirate base: A place where pirates lived under their own rule and maintained their own defense system.

pirate haven: A safe place for pirates to harbor and repair their ships, resupply, and organize raiding parties.

privateer: A private ship or ship owner commissioned by a state or government to attack the merchant ships of an enemy nation.

ransom: A sum of money demanded for the release of someone being held captive.

siege: A military blockade that isolates a city while an attack is underway.

tribute: Payment from one ruler of a state to another, usually for protection or to acknowledge submission.

By 632, the year of Muhammad's death, Muslim believers had established a rapidly growing community that eventually encompassed the Arabian Peninsula and beyond.

In the eighth century the Moors, a people from regions of the Sahara Desert and the Mediterranean coast of Africa, converted to Islam. The Moors invaded the Iberian Peninsula, an area of land belonging to present-day Spain and Portugal in southwest Europe. They established a capital in the southern Spanish kingdom of Cordova. From Cordova, they developed one of the most advanced cultures in Europe at that time, renowned for its great scholars, architects, mathematicians, doctors, and artists. The new Muslim rulers governed non-Muslims in these lands for centuries. At the height of their power, the Moors ruled almost all of the Iberian Peninsula.

Around 1000, the Roman Catholic Church launched the Crusades, a series of military campaigns to take control of the Holy Land (roughly the present-day territory of Israel, the Palestine territories, and parts of Jordan and Lebanon) from the Muslims. Thousands were killed, and the bitterness Muslims felt toward the crusading Christians endured long after the fighting ended near the end of the thirteenth century. During the Crusades, a strong religious fervor swept Europe. The Catholic rulers in the Spanish kingdoms responded by rising up against the Moors. They took control of all the kingdoms on the Iberian Peninsula with the exception of Granada.

Meanwhile, by the thirteenth century, a little-known tribe called the Ottoman Turks emerged in Anatolia (present-day Turkey). First taking over the Muslim countries of the Arabian Peninsula, the Ottomans continued to expand. By the fourteenth century, they had begun making inroads into the Byzantine Empire. By the fifteenth century, they had taken control of Hungary, most of the Balkan Peninsula, and parts of Persia (present-day Iran). In 1453 the Ottomans shocked Europe when they conquered Constantinople and made it their capital, bringing an end to the Byzantine Empire.

Barbary piracy begins

In 1492 Spanish monarchs Isabella (1451–1504) and Ferdinand (1452–1516) captured Granada from the Moors, eliminating the last remaining Muslim kingdom in Spain. Within ten years, they forced the Moors to either leave Spain or convert to Christianity. Tens of thousands of Spanish Muslims, suddenly without a home, migrated across the Mediterranean Sea to the slice of the northern coast of Africa they called the Maghreb, known to Europeans as the Barbary Coast. North Africa had been dominated by the Muslims since the eighth century, but the Ottoman Empire's control over these Barbary states was weak. At the end of the fifteenth century, they were mainly governed by local leaders.

There were already pirate communities on the Barbary Coast. With the immigration of thousands of exiled Moors, these communities grew dramatically. Piracy appealed to many of the newcomers. Sea raiding was one of the few ways to earn a living on the Barbary Coast, where farming was poor and little or no industry existed. And, with bitter memories of their exile from Spain and the brutality of the Crusades, the new corsairs had no qualms about targeting Spanish and Italian vessels and ports. Those who took up sea raiding made arrangements with local rulers. For a percentage of their booty (goods stolen from ships or coastal villages during raids), the ruler would give them use of his ports and a market for their slaves and goods. From the start the corsair raids along the coastlines of Spain and Italy were as successful for the corsairs as they were brutal and terrifying for the Europeans.

Spain responded to the corsair raids by sending its fleets across the Mediterranean to North Africa. The Spanish fleets captured the city of Algiers and built a Spanish fort on the island of Peñon in the city's harbor. For the next seventy-five years, Spain and its allies would struggle desperately with the Ottomans for control of the Mediterranean. The corsairs on the Barbary Coast quickly rose to become a formidable foe.

The Barbarossas

Two brothers from the Greek island of Lesbos, Aruj (c. 1474–1518) and Hizir (c. 1478–1546), appeared in the new pirate communities in the Maghreb in the early sixteenth century. (Both brothers would later become known as Barbarossa, though Hizir would become most famous under this name.) The brothers had excellent naval skills and a determination to attack and steal from Christians in the name of Islam. The brothers initially worked together, with Aruj as the leader. Aruj set up a pirate base, a place where he and his fellow corsairs lived under their own rule and maintained their own defense system, on the island of Djerba, off the coast of Tunis. He made a deal with the ruler of Tunis. Aruj would give him 20 percent of his booty from raiding Christian ships and communities if his corsairs could use the harbor.

Aruj and his crews then proceeded to raid ships and pillage the shores of Spain and Italy. They used money from the goods, human prisoners, and ships captured in their raids to steadily build up their fleet. In 1504 Aruj and his crew, working from two small galleys (long, low ships propelled mainly by oars), attacked and seized two extremely large and well-armed warships belonging to the pope (the head of the Catholic Church). This was a nearly impossible feat that stunned all of Europe. Aruj, a powerful, stocky man with a violent temper and thick red hair and beard, soon became known to Europeans as Barbarossa, a name that means "red beard" in Italian.

Along with many successful raids on ships and coastal villages in Spain and present-day Italy, Aruj made several attempts to seize the forts the Spanish maintained along the Barbary Coast. In one of these raids, he was shot and lost an arm, but this did not stop his raiding. In 1516 he led his forces into the city of Algiers, where he killed the dey (a local ruler in Algiers) and made himself ruler of the city-state. He soon controlled most of the surrounding territory, with the exception of the Spanish fort on Peñon. Aruj was killed by Spanish forces in 1518.

Aruj, one of the Barbarossa brothers, attacked ships belonging to the Pope in 1504.
PRIVATE COLLECTION/PETER NEWARK PICTURES/THE BRIDGEMAN ART LIBRARY INTERNATIONAL.

Upon Aruj's death, his brother Hizir is said to have immediately dyed his beard red as a sign that he would follow in his brother's footsteps. He, too, took on the name of Barbarossa and became even more successful and famous than his brother. Barbarossa shared his brother's hatred of the Christians, but he was a different sort of pirate leader. Barbarossa worked closely with the Ottoman Empire, becoming the recognized ruler of Algiers and an Ottoman commander at sea. From the time of his brother's death until he died in 1547, Barbarossa fought and won many Ottoman battles against Spain and other Europeans. After a successful battle in 1522, the grateful Ottoman sultan gave Barbarossa the title Khayr ad-Din, which means "goodness of the faith" or "gift of God."

Barbarossa captured the Spanish fort on Peñon in 1529. In 1538 he was the commander of the Ottoman fleet when it won an important naval battle, the Battle of Preveza, against renowned Genoese pirate-hunter Admiral Andrea Doria (1466–1560). With Barbarossa's help, the Ottoman Empire further expanded in the Mediterranean. His leadership of the corsairs secured their place in North Africa and left behind a large and highly profitable pirating organization that would endure for centuries.

Although he was an accomplished military leader, Barbarossa was as violent as any of the corsairs. He was responsible for the capture and enslavement of tens of thousands of people. A group of Frenchmen who accompanied him and his corsairs on several violent raids witnessed the corsairs' pillaging of the island of Lipari, off the north coast of Sicily. After the town had surrendered, Barbarossa had the population brought in front of him and ordered that they be cruelly tortured, humiliated, and killed. A French chronicler of the event, as quoted by Tim Travers in *Pirates: A History*, notes, "When we asked them why they treated these people with such cruelty they replied that among them such cruelty was deemed a virtue."

Knights of Malta: the Christian corsairs

The Barbarossa brothers and their corsair fleets had a powerful enemy in their region, the Catholic brotherhood known as the Knights of Malta. The Knights were founded as the Knights Hospitallers of St. John of Jerusalem during the First Crusade (1095–99). The group's original purpose was to care for wounded Christian crusaders in Jerusalem. As the Crusades continued, however, the Knights became a powerful military force against non-Christians. The Catholic pope was the only authority to whom they responded. By the end of the Crusades, the Knights were known for religious fanaticism (extreme intolerance for other views). When the

This painting depicts the siege of Rhodes by the Knights Hospitallers. The Knights held Rhodes until 1522, after which they were allowed to establish a base in Malta and became known as the Knights of Malta.
ART RESOURCE, NY.

Knights sought a new home base after the fall of Jerusalem, many nations did not want them in their territory, because of their fanaticism.

In 1309 the exiled Knights captured the island of Rhodes, an island off present-day Turkey. From their securely defended fortress on the island, the Knights established a profitable trading and piracy business.

Rhodes was in an excellent location in the Mediterranean, allowing the Knights to easily ambush sea-going vessels. The Knights' main goal at sea was to capture Muslims to sell into slavery. The Knights were excellent seamen and highly effective raiders and slave traders, and their raids damaged the Ottoman sea trade. In the early sixteenth century, the Ottomans waged several campaigns to try to force the Knights to leave Rhodes. Although outnumbered, the Knights managed to hold onto the island until 1522, when an Ottoman siege lasting more than six months forced the starving brotherhood into exile once again. (A siege is a military blockade that isolates a city [in this case an island] while an attack is underway.)

Eventually King Charles I of Spain (1500–1558) allowed the Knights to establish a base in Malta, a group of three islands lying in the straits between the Muslim city of Tunis and the Christian island of Sicily, off the coast of Italy. The islands were barren and rocky but they were set "in the path of every corsair raid on the Italian coast," according to Roger Crowley in *Empires of the Sea*. In return for allowing the Knights to settle on Malta, King Charles asked that they also defend the city of Tripoli. In the 1530 lease document granting Malta to the Knights, as quoted by Crowley, Charles required that they "perform the duties of their Religion for the benefit of the Christian community and employ their forces and arms against the perfidious enemies of the Holy Faith."

The Knights of Malta built up a small but strong navy and organized their own fleet of corsairs. The Knights attracted many adventurers from all over the world. These young seamen arrived with the hope of going out raiding and making their fortune on the Maltese galleys—the large, single-decked vessels used in the Mediterranean at that time. The new Christian corsairs flew under the flag of the Knights of Malta and were authorized to raid only Muslim ships. The Knights of Malta, who dedicated themselves to lives of chastity, prayer, and helping Christians in need, were relentless in pillaging Muslims ships and coasts and enslaving Muslim captives. Such treatment was justified, they felt, because the Muslims were infidels, or people who do not follow the Christian religion. Although they differed in religion from the Barbary corsairs, the two groups were alike in many other respects.

The Barbary corsairs vs. the Knights of Malta

The Knights of Malta never had a stronger foe than Dragut Reis (also known as Turgut Reis; 1485–1565), who succeeded Barbarossa as leader of the Barbary corsairs. ("Reis," also spelled "Rais," means "captain" or "chief," and was used as part of many corsair leaders' names.) After his mentor's death, Dragut became known as the "Drawn Sword of Islam." He fought the Spanish and led the Ottoman fleet in an assault on the Knights on their island of Malta. Dragut's forces laid siege to the island in 1551, but the Knights held on. The corsair chief went on to seize Tripoli, and became the bey (a local ruler in Tripoli and Tunis) of that city-state.

In 1557 the Knights of Malta elected French nobleman Jean Parisot de La Valette (c. 1494–1568) as their grand master. La Valette had been captured by the Barbary corsairs in 1541 and forced to serve as a galley slave under the command of Dragut for one year. He hated Dragut and was known as a particularly zealous Christian warrior. In 1565 the Ottoman Empire sent Dragut and his huge corsair fleet to attack Malta again. La Vallette and Dragut were to face each other in battle once again.

The siege of Malta was a lopsided battle from the beginning. There were only about five hundred Knights, aided by an armed group of Maltese residents and a variety of European soldiers, making up a total of between 6,100 and 8,500 combatants on the island. The Ottomans had put together their largest force ever, with as many as 48,000 soldiers and seamen. The brutal battle and following siege lasted three months. Although many were killed on Malta, the determined Knights won out, and the Ottomans and corsairs finally retreated in defeat. Dragut was killed in the battle. The siege of Malta was a huge victory for the Knights of Malta. Many historians consider this Ottoman defeat to be the first sign that the Ottomans would lose the war for control of the Mediterranean.

Uluj Ali (also known as Ochioli; 1520–1587), the Barbary corsair who succeeded Dragut, fought as a leader of Ottoman naval forces in many successful battles. In 1571 he led a force of corsairs and Ottomans against the Holy League—an alliance of Spain, the pope, Venice, Genoa, and the Knights of Malta—in the Battle of Lepanto, one of the major naval battles of that era. The Ottomans lost the battle, although Uluj Ali served with distinction. The loss at Lepanto was devastating to the Ottomans. After this battle, they became far more reluctant to enter into battles in the Mediterranean. It signaled a new era for the corsairs as well. According to pirate historian Philip Gosse in *The History of Piracy*, the loss of the battle meant "the end of the race of pirate kings." The next hundred years was marked by highly successful corsair raiding, but the powerful leadership of the first era would never be duplicated.

The Uskoks: Pirates of the Adriatic

The Barbary corsairs and the Knights of Malta were not the only pirates in the Mediterranean Sea. In the sixteenth century, the Adriatic Sea, the arm of the Mediterranean Sea extending between the Balkan Peninsula and Italy, became the home of a fearsome band of pirates known as the Uskoks.

In the early sixteenth century, the expansion of the Ottoman Empire into the Balkan Peninsula had driven the Uskoks, a group of Christian Serbs and Croats, from their homes. They settled in present-day Croatia on the coast of the Adriatic Sea. The Uskoks, a feisty band of guerilla fighters (irregular forces in armed conflict usually characterized by hit-and-run tactics), had been welcomed there by the Austrian emperor, who offered to pay them to fight the Ottomans and prevent them from encroaching farther into Austrian-held territory.

When the well-armed Ottoman warriors approached the Uskosks' new territory by land, the outnumbered Uskoks quickly learned to attack their enemy at sea. The islands in the surrounding Adriactic provided creeks and inlets that were perfect for the Uskoks to hide in as they waited to ambush Ottoman vessels. Using light, swift boats, the Uskoks raided in a manner similar to the Viking raids of ninth and tenth-century Scandinavia. (For more information, see **Piracy in Medieval Europe**.)

The Austrian emperor failed to pay the Uskoks as promised. They continued to raid Ottoman merchant ships, both for profit and out of hatred for the Ottomans. Piracy became the major economic mainstay of their people.

In 1540 the nearby city-state of Venice, one of the greatest sea powers in the region, entered into a treaty with the Ottomans. The Uskoks felt that anyone who made a pact with the Ottomans was their enemy, and they began to raid Venetian vessels. Venice complained to the Austrian emperor, but he could not stop the Uskoks. Venice's warships then began patrolling the Uskosks' water routes. The determined Uskoks continued to carry out their piracy under the cover of night or bad weather.

Eventually these conflicts at sea resulted in war between Venice and Austria. The two powers arranged a peace treaty in 1617. At that time it was clear to both that the Uskoks were impossible to control. Venice and Austria used their forces to relocate the Uskoks to inland Croatia. The Uskoks, no match for the armies of these powerful nations, had no choice but to comply with the required move to a region where they could no longer carry out their sea raids.

Galleys and galiots

Corsairs could not have gotten away with harassing powerful nations had they not been masters of the sea. Their sea vessels could outmaneuver the ships of kings, popes, and wealthy merchants. Throughout the sixteenth century, Barbary corsairs and the Knights of Malta conducted their raids in large, narrow galleys. They were not very different from the galleys used by pirates in the Mediterranean in ancient times. (For more information, see

A galley of the Barbary corsairs. PRIVATE COLLECTION/THE BRIDGEMAN ART LIBRARY.

Piracy in the Ancient Mediterranean.) The corsairs' galleys usually had from twenty to thirty or more large oars arranged in a single bank, and each oar was powered by three to six men. With all the muscle power at the oars, these lightweight galleys were highly maneuverable.

Corsair galleys had masts and carried along with them sails that could be raised to take advantage of favorable winds. The galleys were enclosed at the back to protect the armed raiders who were carried onboard. At the front end were four or five guns in a strongly built forecastle (the upper deck located at the front of the galley), and there were swivel guns mounted in the midsection. Like many other pirates, the corsairs tried not to use artillery (large weapons such as cannons) when attacking. Artillery fire would damage the ship that they were attacking, and the corsairs wanted to take it home in one piece.

There were problems with corsair galleys. They were not solid enough to sail in the open ocean. As long as the corsairs were using galleys, they stayed close to shore, and raiding was limited to favorable weather conditions. An even more significant limitation was that the galleys did not have the capacity to carry large amounts of water. With as many as 180 oarsmen at work and nearly as many raiders, the need to stop for more drinking water and fresh food was constant; the galleys had to make their way to shore regularly. Another problem was the constant possibility that the many slaves required to power the vessel might at any moment rise up against the corsairs.

Full-size galleys were extremely expensive. Most corsairs used smaller and faster versions called galiots. These had between six and twelve oars, and each oar required only two oarsmen.

Most corsair fleets were owned by investors, who also funded the raiding expeditions. In return the investors received a significant portion of the booty from the corsairs' raids.

Raiding tactics

When the Barbary corsairs spotted a vessel they wished to seize, they usually shot off a cannon to warn the victims they were under attack. Because the corsairs were so feared, most crews did not attempt to fight or flee. Sometimes, though, the approaching corsairs used trickery to make sure the targeted ship did not prepare for battle. They frequently flew the flag of a friendly country and hid below deck, so that their turbans and colorful attire would not give them away. As they approached the victim, the corsairs sometimes shot at the people on deck if they saw signs of resistance to their boarding.

Every corsair galley carried a large troop of armed raiders onboard to carry out the raiding. When they boarded the captured vessel, these raiders screamed and waved their weapons, adding to their captives' fear. If the crew resisted, the fighting corsairs generally overpowered them quickly and sometimes very violently. Soon after securing the vessel, the corsairs would free all Muslim galley slaves from the ship's rowing benches. Next they would examine the ship for its cargo and goods, and if the captain and crew did not tell them where it was, they were likely tortured or killed.

With the cargo investigated, the corsairs turned their attention to the passengers, whose value in terms of potential ransom or price in the slave market was often the biggest prize of the raid. (Ransom is the sum of money demanded for the release of someone being held captive.) The corsairs preferred wealthy captives whose families had money to pay large ransoms. Knowing this, some wealthy passengers traded clothes with their servants as the corsairs approached their ship, hoping to appear poor in order to avoid capture. Other wealthy passengers swallowed their jewelry and coins. The corsairs knew these tricks. They checked their captives' hands to see if there were calluses from working. If there were none, they assumed they had captured a wealthy person. They threatened torture, particularly *bastinado*, or beating the soles of the feet, when looking for valuables. At times they even forced the passengers to drink a liquid that made them vomit up whatever they had swallowed.

After securing the captives and searching the galley for plunder, the pirates determined whether they wanted to keep the vessel they had seized. If so, one of the favored corsairs was chosen to be captain, and he set a course for their home port, drawing from the galley's Christian crew to replace the Muslims on the rowing benches. Finding enough slaves to keep a fleet of galleys in service was an eternal problem for the Barbary corsairs. The need for slaves necessitated that they continue raiding.

After ransacking the ship, the corsairs tallied up the value of the cargo and human captives. They usually owed a portion of the booty to the local bey and another portion might go to the Ottoman Empire. The rest would go to the ship owners to be divided in agreed-upon portions among the ship's crews.

Slavery and redemption

Human captives were the most lucrative prize for the corsairs. Although there are no accurate estimates, some historians contend that well over one million Europeans were captured by the Barbary corsairs and enslaved in the major Barbary states from the early sixteenth century through the early nineteenth century. Slave trading was a huge, well-organized, and highly profitable business.

The threat of being captured and enslaved was not limited to ship passengers. Corsairs raided the coastal villages in western Mediterranean regions, particularly Italy and Spain and their outlying islands, sometimes taking an entire population of a town captive. All along the coasts of the western Mediterranean, communities set up alarm systems to warn of the approach of corsair raiders. When the alarms sounded, residents fled their homes to hide from the corsairs. Sometimes the corsairs would capture a group of inhabitants of a coastal town and then return to the town the next day to bargain with their captives' families about the ransom price. If they were not paid an immediate ransom, the corsairs took the captives to a slave-trade port to be sold.

Captives of corsair raids faced a miserable journey to the North African slave-trade ports. When they arrived, they were held in damp, filthy underground prisons called *bagnios* while their captors determined their

Captives of the Barbary corsairs who could not be ransomed became slaves. Being a galley slave was the worst fate of all. PRIVATE COLLECTION/PETER NEWARK HISTORICAL PICTURES/THE BRIDGEMAN ART LIBRARY INTERNATIONAL.

value. Wealthy captives and captives that were trained in a specialized trade were most valuable. Once the backgrounds of the captives had been determined, the bey of the port city viewed the group and selected for himself the best of the bunch. The rest were taken to the slave auction, a humiliating experience of being paraded through the city streets.

The lives of slaves in the Barbary Coast varied greatly. For people who went to work in a specialized trade or as a household servant, the life was, according to most reports, generally tolerable. Many of these slaves were paid a small amount for their work, and some were eventually able to buy their way out of slavery. Others used their savings to create their own businesses. Some married local women and raised families.

The lives of general laborers were more difficult. They lived in the bagnios with barely enough food to survive. By day they were forced to do back-breaking work on public projects, such as hauling huge stones to build up a harbor, breaking rocks in a quarry, or hauling building materials. By Islamic law, though, the laborers' work stopped three hours before sundown every day, and there was no work on Friday, the Sabbath, a day of rest and worship for Muslims.

Being a slave in a galley was the worst fate of all. By many accounts, galley slaves were chained, nearly naked, to their one-foot-wide benches for the duration of an expedition—sometimes a month or two at a time. When the galley was in pursuit of another ship, they were driven to row full force, pushed well past the point of exhaustion by the overseer's whip upon their backs. They were fed just enough food and water to be able to keep rowing without fainting, and they were frequently deprived of sleep. Observers said they could smell the galleys from a distance because, being chained in place and having no bathroom facilities, the slaves frequently sat in their own waste. Overwork and rampant disease killed many galley slaves. When they died, they were thrown overboard and the corsairs found a replacement for their post.

People in Europe were greatly concerned for the Christians in Barbary captivity. Paying ransom to obtain their release became a popular cause. Pamphlets describing the ordeals of the captives, and particularly the adventures of the few who were able to escape captivity, were widely read and often highly sensational. Bargaining for ransom required intermediaries (go-betweens), and this role was often fulfilled by religious orders. The Order of the Holy Trinity for Redemption of Captives, founded in Provence (in present-day France) during the Crusades, was one of the largest orders to take on the task of freeing Barbary captives. The priests of the Trinity claimed to have freed more than thirty thousand captives (although many historians consider this an exaggeration). In England redemption of captives generally fell to taxpayers or charitable groups. Unfortunately, the majority of the money raised was squandered on publicity and other misguided expenses in Europe and never made it to North Africa.

For all captives, one way out of slavery was to accept Islam as their religion. Not surprisingly, thousands of captured Europeans did exactly that. Some only professed their religious conversion. They pretended to live as Muslims in the Barbary states and waited for a chance to return to Europe. A large number of captives willingly converted to Islam and became Barbary corsairs themselves.

Miguel de Cervantes and the Barbary Corsairs

In 1575 two young Spanish soldiers were among the many people captured and sold into slavery by the Barbary corsairs. Miguel de Cervantes y Saavedra (1547–1616) and his brother Rodrigo were captured while they were traveling home after fighting in the Battle of Lepanto (1571), a huge naval battle off the southern coast of Greece, in which Spain and its allies fought against the Ottoman naval forces and the Barbary corsairs.

After capture, the Cervantes brothers were taken to Algiers. From there, their purchasers made ransom demands of their family. The Cervantes, a family of modest means, were only able to come up with enough money to pay the ransom on Rodrigo. Miguel remained captive in Algiers for five years. He made three or four escape attempts, but each time he was caught and returned to captivity. Like other captives, Cervantes was frequently shackled and threatened with death by impalement, or execution by driving a long stake through the length of a person's body and then leaving the person to die a slow and painful death. Finally, in 1580, the priests of a Christian religious group called the Order of the Holy Trinity for Redemption of Captives were able to pay his ransom. Cervantes returned home to Spain,

Miguel de Cervantes y Saavedra was the most famous captive of the Barbary corsairs. PUBLIC DOMAIN.

where he would eventually write the book *Don Quixote*, which is considered the first novel and one of the greatest classics of Western literature. Cervantes was the most famous captive of the Barbary corsairs.

Renegades

By the last quarter of the sixteenth century, the Barbary corsairs were a multinational lot, with English, French, Flemish, Dutch, Italian, and many other nationalities among them. Some were initially captured by the corsairs and persuaded to convert, but others made their way to North Africa voluntarily, only too glad to join the corsairs and try their hands at making a fortune at sea. In fact, by the end of the sixteenth century, Christian converts from European countries made up almost two-thirds of the corsairs on the Barbary Coast. Many descriptions of these renegades, as the Christian converts were called, are far from flattering. Visiting Europeans and local residents alike viewed them as foul-mouthed, drunken, unruly, and often violent.

Two prominent renegades in the first years of the seventeenth century were the English pirate captain John (Jack) Ward (c. 1533–1622) and the Dutch pirate Simon de Danser (also known as Siemen Danziger or Zymen Danseker; c. 1579–c. 1611). As a young seaman, Ward had hopes of being a privateer in the service of England. (A privateer is a ship owner commissioned by a state or government to attack the merchant ships of an enemy nation.) He, as quoted by Christopher Lloyd in *English Corsairs on the Barbary Coast*, was known to lament about the "good old days" of piracy, "when we might sing, drab [spend time with prostitutes], swear and kill men as freely as your cakemakers do flies; when the whole sea was our empire where we robbed at will."

Ward seized a French ship and made his way to Tunis in the early seventeenth century. There he obtained the protection of a powerful Ottoman military leader. Soon he had a huge fleet of corsairs and was capturing large, richly laden ships all over the Mediterranean. His reputation drew many renegades to Tunis to serve in his fleet. Ward was a colorful but extremely immoral person. When asked if he would work in the service of France, Ward replied, as quoted by Lloyd, "I favour the French? I tell you if I should meet my own father at sea I would rob him and sell him when I had done." In 1608 he tried to purchase a pardon in England so that he could return to his home without being arrested for his piracy. When that failed, he led a life of luxury in a castle in Tunis, where he remained until his death.

Simon de Danser had worked his way from common seaman to commander of a ship before the temptation to become a pirate overtook him. Like Ward, he began his life of sea raiding by stealing a ship. In 1606 he arrived in Algiers, where his pirating exploits were already famous. He teamed up with Ward for a time, but based his piracy in Algiers, while Ward anchored in Tunis. In three years of raiding from Algiers, Danser is said to have brought in or sunk an estimated forty ships, earning him the name of "Devil Captain" among the locals. He had a reputation for treating the local corsairs with cruelty and was known on at least one occasion to have abandoned his entire crew when it served his purpose.

After three years on the Barbary Coast, Danser received a pardon from France and returned, a wealthy man, to his former home in Marseilles. He brought with him goods he had stolen from Algiers. In 1622 the French king requested that Danser return to Tunis to negotiate for the return of some captured ships. When Danser arrived, the bey of Tunis pretended to welcome him and invited him into his castle. As Danser entered, the castle's gates slammed shut. The bey had Danser beheaded and his body was thrown into a ditch to repay him for his thievery and abuse of Tunisian seamen.

Round ships

When Danser came to the Barbary Coast, he brought with him an extensive knowledge of the latest advances in shipbuilding and navigation, and he shared this information freely with the corsairs at Algiers. He promoted the use of the "round ship," a large sailing ship that could be operated with a small crew, eliminating the constant need for galley slaves. Soon the Barbary Coast became a center of shipbuilding, and the new round ships changed the way Barbary corsairs operated. Although they continued to use galleys for some of their local raids, with round ships the corsairs were able to pass through the Straits of Gibraltar and into the Atlantic Ocean for the first time. They quickly became as skillful at raiding on the high seas as they had been in the Mediterranean.

Using their new round ships, the Barbary corsairs traveled as far as England, and between 1609 and 1625, the corsairs captured nearly five hundred English vessels. In 1631 an adviser to the king of England wrote to the king to plead for ransom money for captured English seamen. He noted, as quoted by Gosse, "They say that unless you send speedily they will go to England and fetch men out of their beds as they commonly used to in Spain." It was not long before corsair fleets arrived in the Thames River and raided the coasts of western England.

One renegade who took advantage of the new round ships was Dutch pirate Jan Janszoon van Haarlem (c. 1570–c. 1641), a young seaman drawn to the Barbary Coast by the prospect of making his fortune as a corsair. He converted to Islam and became known as Murat Reis (also spelled Rais). Murat was settled in the relatively new pirate haven of Salé (also spelled Sallee), in Morocco. (A pirate haven is a safe place for pirates to harbor and repair their ships, resupply, and organize raiding parties.) There he made a successful career of sea raiding. Until 1627 Salé had been at least nominally governed by the sultan of Morocco, but Salé's large population of corsairs—and the businessmen who thrived on their booty—revolted and set up their own republic. Murat became the first president of the new and thriving pirate republic of Salé. The corsairs based there, known as the Sallee Rovers, were feared throughout vast regions along the Mediterranean Sea and Atlantic Ocean.

After a time, Murat grew weary of leading the republic. He moved to Algiers and returned to raiding. In 1627 he organized an expedition to the faraway island of Iceland in the North Atlantic. There, finding few riches to raid, Murat and his crew took hundreds of Icelanders captive and brought them back to the Barbary Coast. In 1631 Murat and his crews raided the village of Baltimore, in West Cork, Ireland, taking more than one hundred people back to Algeria in chains.

The decline of the corsairs and their legacy

Although the Barbary corsairs disrupted trade, destroyed entire towns, and caused great misery, the European nations were often too busy fighting with each other to make serious attempts to stop them. Instead, European nations entered into treaties with the corsairs that required the Europeans to pay tribute to the corsairs and Barbary Coast rulers. (A tribute is payment from one ruler of a state to another, usually for protection or to acknowledge submission.) The Europeans paid handsomely for the corsairs not to raid their merchant vessels at sea. Even with tribute payments coming in, however, the corsairs continued their raiding.

In the second half of the seventeenth century, England began sending out naval forces to fight pirates. These campaigns greatly damaged corsair fleets and the ports of the Barbary Coast. Toward the end of the century, the French also launched antipiracy campaigns. Although the Europeans won the battles and the corsairs signed treaties promising to stop their raiding, within a short time they resumed their piracy.

Around this time the English colonies in North America won their independence from England and formed the United States. The new nation's merchants, like European merchants, were frequently raided by the Barbary corsairs. To maintain trade, the United States was compelled to pay a huge tribute to Algiers to protect its ships from Barbary piracy. In 1799, for example, the United States sent Algiers a payment of fifty thousand dollars, as well as twenty-eight guns, ten thousand cannon balls, and much more. Tunis and Tripoli also demanded tribute. Tensions increased, and when the United States fell behind in its tribute payments to Tripoli, the ruler of that city declared war. In 1804 the United States dispatched a squadron from its new navy. A U.S. blockade at Tripoli convinced the leaders there to sign a treaty ending U.S. tribute payments.

This painting depicts the attack on the Barbary corsairs at Algiers by the British in 1816. PRIVATE COLLECTION/THE STAPLETON COLLECTION/THE BRIDGEMAN ART LIBRARY INTERNATIONAL.

The treaty broke down in 1812 as the United States and Great Britain fought each other in the War of 1812 (1812–15).

By 1815 Europe and the United States were at peace and agreed to renew their efforts against the Barbary corsairs. The United States won an initial victory over the Barbary states. Great Britain followed in 1816 in an assault that left the corsair fleets and much of the harbor of Algiers in flames. These victories diminished but did not stop the corsair raiding. In 1820 France finished the job. It sent a huge fleet to Algiers, bombed the port, and moved in 37,000 soldiers to occupy the city. Over time, the French conquered Tunis as well. Although random pirate raids continued, the age of the Barbary corsair ended with the French occupation of the Barbary Coast.

For More Information

BOOKS

Cordingly, David, ed. *Pirates: Terror on the High Seas from the Carribean to the South China Sea.* East Bridgewater, MA: World Publications Group, 1998, 2008.

Crowley, Roger. *Empires of the Sea: The Siege of Malta, the Battle of Lepanto, and the Contest for the Center of the World.* New York: Random House, 2008, p. 43.

Gosse, Philip. *The History of Piracy.* New York: Tudor, 1932, 1995, p. 40.

Lloyd, Christopher. *English Corsairs on the Barbary Coast.* London: William Collins Sons, 1981, p. 49.

Travers, Tim. *Pirates: A History.* Stroud, Gloucestershire, UK: Tempus, 2007, p. 208.

PERIODICALS

Lunsford, Virginia. "What Makes Piracy Work?" *USNI (U.S. Naval Institute) Proceedings Magazine* (December 2008). Available online at www.usni.org/magazines/proceedings/story.asp?STORY_ID=1693 (accessed on January 3, 2011).

WEB SITES

Davis, Robert. "British Slaves on the Barbary Coast." *BBC: British History in Depth.* www.bbc.co.uk/history/british/empire_seapower/white_slaves_01.shtml (accessed on January 3, 2011).

Drye, Willie. "Pirate Coast Campaign Was U.S.'s First War on Terror, Authors Say." *National Geographic News.* www.nohum.k12.ca.us/tah/learninglabs/BarbaryPirates/barbary_pirates.htm (accessed on January 3, 2011).

The Privateers of the Spanish Main

In the sixteenth century Spain was caught up in seemingly endless wars. The nation was involved in wars with France, England, and the Netherlands. Spain also had to defend itself in the Mediterranean Sea against the Barbary corsairs, pirates from the southern coast of the Mediterranean Sea in northern Africa. (For more information, see **The Barbary Corsairs**.) On top of all this, Spain was targeted by sea raiders who had been licensed by its European enemies to attack its ships and coastal cities in the distant seas of the Americas.

Sea raiding in the sixteenth-century Americas was rooted in the ongoing wars in Europe, but it was also a response to Spain's unrelenting hold over the resources of the New World. After finding vast stores of gold, silver, and other treasures (much of which were stolen from native civilizations), Spain enforced a strict monopoly, or exclusive control, on colonization and trade in the Americas. France, England, and the Netherlands wanted to gain access to the New World for their own exploration and profit. Spain was already Europe's leading power, and these countries sought to thwart its expanding empire and wealth. During their wars with Spain, all three countries licensed private ship owners to attack Spanish ships and ports. The licenses allowed the ship owners, called privateers, to legally seize shiploads of silver, gold, and other treasures being shipped back to Spain from the Americas.

The region in the Americas from which the treasures were transported was known as the Spanish Main. This region spanned from the Isthmus of Panama, the narrow piece of land between the Caribbean Sea and the Pacific Ocean that joins the North American continent to the South American continent in present-day Panama, to the mouth of the Orinoco River in Venezuela, and included some of the outlying Caribbean Islands. The Spanish Main was a perfect place for sea raiding. There were abundant riches, scarce naval forces to patrol the coasts and waters, and many

WORDS TO KNOW

act of reprisal: A document granting permission to individuals to raid the vessels of an enemy in response to some harm that enemy had done.

admiralty court: A court that administers laws and regulations pertaining to the sea.

booty: Goods stolen from ships or coastal villages during pirate raids or attacks on enemies in time of war.

caravel: A small, highly maneuverable sailing ship.

convoy: A collection of merchant ships traveling together for protection, often escorted by warships.

flota: A Spanish treasure fleet that transported goods and riches from the New World to Spain every year.

galleon: A large, square-rigged sailing ship with three or more masts that was used for commerce and war.

knight: A man granted a rank of honor by the monarch for his personal merit or service to the country.

letter of marque: A document licensing a private ship owner to the seize ships or goods of an enemy nation.

maritime: Relating to the sea.

monopoly: Exclusive control or possession of something.

musket: A muzzle-loading shoulder gun with a long barrel.

privateer: A private ship or ship owner commissioned by a state or government to attack the merchant ships of an enemy nation.

prize: The goods, human captives, and ships captured in pirate raids.

ransom: A sum of money demanded for the release of someone being held captive.

reprisal: An act of revenge against an enemy in wartime.

unsettled islands where raiders could anchor their ships and lay in wait for their prey.

Origins of the Spanish Main

Spain's empire in the New World began in 1492 when Christopher Columbus (1451–1506), an Italian seafarer in the service of Spain, arrived on islands in the Caribbean Sea. Mistakenly thinking he had found a route to Asia, Columbus called the islands the West Indies. When he returned to Spain to report his findings, a new era of Spanish exploration and conquest began.

One of the most immediate issues facing Spain after Columbus's discovery was its right to claim the New World lands. This worried some

Europeans. Spain had long been attempting to compete with Portugal's highly profitable trade with Africa and Asia, and competition for trade had caused many wars in the past. Thus the pope, the head of the Roman Catholic Church, established the Treaty of Tordesillas in 1494. The treaty divided the world in half with an imaginary line running from north to south. Portugal was granted authority to control the non-Christian lands to the east of the line and Spain was granted control of the lands to the west. At the time, no one knew that beyond the western line lay the North and South American continents. (Present-day Brazil, which extended to the east of the line, would become Portuguese territory.) Spain and Portugal signed the treaty. Because it was issued by the pope, they believed they had a God-given right to build empires on their sides of the world. The other major powers of Europe were not included in the treaty and did not sign it.

The Spanish exploration of the Americas that followed was bold and rapid. By the early 1500s explorers and conquistadors (conquerors) had created rough outposts on the Caribbean islands of Cuba, Hispaniola (present-day Haiti and the Dominican Republic), Jamaica, and Puerto Rico. Most explorers were searching for riches, however, and in terms of gold and silver, the islands were disappointing. In fact, the Spanish called many of the Caribbean islands *Islas Inútiles* (useless islands) and did not establish settlements on them. The explorers continued their search for riches on the continent.

In 1519 Spanish conquistadors under the leadership of Hernán Cortés (1485–1547) marched into the lands of the wealthy and sophisticated Aztec civilization of present-day Mexico. Here they found what they were looking for—evidence of abundant gold and precious gems in the glittering Aztec artwork and buildings. Within two years the conquistadors attacked the Aztec city of Tenochtitlán. After a long and brutal battle, the Spaniards defeated the Aztecs and destroyed the city, building Mexico City on top of the ruins.

Riches abound

In Spain the news of Cortés's discovery of abundant riches stimulated more exploration and conquest. In fact, during the sixteenth century, an estimated two to three hundred thousand Spaniards traveled to the New World to make their fortune. In 1532–1533 Spanish conquistadors, led by Francisco Pizarro (c. 1475–1541), destroyed the wealthy Inca Empire in Peru. Once again the conquest yielded enormous treasures. Massive amounts of gold were melted down and shipped back to Spain.

Later Spanish expeditions revealed productive silver mines, notably in Potosí (in present-day Bolivia), and in Zacatecas, Mexico. Potosí, discovered in 1545, became the world's largest source of silver. There Native Americans and, later, African slaves were forced to mine silver ore from Cerro Rica ("Rich Hill"). The slaves also labored in the processing mills that turned the ore into ingots, or metal bars. Slaves loaded the bars onto mules that carried them overland to the ports of Cartagena (in present-day Colombia) and Portobelo, on the Isthmus of Panama. The silver was stored in the port cities, awaiting shipment to Spain. Cartagena, which was founded in 1533, became one of the major ports of the Spanish Main. Other major port settlements included Havana, Cuba, and Santo Domingo, Hispaniola.

Spain strictly enforced its Treaty of Tordesillas rights in the New World. It viewed the vast region extending from South America all the way up to Canada as the exclusive property of Spain. People in Spanish settlements were not allowed to trade with other nations. Foreign ships that were seized and found to be holding goods that had been purchased in the Spanish New World were treated as pirate ships.

French privateers

After Cortés and his troops ransacked the Aztecs, it was their duty to send a large portion of the treasures to their king in Spain. In 1523 Cortés loaded three caravels (small, highly maneuverable sailing ships) full of treasures seized from Tenochtitlán, including: gold, silver, jade, and pearls as well as statues, jewelry, and exquisite robes and masks. The treasure ships sailed for Spain, but two of them never made it. As they passed the southern coast of Portugal, a ship owner named Jean Fleury (or Florin) of Honfleur (d. 1527) spotted them. At that time, France and Spain were fighting each other in the Four Years' War (1521–27), and Fleury was serving as a privateer for the French. Knowing nothing of the treasures that the ships carried, Fleury led the capture of two of them. He was astonished to find the holds full of Aztec gold and jewels. News of Fleury's raid soon reached France, where the idea of the exotic and immense Aztec treasure dazzled the French public. To many seafarers, the life of a privateer suddenly looked very appealing.

In his raid on the caravels, Fleury had acted as a licensed privateer. The French viewed his seizure of the Spanish treasure as a legitimate act of war. The Spanish, on the other hand, claimed their treasure had been stolen. They captured Fleury in 1527 and hanged him as a pirate, along with 150 of his men. Fleury's hanging infuriated the French king, who refused to accept Spain's monopoly on the American continents. The king began to issue letters of marque to private ship owners. These documents granted them the right to attack the Spanish ships and coastal settlements in the Spanish Main.

Few records of the French privateers have survived; they are best known for the destruction they caused in their raids. The French privateers started their raiding in the Spanish Main slowly, capturing a Spanish ship near Panama in 1536. In 1537 French privateers raided several Spanish ships and the major port cities of Cartagena, Nombre de Dios in Panama, Havana, and Santo Domingo.

Two sixteenth-century French privateers did gain notoriety. François Le Clerc (often called Jambe de Bois, or "peg leg," because of his wooden leg) and Jacques de Sores were responsible for devastating attacks on Cuba in 1554 and 1555. Before arriving in the Caribbean, Le Clerc had lost his leg and the use of one of his arms in a pirating raid off the English coast. He was already known for a vicious attack on a port in the Canary Islands. De Sores was a Huguenot, a French Protestant. The Huguenots had been severely persecuted by the Catholics who ruled France, and de Sores detested Catholics.

As war between the French and Spanish raged in 1553, Le Clerc and de Sores received a commission from the French king to raid in the Spanish Main. They gathered a fleet of three royal ships and several private vessels and sailed with a crew of three hundred men to the Caribbean. In 1554 Le Clerc led the fleet into the harbor of Santiago, at that time Spain's largest settlement on Cuba. Le Clerc's men crushed the settlement's defenses and spent over a month destroying the port. Their attack on Santiago was so devastating the city never fully recovered.

The next year de Sores led a large-scale attack on the weakly defended port of Havana, which was quickly captured. Although accounts of the raid on Havana differ, apparently de Sores did not find the treasure he was seeking there and so demanded a ransom to be paid to free the town and his prisoners there. (A ransom is a sum of money demanded for the release of someone being held captive.) When he did not receive the ransom money, he and his men went on a rampage, brutally murdering some of the

The Privateer System in Sixteenth-Century Europe

Privateers were private ships and ship owners who were commissioned by their governments to attack the merchant ships of an enemy nation. The practice dated back to the system of reprisal (retaliation or revenge), which originated in ancient times. Under the system of reprisal, when a merchant ship or other private vessel was attacked and plundered by a foreigner at sea, the ship owner could apply to the king or queen for a license granting him permission to obtain compensation for his loss. The monarch then issued the license, often called an act of reprisal, which authorized the ship owner to seize the property of the party that had stolen from him— or to take the same amount of property from any ship flying under the flag of the same nation as that of the wrongdoer. Monarchs who used the system of reprisal were generally not interested in the ship owners' losses. They wanted to hurt their enemies by attacking their merchant ships. Perhaps even more importantly, they wished to bring their enemies' money into their own treasuries.

Most sixteenth-century privateers were seamen who had the courage and the necessary skills to inflict damage on an enemy's navy and merchant ships. The ships they sailed varied. Some were warships and some were merchant ships converted to their uses; others were much smaller. A privateer might do its raiding alone or join a squadron of private ships. Throughout the sixteenth century, privateers were frequently called on to assist the royal navies of their countries.

Some privateers were responsible for equipping their own vessels and hiring their own crews, although many were sponsored by their monarchs or by investors who took a part of the prize. In most cases, the monarch received one-fifth of the prize. Privateers, unlike pirates, worked within their country's legal system. Admiralty courts (courts that administer laws and regulations pertaining to the sea) judged their prizes and divided them up among the captain (who divided it further to pay the crew), owners or investors, and the monarch.

By the sixteenth century, the privateering system had evolved. Letters of marque and other commissions were usually issued to privateers to redress the nation's injuries from an enemy rather than the privateers' personal losses. Authorization for privateering was, at least in theory, only issued when the country of the raiding party was at war with the country of the seized ship. When wars ceased, however briefly, the privateers were no longer licensed to raid. Although there were many exceptions to this rule, it was a very important distinction. For a privateer, possessing a legitimate letter of marque or any other form of license from his country distinguished him from a pirate, and pirates were usually hanged if captured.

captives, including some African slaves. The privateers burned the town to the ground, caused massive damage to the surrounding countryside, and vandalized the Catholic church. De Sores's hatred of Catholics and his cruelty again became apparent in 1570, when he captured a Portuguese ship. Onboard were thirty-eight Jesuits (members of a Roman

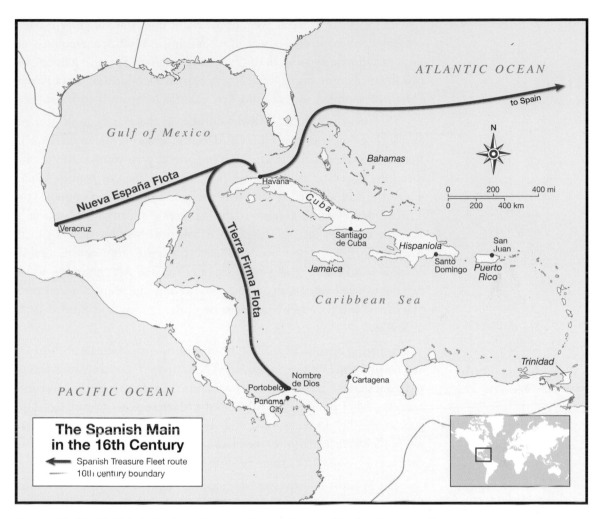

A map of the Spanish Main in the sixteenth century, showing the route of the Spanish treasure fleets. MAP BY XNR PRODUCTIONS INC./CENGAGE LEARNING.

Catholic religious order), and de Sores cold-bloodedly threw all of them overboard to drown.

Safety in numbers: the Spanish flotas

Spain was outraged by the privateer attacks on its ships and colonies. But with its many ongoing wars, it did not have enough money or forces to adequately protect its colonies, and the region was too vast to patrol. After suffering losses in the French raids, Spain decided to institute a convoy system. (A convoy is a collection of merchant ships traveling together for protection, often escorted by warships.) Starting in 1562, Spain required all ships carrying trade goods from the Spanish Main to Spain to join one of two flotas (treasure fleets)—the Nueva España Flota or the Tierra Firma Flota—that formed annually and were escorted by Spanish warships.

The two convoys began their journeys in the rich Spanish port of Seville. The Nueva España Flota sailed for the coasts of Mexico each April. Initially it anchored at Veracruz, but because of poor weather conditions there, the flota later made landfall near the island of San Juan de Ulúa. There, the fleet was loaded with silver and gold from Mexico's mines. The Tierra Firma Flota, also known as the "Galeones" (Spanish for "galleon") after the warships that accompanied it, sailed to Nombre de Dios each August. This destination, too, was later changed to the more favorable conditions at Portobelo, also on the coast of Panama. After the ships of the two flotas were loaded with goods at the two separate ports, they sailed to Havana, where they combined into one huge convoy and headed back to Seville.

In 1561 a Spanish expedition from Mexico crossed the Pacific Ocean and occupied the Philippine Islands. There, Spanish traders gained access to Japanese and Chinese goods. They shipped products such as silk, ivory, and porcelain from the Philippines to the Mexican port of Acapulco. The goods were then loaded onto a mule train bound for San Juan de Ulúa, where they were loaded with the silver and other goods from Mexico onto the Nueva España Flota ships heading back to Seville.

The Spanish galleons were large sailing ships, weighing from 300 to 500 tons (272 to 454 metric tons). Each ship had three masts and square sails that required them to sail with the wind coming from behind them, which caused delays during unfavorable weather. The galleons had large forecastles (upper decks with shelters located at the front of the ship) and raised decks at the rear of the ships, and they were built to hold large amounts of cargo. They were equipped with fifty or sixty heavy cannons and carried up to two hundred crew members. As a consequence, the Spanish galleons could be slow and difficult to maneuver.

By some estimates, Spanish ships carried more than 180 tons (163 metric tons) of gold and 16,000 tons (14,515 metric tons) of silver from the New World to Spain in the period between 1500 and 1650—more than anyone could have previously imagined. Estimates of the wealth taken from the Americas are staggering. John Christopher Fine, author of

A Spanish galleon. These large, heavy ships were slow and difficult to maneuver. © BETTMANN/CORBIS.

Treasures of the Spanish Main: Shipwrecked Galleons in the New World, cites estimates of twenty billion dollars worth of gold and silver shipped from the Spanish Main to Spain in the period from the early sixteenth century to the early nineteenth century. According to pirate historian David Cordingly, the treasures shipped to Spain from the New World in the four-year period between 1596 and 1600 were worth 34,428,500 pesos, which would be valued at about $774 million in the twenty-first century.

The flota system, which continued into the eighteenth century, was expensive and limiting to merchants, who could not ship goods as often as they liked. But as a protection against pirates and privateers, the system worked well. In its entire history, there were only two incidents of ships in the convoys being seized.

The English sea dogs

Forty years of French and Spanish warfare ended in 1559. While French privateers had been the main threat to Spanish ports and ships in the early part of the sixteenth century, English privateers took over in force in the second half of the century.

England had gotten a late start in developing its empire in the New World, mainly due to a lack of money for exploration. In addition, England and Spain had been allies for many years so there was little incentive for England to disrupt Spanish interests in the Americas. In 1554 England's Catholic queen Mary I (1516–1558) married the Spanish heir to the throne, Philip II (1527–1598), creating a temporary, but strong, Catholic alliance between the nations. But when Mary died in 1558, her half sister, the Protestant Elizabeth I (1533–1603), took the throne. Philip, who viewed Spain as the protector of the Roman Catholic Church, began to conspire to undermine the rule of Elizabeth. The English queen responded by secretly engaging privateers to harass Spain's ships. In time she would build up the Royal Navy to fight the Spanish, but in the meantime, Elizabeth's "sea dogs," or privateers, private seamen such as John Hawkins (1532–1598) and Francis Drake (c. 1540–1596), became some of the most accomplished and feared forces on the seas.

John Hawkins and the Battle of San Juan de Ulúa

In 1562 John Hawkins obtained financing from a group of wealthy merchants for a venture in which he would obtain slaves from Africa and trade them in the New World. Despite the Spanish ban on trading in the Americas, Hawkins was confident that he could trade with the settlers, because they desperately needed laborers for their mining and agricultural plantations. Hawkins set off for Africa, equipped with three ships. Off the coast of Sierra Leone, Hawkins's small fleet raided Spanish and Portuguese ships, stealing slaves and other goods from them. The trading in the Caribbean went well, but the Spanish caught up with Hawkins on his way home and captured two of his ships. Even with only one ship left on his return, Hawkins's expedition proved profitable.

Hawkins ventured on a second slave trading expedition in 1564. The queen, impressed with the success of his first trip, loaned him a royal ship, which was a sign that she approved of his raiding. Hawkins arrived on the

Venezuelan coast with a shipload of African men and women to be sold as slaves, only to find that the Spanish government, protecting its monopoly on trade with the colonies, had forbidden the colonists to trade with him. Partly by force, and partly because the colonists wanted to trade, Hawkins was able to sell the slaves to them anyway, and on this excursion he made an even bigger profit than on his first.

Hawkins's third expedition in 1567 went badly. This time he had a fleet of six ships, including two supplied by the queen. He brought along his young cousin, Francis Drake, to command one of the ships. When he arrived with a shipment of slaves on the coasts of the Spanish Main, Hawkins found that the king of Spain had sent out strict orders, again forbidding the settlers to trade with Hawkins's fleet. Despite the ban, Hawkins had some success in trading, but as his fleet approached Mexico, it was hit by a bad storm and forced to take shelter in the Spanish port of San Juan de Ulúa.

Soon after Hawkins's damaged fleet anchored in the Spanish port, the Nueva España Flota arrived there on its annual trip, accompanied by two warships. Onboard one of the ships was the Spanish viceroy (governor) of New Spain, the district of Spanish America comprised mainly of Mexico and it surroundings. The Spanish pretended to negotiate with the English captains, but in reality they were preparing to attack them. Suddenly and violently, they set upon the English fleets. Drake managed to escape with his ship. Hawkins fought on in a hopeless battle, watching the Spaniards kill many of his crew and sink his ships. Finally he gathered the survivors on his last remaining ship and fled. After an agonizing journey home, in which many of the crew starved or died of thirst, Hawkins arrived back in England in 1569. The former slave trader and sea raider went on to a distinguished career as lord treasurer of the navy. He never ventured out as a privateer again.

The Battle of San Juan de Ulúa was a pivotal moment in the history of English privateering and piracy. Cordingly writes in *Under the Black Flag: the Romance and the Reality of Life among the Pirates* that the battle "showed Hawkins and his countrymen that peaceful trade with the Spaniards in the West Indies was no longer possible." For Drake the experience of Spanish treachery at San Juan de Ulúa determined his course. From then on, he spent his life fearlessly attacking Spain at sea.

The defeat of John Hawkins at San Juan de Ulúa. This battle was a pivotal moment in the history of English privateering and piracy. HULTON ARCHIVE/GETTY IMAGES.

Francis Drake in Panama

Drake received a privateering license in 1572. For his first target, he chose the Spanish port of Nombre de Dios in Panama, an unassuming town consisting of only about two hundred houses. Spanish mule trains brought gold and silver ingots from the inland mountains to Nombre de Dios on a regular basis. Great quantities of the precious metals were stored there until the galleons of the Tierra Firma Flota came on its annual run to carry them back to Spain.

Drake attacked Nombre de Dios in July 1572. He split his crew into two groups that marched into the city in the dead of night. They approached from different directions banging drums, sounding trumpets, and generally making enough noise to frighten the residents into thinking they were being attacked by a much larger force. At first, the plan seemed to work, and many guards fled. But as Drake and his men approached the king's treasure house, a group of Spaniards launched a volley of musket fire

Pieces of Eight

With rich sources of gold and silver in its New World colonies, Spain was faced with the problem of shaping enormous quantities of precious metals into transportable form. In the early part of the sixteenth century, Spaniards melted down the gold and silver and shaped it into ingots, metal blocks that would later be processed into coins in Spain. But with so much precious metal, it made sense to make the metal into money at the source. The Spaniards' first New World mint, a place where money is made under the authority of the government, was established in 1536 in Mexico City. A few decades later, mints were established in Lima, Peru, and Potosí (in present-day Bolivia).

The Spanish coin system had gold and silver coins. The gold doubloon, a coin that weighed approximately 1 ounce (28 grams), was the highest valued of the coins. The more common silver peso or dollar coin was worth eight Spanish *reales*, and so became known as the "piece of eight." One piece of eight would be worth about twenty-three U.S. dollars.

In the Spanish Main privateers and pirates attacked ships laden with pieces of eight being transported back to Spain, and so there has long been an association between piracy and the coin. The connection was probably more strongly forged, however, in fictional representations of piracy. It is featured throughout Scottish writer Robert Louis Stevenson's 1883 pirate novel *Treasure Island*, in which a parrot named Captain Flint repeatedly shrieks, "Pieces of Eight! Pieces of Eight!" More recently, the coin played a central role in the popular *Pirates of the Caribbean* films, in which the nine pirate lords, including Captain Jack Sparrow, each agree to present a piece of eight at the Brethren Court meetings that occur over the centuries.

Gold Spanish doubloons and silver pieces of eight. IRA BLOCK/NATIONAL GEOGRAPHIC/GETTY IMAGES.

at Drake and his crew. (A musket is a muzzle-loading shoulder gun with a long barrel.) Hit in the thigh and bleeding profusely, Drake continued to lead his men on to the treasure house. By the time they got there, he lost consciousness. His crew forced open the storehouse only to find that the fleet had already arrived and taken the treasure. They carried their collapsed commander back to the safety of the ship.

Drake's men sailed to the coasts of Panama, and there Drake recovered from his wound. The expedition found refuge with the Cimaroons, former African slaves who had escaped from Spanish bondage and lived in the forests off the coast with the native peoples. For several months, the fleet went out on raiding trips, but most of their prizes were small. (Prizes are the goods, human captives, and ships captured in pirate raids.) In the spring of 1573 they met up with Huguenot privateer Guillaume Le Testu (c. 1509–1573) cruising the seas off Panama. Le Testu told Drake about a mule train carrying silver to Nombre de Dios that was poorly defended against raiders. Drake jumped at the opportunity. With the combined forces of Le Testu's crew, his own crew, and the Cimarroons, he led a successful ambush on the mule train, seizing a large load of silver. With great difficulty, Drake and his men managed to transport the heavy silver back to their ship, and they returned to England with their enormous prize. Drake instantly became a national hero in England.

Drake sails around the world as a privateer

In December 1577 Drake set out on a long-planned voyage, secretly sponsored by Queen Elizabeth, to explore the Pacific coast of South America. His fleet consisted of five large and well-armed galleons. Drake sailed in the *Golden Hind*, a galleon about 120 feet (37 meters) long and 22 feet (7 meters) wide, with three masts for sails and a crew of eighty men. The entire fleet made it as far as the east coast of South America, but after wintering in present-day Argentina, only three ships were in good enough shape to continue on. By the time Drake got to the Pacific coast of South America, only the *Golden Hind* was left.

When Drake reached the Pacific, he found that the ports along the coast were almost entirely unguarded. Up to this time, the Spanish had been the sole European settlers on the Pacific coast of South America and had never been attacked there. Drake proceeded up the coast, capturing one trading vessel after another and raiding port towns such as Arica, Chile, and Lima, Peru. After capturing the *Cacafuego*, a large treasure ship filled with gold, silver, and jewels, Drake had enough booty to return to England. (Booty is the goods stolen from ships or coastal villages during pirate raids or attacks on enemies in time of war.) But he could not sail back down the Spanish-held coast for fear of Spanish reprisal. Instead he set his course across the Pacific Ocean and around Africa.

Drake finally arrived in England three years after his voyage began. His expedition was only the second ever to have circumnavigated, or sailed all the way around, the globe, and Drake had made significant geographic discoveries along the way. England, though, was more interested in the immense booty he brought home, valued at £326,580. A good portion of his prize went to the queen. Six months after his return, Queen Elizabeth knighted Drake, who she affectionately called "her pirate." (A knight is a man granted a rank of honor by the monarch for his personal merit or service to the country.) It was an unusual rise in position and fortune for the son of a humble farmer.

The privateer at war

Relations between Spain and England deteriorated in the decade after Drake's long voyage. Hostilities mounted for several reasons, many having to do with the balance of power in Europe and the Spanish king's intolerance of Protestantism. English privateers, too, played a large role in incurring the Spanish king's wrath.

Witnessing Drake's success, many English seamen headed for the Caribbean as privateers. King Philip, enraged by English raids on his ships, resorted to trickery to fight back. In 1585 his ministers spread the word that Spain needed wheat to feed its troops. English merchants, wanting to do business, quickly sent ships filled with wheat to Spanish ports. To their dismay, Spanish soldiers were waiting to seize their ships and cargoes. It was Queen Elizabeth's turn for fury. She began to issue multiple letters of marque to ship owners.

Drake was ready to fight. He outfitted a twenty-five-ship fleet, including two royal vessels. In 1585 he set off for the Caribbean. There he attacked the large Spanish ports of Cartagena, Columbia, and Santo Domingo, Hispaniola, and the Spanish settlement at St. Augustine, Florida. Two years later Drake attacked again, this time targeting the huge Spanish fleet anchored at the port of Cadiz in Spain. With only a small fleet, he was able to burn and sink several ships. In these raids, Drake and the other privateers badly disrupted the Spanish economy. Merchants and traders, fearing privateer raids, stopped transporting goods from the New World that were badly needed in Spain. The privateers were a large factor in King Philip's final decision to initiate war with England.

In 1588 the huge Spanish armada of 130 ships sailed to the English Channel in an attempt to invade England. Spain had the most powerful navy in the world. Queen Elizabeth's navy numbered thirty-four ships; these were matched by a force of private vessels armed for war. Drake functioned as second in command of the Royal Navy rather than as privateer.

Most of Spain's ships were converted merchant ships designed to carry heavy cargo. They were heavy and did not maneuver easily. Although England did not have nearly as many ships as Spain, the English galleons were better suited to naval fighting. The British ship design had been strongly influenced by Hawkins, who understood from his years of raiding that the ships needed to be fast and easy to handle. The English ships were sleek and low in the water. Their rigging was more advanced, allowing them to sail almost directly into the wind, while Spain's ships needed to have the wind behind them. Hawkins had also trained sailors, making the English fleet the most modern navy in the world.

England won an unexpected victory against the mighty Spanish Armada, forever changing the dynamics of European power. Although Drake did not play a defining role in the victory, the privateer's contribution to England's rise to power was remarkable.

The Dutch privateers

During the first half of the sixteenth century, the king of Spain, Charles V (1500–1558), was also the Holy Roman Emperor, the leader of a loose confederation of states and territories that included the states of present-day Germany and most of central Europe. In 1554 Charles divided his empire, giving Spain and the Seventeen Provinces, which included present-day Belgium, Luxembourg, and the Netherlands, to his son, Philip II. Economic and religious tensions soon began to build between the Dutch and the Spanish. The Netherlands was a prosperous center of international trade, and Spain had imposed harsh taxes on it. The Netherlands had also become largely Protestant after the Reformation. (The Reformation was a sixteenth-century religious movement that aimed to reform the Catholic Church and resulted in the establishment of Protestant churches.) Philip took measures to stamp out the new religion. In

1568 the Netherlands rose in rebellion. The long war for independence that erupted came to be known as the Eighty Years' War (1568–1648).

During the Eighty Years' War, Dutch seamen began to roam distant ports looking for ways to make money. Since Spain refused to allow foreigners to trade in its New World ports, the Dutch followed the example of the French and English. Many created routes in which they picked up slaves and other goods in African ports and then smuggled them to willing buyers on the Spanish Main. Spain reacted with harsh measures. For example, in 1593 a Spanish commander captured ten Dutch merchant ships that had been trading illegally in the colonies. He had the captains hanged and forced the crew members into slavery.

By the early seventeenth century, Dutch privateers were successfully harassing and raiding Spanish ports and ships on the Spanish Main. Many were employed by the Dutch West Indies Company, which had been granted a charter for a trade monopoly on the Caribbean islands by the Netherlands. One of the early Dutch privateers commissioned by the company was Pieter Schouten. In 1624 Schouten attacked port cities on the coast of the Yucatán in Mexico and captured a Spanish galleon loaded with treasures from Honduras. The booty Schouten brought back to the Netherlands prompted the Dutch West Indies Company to sponsor more privateers.

The most famous of the Dutch privateers was Pieter Pieterszoon Heyn (commonly called Piet Heyn; 1577–1629). During the Dutch war for independence, Heyn was captured by the Spanish in 1600 and forced to serve as a galley slave for two years. After his release, he took a position with the Dutch West Indies Company and rose in its ranks. Heading to the Caribbean in 1623, he carried out a series of strikes against Spanish and Portuguese settlements.

In 1628 Heyn took command of a mission to capture the full Spanish flota as it sailed from the Spanish Main. He had an enormous fleet of thirty-one ships equipped with 679 cannons and carrying 2,300 sailors and 1,000 soldiers. As his fleet approached Cuba, where the two flotas were scheduled to meet, the Tierra Firma Flota learned of his mission and changed its course. The Nueva España Flota from Mexico, however, was unprepared for the raid and was captured. Heyn, an honest and strict commander, allowed no unnecessary violence in the raid and released all the crew unharmed from the Spanish ships. But he returned to the Netherlands with an enormous booty, and there he was greeted as a hero. According to historian David F. Marley "it took five days for the

A statue of Piet Heyn in
Rotterdam, Netherlands.
© HUGO NIENHUIS/ALAMY.

thousands of chests of bullion and coins to be loaded onto more than a thousand mule carts that followed Heyn's coach on a triumphal march through the city of Amsterdam. Privateers everywhere must have exulted, as the lure of Spanish gold shone brighter than before."

For More Information

BOOKS

Cordingly, David. *Under the Black Flag: The Romance and the Reality of Life Among the Pirates.* New York: Random House, 2006, p. 39.

Fine, John Christopher. *Treasures of the Spanish Main: Shipwrecked Galleons in the New World.* Guilford, CT: Lyons Press, 2006.

Lane, Kris E. *Pillaging the Empire: Piracy in the Americas, 1500–1750.* Armonk, NY: Sharpe, 1998.

Marley, David F. "The Lure of Spanish Gold." In *Pirates: Terror on the High Seas from the Caribbean to the South China Sea.* Edited by David Cordingly. East Bridgewater, MA: World Publications Group, 1998, 2007, p. 35.

Miller, Helen Hill. *Captains from Devon: The Great Elizabethan Seafarers Who Won the Ocean for England.* Chapel Hill, NC: Algonquin, 1985.

WEB SITES

"All About Pirates." *Candlelight Stories.* www.candlelightstories.com/storybooks/all-about-pirates (accessed on January 3, 2011).

Privateer Dragons of the Caribbean. www.privateerdragons.com (accessed on January 3, 2011).

Reefs, Wrecks, and Rascals: The Pirate Legacy of the Spanish Main. www.mdpls.org/county_internet/virtual (accessed on January 3, 2011).

5

The Buccaneers of the New World

The word *buccaneer* has come to be used interchangeably with the word *pirate*, but it originally referred to a particular group of seventeenth-century sea raiders in the Caribbean Sea. The buccaneers were hunters on Hispaniola (present-day Haiti and the Dominican Republic) who turned to sea raiding. They were based in two ports: the island of Tortuga, off the coast of Hispaniola, and Port Royal, Jamaica.

Buccaneers frequently acted as pirates, robbing ships at sea or pillaging coastal communities for their own gain. Throughout the seventeenth century, however, major European powers struggled against each other for control of the Caribbean colonies, and the buccaneers were constantly sought by one country or another to serve as privateers, or private ship owners commissioned by a state or government to attack the merchant ships of an enemy nation. A buccaneer could be either a pirate or a privateer. Most were, at one time or another, both.

The buccaneers were often cruel and ruthless to their victims, but they were usually loyal to each other and they achieved a remarkably organized method of carrying out the business of sea raiding on a large scale. A significant number of buccaneers rose from dire poverty to wealth and high positions. Despite their scorn of European governments, the buccaneers were willing to work for the French, English, and Dutch and helped them to open colonies in the Caribbean.

The Caribbean in the early seventeenth century

In the early seventeenth century Spain was a major world power, and it tried to maintain complete control over the Americas, as it had been doing since the end of the fifteenth century. Spain's flotas (treasure fleets that transported goods and riches from the New World to Spain) were essential to the nation's economy. But Spain managed its colonial trade and industry poorly. Involved in numerous ongoing wars in Europe, it

WORDS TO KNOW

barque: A simple vessel with one mast and triangular sails.

booty: Goods stolen from ships or coastal villages during pirate raids or attacks on enemies in time of war.

buccaneer: A seventeenth-century sea raider based in the Caribbean Sea.

flota: A Spanish treasure fleet that transported goods and riches from the New World to Spain every year.

indentured servant: A person working under a contract that commits him or her to an employer for a fixed period of time, typically three to seven years.

knight: A man granted a rank of honor by the monarch for his personal merit or service to the country.

letter of marque: A document licensing a private ship owner to the seize ships or goods of an enemy nation.

maroon: To strand an individual on a deserted island or shore with few provisions.

pirate haven: A safe place for pirates to harbor and repair their ships, resupply, and organize raiding parties.

plunder: To rob of goods by force, in a raid or in wartime.

privateer: A private ship or ship owner commissioned by a state or government to attack the merchant ships of a hostile power.

rack: A piece of equipment used for torture; a person tied on a rack is slowly stretched by the wrists and ankles, causing extreme pain.

ransom: A sum of money demanded for the release of someone being held captive.

ship's articles: The written sets of rules and conditions under which pirates operated on any given expedition.

did not have enough money or naval power to properly defend most of its New World possessions. The defense efforts it did manage in the New World were focused on its major port cities in the Caribbean, primarily Havana, Cuba; Portobelo, Panama; Santo Domingo, Hispaniola; Veracruz, Mexico; and Cartagena, in present-day Colombia.

Spain's inability to defend its vast New World territory tempted other European countries, particularly France, England, and Holland (present-day Netherlands) to establish their own Caribbean colonies. During the first half of the seventeenth century, non-Spanish European settlers established colonies on the Caribbean islands of Saint Kitts, Nevis, Barbados, Antigua, Curaçao, Tortuga, and Jamaica. To populate their new colonies and at the same time rid their countries of unwanted people, the European countries transported convicted criminals, homeless vagrants, and prostitutes to the colonies. Many of the transported colonists were political prisoners from the English Civil War (1642–1651; a war in which the English monarchy was replaced by a republican commonwealth). As a result of the war, King Charles I (1600–1649) was executed and Oliver Cromwell (1599–1658) became head of state. Cromwell sent thousands of Irish and Scottish dissenters, or people who did not accept the new government's religion or policies, to the islands of Saint Kitts and Barbados. In France the persecution of the Huguenots (French Protestants) forced thousands into exile, and a significant number headed for the Americas.

A large number of Caribbean settlers arrived as indentured servants, who worked under contracts that committed them to an employer for a fixed period of time, typically three to seven years. Some people voluntarily signed these contracts in exchange for transportation to the New World. Others, like the political prisoners and religious dissenters, were transported involuntarily and forced into indentured servitude because they had no other way to support themselves. In France and England smugglers (people who imported illegal goods) and human traffickers kidnapped children from poor city neighborhoods and shipped them off to the Caribbean as indentured servants. Historians argue that many indentured servants were treated even worse than slaves. Since people had to purchase slaves, they tended to maintain the slaves' health in order to protect their investment and get a lifetime of work from the slaves. But if an indentured servant died from lack of nutrition or overwork, it was a minor loss to the employer.

The first English and French settlers in the Caribbean tended to employ indentured servants to labor on tobacco plantations, but the results of tobacco farming were poor. By midcentury sugar plantations replaced the failing tobacco plantations. The sugar crops demanded even more laborers, and traders began to bring in increasing numbers of African slaves to the Caribbean. Thus, when indentured servants completed their contract or ran away from their employers, they often faced utter poverty. There were few jobs for paid laborers and, without money to invest in land, it was difficult to survive.

The early buccaneers

As the seventeenth century began, England, Holland, and France were often at war with each other, but they mostly fought Spain. One of the battlegrounds was the Caribbean, where the European nations hoped to strike at Spain's power, establish their own colonies, spread their religion, and more than anything else, bring home some of the New World wealth. With smaller navies than Spain's, England, France, and Holland relied on the practice of privateering that had developed in earlier centuries, and the waters of the Caribbean became infested with privateers that targeted Spanish shipping.

Naturally the Spanish government was alarmed by the pirates in their midst. (The Spanish did not distinguish between privateers that attacked them and pirates.) Knowing they could not defend their entire territory from pirates, Spanish officials ordered residents to leave the more remote areas in the Caribbean. In 1605 the Spanish residents of the northwestern portion of Hispaniola were removed from their homes, and large herds of livestock were left behind. Without any predators, horses, pigs, and cattle multiplied in the abandoned lands.

Over the next couple of decades, the abundance of wild livestock attracted a group of hunters to the northwest regions of Hispaniola. These hunters were a motley crew, mainly French, made up of runaway indentured servants, former pirates, escaped African slaves, and other outcasts desperate to sustain themselves without suffering in servitude.

This group of men survived by conducting long hunting trips, often one or two years long, on Hispaniola, where they killed large quantities of the wild animals. The few surviving native people of the region taught the hunters a method of curing their meat to prevent it from rotting in the tropical heat. The oven they used for smoking strips of beef or pork was called a *boucan* and the hunters soon came to be known as *boucaniers* or *buccaneers* in English. They traded with smugglers and traders along the coast, exchanging bundles of the smoked beef and pork as well as animal hides for guns, ammunition, tobacco, and alcohol. They traded on Tortuga Island, a 25-mile (40-kilometer) long island off the northwest coast of Hispaniola, which they reached by canoe. On Tortuga they went on long, drunken, brawling sprees. When their money and alcohol ran out, they returned to the woods of Hispaniola to hunt.

During the hunt, the early buccaneers usually lived in groups of six or eight men. They lived in primitive huts with roofs made from palm leaves. Their favorite foods were meats, but they particularly enjoyed sucking the warm marrow out of the bones of freshly killed cows. To outside observers, the buccaneers seemed like savages. They were so splattered with grease and blood from killing and butchering animals that they appeared to have been tarred. Their clothes were rough, sticky

A buccaneer. PRIVATE COLLECTION/PETER NEWARK AMERICAN PICTURES/THE BRIDGEMAN ART LIBRARY INTERNATIONAL.

with dried blood, and filthy. Many lived in homosexual unions called *matelotage*, a type of marriage. Later, as Tortuga developed, the island's officials tried to stop the homosexual unions by bringing in female prostitutes. At first, though, when one partner in a matelotage union married, he simply brought the new wife into the existing union. Despite their rough qualities, the buccaneers lived together under a form of self-government and managed to exchange a life of servitude for one of adventure.

Buccaneers as sea raiders

A good deal of what is known of the buccaneers comes from Alexander O. Exquemelin's book, *The Buccaneers of America*, first published in Holland in 1678. Exquemelin, who arrived in the Caribbean as an indentured servant in 1666, spent twelve years accompanying buccaneers on sea raids.

Exquemelin claims the first buccaneer to begin sea raiding was a Frenchman named Pierre le Grand. In 1602 le Grand and his crew of twenty-eight men were sailing on a badly damaged barque (a simple vessel with one mast and triangular sails) off the shores of western Hispaniola. They were nearly starving when they spotted a Spanish ship and decided to attack. As they approached the ship, le Grand ordered his crew to pierce the bottom of the barque with holes so there could be no turning back. Only lightly armed, the pirates boarded the Spanish ship as their own boat sank. The ship's captain, who was playing cards at the time of the attack, quickly surrendered. With his prize of the ship and its cargo, le Grand arrived back in Europe a rich man. According to Exquemelin, this incident inspired the early buccaneers of Hispaniola and Tortuga to raid Spanish ships during the hunting off-season. Over the years their raiding increased.

The buccaneers initially conducted their sea raids in long canoes made from hollowed-out tree trunks or in barques. In groups of about twenty men, they rowed up to Spanish barques that were trading along the coasts. Sometimes, under cover of darkness, they targeted large Spanish ships leaving the ports loaded with riches. The buccaneers usually attacked the ships from the rear, to avoid the big guns, and boarded quickly, taking the crew by surprise. The buccaneers were not good seamen, but they were excellent marksmen (skilled at shooting) and equally good with their knives. They often overpowered Spanish crews that far outnumbered them, and they frequently shot, stabbed, or threw overboard entire Spanish crews.

After seizing a ship and its cargo, the buccaneers divided their booty equally. (Booty is the goods stolen from ships or coastal villages during

French buccaneer Pierre le Grand captures a Spanish galleon in 1602. © 2D ALAN KING/ALAMY.

pirate raids or attacks on enemies in time of war.) They usually kept the Spanish ships, and these new vessels enabled them to undertake raids farther out at sea. Still, the buccaneers were not true seamen and preferred simpler ships. What made them exceptional pirates was their expertise at the hunt, whether the prey was an animal or a ship.

Tortuga becomes a buccaneer haven

The Spanish government on Hispaniola was infuriated that buccaneers were living among them. Toward the end of the 1620s colonial officials decided to kill all of the wild livestock in the northwestern region of Hispaniola. They hoped that, deprived of prey to hunt, the buccaneers would leave the region. But the buccaneers simply exchanged one form of prey for another. Without hides and jerky to trade, many buccaneers became full-time sea raiders. No longer satisfied with plundering (robbing of goods by force) passing ships, they began to raid the Spanish coastal regions as well.

With little reason to return to Hispaniola, the buccaneers made Tortuga their base of operations. Throughout the 1630s the Spanish repeatedly raided Tortuga. The buccaneers simply fled, either hiding in the woods or taking refuge on Hispaniola. When the Spanish left, the buccaneers returned.

Two local residents inspect the ruins of a fort built by pirate leader François Levasseur on Tortuga Island, in present-day Haiti. © LARRY MANGINO/ THE IMAGE WORKS.

In 1642 a new governor arrived in Tortuga. François Levasseur (d. 1652), an exiled Huguenot, built a secure fort on a hill overlooking Tortuga's harbor. The fort was capable of holding several hundred men and had its own source of water. Levasseur declared independence from

France, built a palace at the center of the fort, and ruled Tortuga as a king of the pirates. Levasseur detested Catholics and burned the island's Catholic chapel, permitting only Protestant worship. He was a strict ruler known for his cruelty.

In 1643 the Spanish mounted a major attack on Tortuga to drive the buccaneers out, but the fort Levasseur had erected was impossible for them to penetrate and they were forced to retreat. Spain never attempted another attack on Tortuga. For the next decade, Levasseur encouraged buccaneer raiding and grew rich by collecting a percentage of the booty. He was murdered by his own men in 1652, but Tortuga continued to thrive as a pirate haven, attracting adventurers and criminals to its harbor. (A pirate haven is a safe place for pirates to harbor and repair their ships, resupply, and organize raiding parties.)

The Brethren of the Coast

The buccaneers began to call themselves the "Brethren of the Coast" around 1640. They had become an organized, democratic group in which all members had a right to participate in governing. The buccaneers lived under the Custom of the Coast, a set of rules they established among themselves. They placed their membership in the Brethren ahead of their ties to the nations in which they were born. In fact, when a man joined the Brethren of the Coast, he often took a new name. Few buccaneers talked about the lives they led prior to joining the Brethren.

When a buccaneer leader decided to launch a raid, he started by spreading word of his plan. When fifty or so men had agreed to participate in the raid, the group would obtain enough meat to feed themselves for several days, usually by stealing it from local farmers. Then they elected a captain and agreed to a set of ship's articles, which specified how the booty was to be divided among them. (Ship's articles are the written sets of rules and conditions under which pirates operated on any given expedition.) All raiding expeditions were on a "no prey, no pay" basis, meaning that the raiders were paid only when their mission succeeded and provided them with booty to share. Although they gave little thought to stealing from outsiders, buccaneers had strict rules about cheating each other. The punishments for taking booty before it had been tallied or stealing from each other were severe. The first time a buccaneer violated the code, his nose and ears were sliced off; the second time, the buccaneer was marooned, or stranded on a deserted island or shore with few provisions.

François L'Olonnais

One of the most famous buccaneers from Tortuga was a Frenchman named Jean-David Nau (c. 1635–1668), better known as François L'Olonnais. L'Olonnais arrived in the Caribbean as an indentured servant around 1660. He joined the hunters in Tortuga and soon began a career of raiding ships. L'Olonnais's fearlessness so impressed Tortuga's governor that he gave him a ship and a small crew to plunder Spanish ships.

Through raiding, L'Olonnais soon added several ships to his fleet, but he did not hold onto his fleet long. During an assault on the port of Campeche, a city on the west coast of the Yucatán Peninsula in Mexico, L'Olonnais's fleet was shipwrecked. Spanish forces attacked and killed almost all the crew. L'Olonnais survived only by smearing blood on his face and lying in a pile of dead bodies. He eventually stole a canoe and returned to Tortuga.

In 1667 L'Olonnais and French pirate Michel Le Basque fitted a fleet of eight ships with a crew of about eight hundred buccaneers and headed to the trading city of Maracaibo, Venezuela, located on the western side of the channel between the Gulf of Venezuela and Lake Maracaibo. News of his approach reached Maracaibo before the fleet arrived. The buccaneers found the town abandoned and its treasures gone. L'Olonnais sent out search parties seeking Spanish residents or soldiers. All who were found were tortured over and over again to force them to disclose the location of treasures.

L'Olonnais terrorized Maracaibo for two weeks. Finding little of worth, he and his crew decided to cross Lake Maracaibo to raid the town of Gibraltar. There, Spanish troops met them. L'Olonnais led the assault on the Spaniards, crying, as quoted by Exquemelin, "Come on, brothers, follow me, and let's have no cowardice." After a fierce battle in which many were killed on both sides, L'Olonnais captured Gibraltar and pillaged it, displaying extreme cruelty to its residents. He demanded a large ransom for the courtesy of not burning down the town. (A ransom is a sum of money demanded for the release of someone being held captive or, in this case, for some other consideration.) He then returned to Maracaibo to demand an even larger ransom there.

The pirates returned to Tortuga, where they divided up their enormous booty according to their ship's articles. News of L'Olonnais's success traveled throughout the Caribbean, and despite disturbing tales of his cruelty, many young sailors signed on for his next expedition. He launched several more expeditions, although none were as rewarding as Maracaibo.

The Practice of Torture

In written accounts about buccaneers, references to torture are so frequent that they are almost casual. Buccaneers were not the only violent men in the seventeenth century. Warfare among the Spanish, French, English, and Dutch was often brutal, and sometimes the naval and military forces carried out acts that were just as shockingly cruel and inhumane as those of the buccaneers. But by all accounts, the buccaneers of the seventeenth century were an especially vicious lot. Popular literature and film, however, does not always portray this extreme violence.

In 1669 John Style, a witness in the Caribbean quoted by Jack Beeching in his introduction to Alexander O. Exquemelin's book *The Buccaneers of America*, said, "It is a common thing among the privateers ... to cut a man in pieces, first some flesh, then a hand, an arm, a leg, sometimes tying a cord about his head, and with a stick twisting it until the eyes shoot out, which is called 'woolding.'"

Some pirates were clearly psychopaths and being a pirate allowed them to act out their worst tendencies. For example, Dutch buccaneer Roche Brasiliano (c. 1630–1671) was known for his violent temper and his utter hatred of Spaniards. According to Exquemelin:

> He had no self-control at all, but behaved as if possessed by a sullen fury. When he was drunk, he would roam the town like a madman. The first person he came across, he would chop off his arm or leg, without anyone daring to intervene, for he was like a maniac. He perpetrated the greatest atrocities possible against the Spaniards. Some of them he tied or spitted on wooden stakes and roasted them alive between two fires, like killing a pig—and all because they refused to show him the road to the hog-yards he wanted to plunder.

Henry Morgan's buccaneers torture prisoners in Panama.
© INTERFOTO/ALAMY.

Most historians describe L'Olonnais as a psychopath or sociopath, someone with a personality disorder characterized by an abnormal lack of feelings for others and an ability to appear normal while conducting extremely immoral acts. Exquemelin chronicled L'Olonnais's vicious habits. He writes:

> When [L'Olonnais] had a victim on the rack [a piece of equipment used for torture on which a person is slowly stretched by the wrists and ankles], if the wretch did not instantly answer his questions he would hack the man to pieces with his cutlass [sword] and lick the blood from the blade with his tongue, wishing it might have been the last Spaniard in the world that he had killed.

Pirates throughout history have used terror to obtain their goals, but L'Olonnais's cruelty was too much even for many of the hardened pirates he sailed with. In one example provided by Exquemelin, L'Olonnais forced two Spanish prisoners to guide him to San Pedro, which he planned to attack. Along the way, they were ambushed by Spanish soldiers and L'Olonnais accused the soldiers of deliberately misleading him. Exquemelin writes, "[L'Olonnais], being possessed of a devil's fury, ripped open one of the prisoners with his cutlass, tore the living heart out of his body, gnawed at it, and then hurled it in the face of the others, saying, 'Show me another way, or I will do the same to you.'"

In 1668 L'Olonnais and his crew ran aground in some islands off the coast of Nicaragua. For six months they barely managed to survive on shore. Finally with a canoe made from a log, they set out for home. On the way, they were attacked by the Spanish. After escaping that attack, they were then attacked by a group of natives. Exquemelin records that the Indians hacked L'Olonnais to pieces and roasted his body "limb by limb."

The Brethren expand

As the years passed, the Brethren of the Coast became an international group with English, Dutch, Flemish, and Danish members. The buccaneers frequently gained new recruits when they raided a ship. They gave the captured crew only two alternatives: to join the buccaneers or serve them as slaves. The life of a sailor was harsh and the pay was low. Many sailors gladly joined, hoping for a better future.

Most buccaneers came from humble origins, but there were a few exceptions. Michel de Grammont (c. 1645–1686) was a nobleman from Paris, France, who arrived in the Caribbean as a privateer. He ran afoul of French law when he captured a rich Dutch vessel. Since France was not at war with the Dutch, the raid was not legal. He spent the proceeds of this raid on weeks of debauchery on Hispaniola. After the money was gone, de Grammont joined the Brethren of the Coast. He became an outstanding leader of the buccaneers, who called him Chevalier (a French word meaning "knight") de Grammont.

Laurens de Graaf (c. 1653–1704) was a Dutch seaman who had been captured in his native country by the Spanish and forced to work as a slave on a plantation in the Canary Islands. He escaped and made his way to the Caribbean in the 1670s to become a buccaneer. De Graaf joined forces with de Grammont and another Dutch pirate, Nicolas van Hoorn (c. 1635–1683) who had also broken ties with his native country. All were based on Tortuga.

In 1683 the three buccaneer chiefs organized a large-scale raid on the Spanish treasure port at Veracruz, Mexico. They approached the well-defended port in two ships, with over one thousand buccaneers onboard. Then they raised the Spanish flag. As the two ships were welcomed into port, the buccaneers attacked, taking the Spanish by surprise. For the next four days, the pirates looted the city of Veracruz. The booty from the violent raid was enormous.

Port Royal, Jamaica

Soon after the English Civil War, Cromwell developed a strategy known as the Western Design. His goal was to establish overseas colonies in the Caribbean and spread Protestantism while destroying Spain's monopoly (exclusive control) on trade with the New World. His greatest hope, according to historians, was that his ships would raid the Spanish treasure fleets and bring home enough booty to fill England's treasury. In 1655 Cromwell mounted an expedition of warships carrying thirty-six hundred English soldiers to attack Santo Domingo, Hispaniola.

The English forces failed miserably in their attack on Santo Domingo. Afterward they seized the island of Jamaica for England. The Spanish had never had much interest in Jamaica. Its population was small, and it was poorly defended. But Spain did not want an English settlement in its territory. After the English took the island, Spain mounted several counter-attacks to try to get it back. The new English colony of Jamaica needed help defending itself. Its first governor, Edward D'Oyley (1617–1675), welcomed French, English, and Dutch buccaneers in the city of Port Royal. He freely issued them letters of marque against the Spanish, hoping to keep the Spanish at bay. (A letter of marque is a document licensing a private ship owner to the seize ships or goods of an enemy nation.)

Port Royal, Jamaica, turned out to be a perfect pirate haven. It had a large harbor that could accommodate up to five hundred ships, and it was strategically located among the various Caribbean shipping lanes. According to Jenifer Marx in *Pirates: Terror on the High Seas from the Caribbean to the South China Sea*, "In the six years following the English occupation of Jamaica, Port Royal buccaneers ravaged eighteen [Spanish colonial] cities, four towns, and some three dozen smaller settlements. Some villages were raided again and again, including a fair number far inland."

Port Royal grew rapidly. A multitude of taverns, brothels, and gambling dens were established for pirates to spend their booty. The economy of the island became dependent on the buccaneers' stolen goods. The city developed a reputation for extreme debauchery. Nevertheless, Port Royal flourished and remained the primary pirate haven of the Caribbean for nearly fifty years.

Christopher Myngs

In 1656 England sent navy captain Christopher Myngs (also spelled Mings; 1625–1666) to Jamaica to help protect the island from Spanish attacks. Myngs's strategy was to attack Spain's ships and raid its Caribbean settlements, thereby weakening the Spanish so they could not mount attacks on Jamaica. He recruited buccaneers to assist him. In 1656 Myngs took part in a successful raid on Santa Marta, Venezuela. The raid proved that using a force of buccaneers for an assault worked.

In 1658 Myngs's fleet attacked several places along the coast of South America, burning and destroying the coastal town of Tolú in present-day Colombia and once again plundering Santa Marta. He sailed to the shores of present-day Venezuela to attack the old port city of Cumana and then Puerto Caballo. Then, at Coro, Myngs seized what every pirate dreamed of: a Spanish silver shipment with an estimated value of approximately £250,000. Myngs decided not to take the huge booty back to the colonial government in Jamaica, as his service in the English navy obliged him to do. Instead, he divided the prize among himself and his buccaneers. When he returned to Port Royal, he was arrested for embezzlement, or the theft of money or property entrusted to one's care but owned by someone else. He was sent back to England in 1660. Fortunately for Myngs, England was undergoing a dramatic change at that time. The death of Oliver Cromwell had resulted in a crisis. The monarchy was restored under King Charles II (1630–1685) and the case against Myngs was dropped in 1660 amid the events of the English Restoration.

Under Charles II, England entered an uneasy peace with Spain. Myngs, who had returned to Jamaica, did not let the events in Europe stop him from harassing the Spanish colonies in the Caribbean. In 1662 his fleet attacked Santiago, Cuba. From there, with a squadron of about fifteen hundred buccaneers, Myngs attacked the town of San Francisco on the Bay of Campeche, in Mexico. In both Cuba and Mexico, Myngs wreaked great damage on the Spanish fleets and towns. Spain complained bitterly to King Charles, and the peace-oriented English king forbade Myngs to make any more raids. He returned to England in 1665.

Thomas Modyford and Henry Morgan

In 1664 King Charles appointed a wealthy plantation owner from Barbados, Thomas Modyford (c. 1620–1679), as governor of Jamaica. Despite England's trend toward peace with Spain, Modyford believed that privateer raids were necessary to stop the Spanish forces in Cuba from taking over Jamaica. The government of England had ordered the colony to stop granting letters of marque and to call in those that had already been issued. The governor decided to ignore orders and continued to enlist privateers in his fight against Spanish colonial forces.

Around 1665, a Welshman named Henry Morgan (1635–1688) became the chief of the buccaneers in Port Royal. He had been the captain of one of the buccaneer ships in Myngs's raids, and he had also led successful attacks on the coast of Central America. It was clear to Modyford that Morgan was a brave and talented, if ruthless, buccaneer. In 1668 the governor commissioned Morgan to lead a raid on Cuba.

Morgan's raid on Portobelo

Morgan set out in command of a force of seven hundred men in twelve ships. They landed in Cuba and marched 50 miles (80 kilometers) inland to the town of Puerto del Principe. There they easily captured the town and set about torturing prisoners to find their valuables. Then they sailed to the Isthmus of Panama to raid the large and well-defended city of Portobelo, where treasure from Peru was waiting to be shipped to Spain.

Because the raid on Portobelo was to be a sneak attack, the band of buccaneers anchored at an inlet about 150 miles (241 kilometers) from the city. They marched to the city over land, carrying twenty-three canoes that they paddled along rivers whenever possible. They reached the city after four days and attacked under the cover of night. However, as they approached the town, several guards spotted them and began shooting. Nevertheless, the buccaneers entered the residential part of the city and quickly herded the frightened townspeople into a church.

The challenge lay in the next step: to storm Portobelo's three strong forts, which were defended by heavily armed Spanish troops. One of the forts was taken easily. Advancing across the fields in front of the other forts, where the Spaniards would have a clear shot at them, was more difficult. Morgan decided to round up a group of nuns, monks, and elderly people to serve as human shields. The buccaneers crossed the fields with the captives directly in front of them. The Spanish fired a few initial shots, wounding a couple of monks, and then stopped shooting. Morgan's buccaneers brought in ladders and soon overwhelmed the forts. They killed more than half of the eighty soldiers inside.

After this victory, the buccaneers locked up their prisoners and began drinking and pillaging the town. They raped the women and tortured prisoners to learn where valuables were stored. Morgan and his men held Portobelo for thirty-one days. From there, Morgan wrote to the president of Panama, asking for an enormous ransom. Panama sent forces to rescue the city, but the buccaneers repelled them. In the end, Panama's president was forced to pay the ransom. The buccaneers returned to Jamaica with a tremendous booty and were greeted as heroes.

The raid of Portobelo was one of the most daring pirate feats of the seventeenth century. Although Morgan's letters of marque only authorized him to attack Spanish ships, the governor gave the buccaneer only a slight reprimand for his attacks on Spanish cities. In truth, Modyford was grateful for Morgan's excesses, which kept Spanish forces on the defensive.

Morgan's quick wits

In 1669 Morgan launched an expedition to raid Maracaibo. He gathered a force of some two thousand men on thirty-six ships, ranging from a flagship (the commander's ship) of 120 tons (109 metric tons) and twenty-two guns to an unarmed sloop of 12 tons (11 metric tons). In March 1669 Morgan and his men were plundering undefended coastal towns near Maracaibo when a Spanish fleet of three warships learned of their arrival. The Spanish ships blocked the harbor so Morgan's fleet could not escape.

Henry Morgan sends a fireship into the Spanish fleet at Maracaibo. PRIVATE COLLECTION/PETER NEWARK PICTURES/THE BRIDGEMAN ART LIBRARY.

The quick-witted buccaneer quickly devised a scheme. His men rigged a large merchant ship to look like a warship, using logs that looked like cannons to add to the effect. He also decorated logs on the decks to look like buccaneers. Then he sent the ship, piloted by a few men, directly into the largest of the Spanish ships. The crew lit fuses and then escaped as both ships exploded into flames. Morgan's fleet captured the other two ships. Morgan once again returned to Port Royal a hero.

Morgan's raid on Panama City

In December 1670 Morgan set out with a huge fleet to raid Panama City, the richest port in the Caribbean. His expedition directly violated a peace treaty between Spain and England, but it was undertaken with Governor Modyford's full knowledge. Morgan's forces of about two thousand buccaneers first captured the fortress of San Lorenzo, on the Caribbean coast of Panama, after a vicious battle with the Spanish forces there. The fortress gave them access to the Chagres River, and the remaining fifteen hundred buccaneers paddled up the river in canoes to Panama City. They reached the city on January 18, 1671, to find it fiercely defended by sixteen hundred Spanish troops. The buccaneers were instantly engaged in a long and difficult battle. Their superior marksmanship gave them the advantage, and after much bloodshed, they gained control of the port, suffering only a few casualties of their own.

Surviving Spanish soldiers had set fire to the city's buildings, unwilling to leave anything for the buccaneers. Most of the city burned to the ground. The buccaneers found to their dismay that most of the city's treasures had been loaded onto a Spanish treasure ship that was already far out to sea. The crew searched for wealthy residents of the city and tortured them to find more valuables. After a month of searching, the privateers collected a fairly large booty. When it came time to divide the prize, however, the buccaneers were not satisfied with their share, and they turned on Morgan, calling him a cheater. In response, Morgan left most of his fleet behind, sailing off in his flagship to raid other sites.

By the time Morgan returned to Jamaica, Modyford had been arrested and sent back to England for violating the treaty. Six months later, Morgan was also sent to London. Modyford and Morgan were both detained there for three years, although neither was punished. In fact, both were knighted, and they returned to Jamaica in high positions. (A knight is a man granted a rank of honor by the monarch for his personal merit or service to the country.) Modyford became Jamaica's chief justice, and Morgan received the post of lieutenant governor. Oddly, Morgan, the former buccaneer captain, was placed in charge of hunting down buccaneers. He died a wealthy man three years later.

Cartagena: the last major buccaneer attack

After Panama City burned to the ground, Cartagena became the richest treasure port in the Americas. After English privateer Francis Drake (1540–1596) had successfully raided the city in 1586, Spain had taken pains to build strong defenses around Cartagena, using its best engineers to design an impenetrable fort. Every buccaneer in the Caribbean wanted to raid Cartagena, but none dared.

In 1688 France, England, Holland, and Spain entered a bitter war known as the Nine Years' War (1688–97). Like most European wars of the era, the Nine Years' War extended to the Caribbean colonies. France had taken control of the western third of Hispaniola in 1659, establishing a colony called Saint Domingue (present-day Haiti). This became the base for a French privateer war against the Spanish. Saint Domingue's governor, Jean du Casse (1646–1715), a former privateer, commissioned fleets of French buccaneers to raid Spanish targets.

To strike out against Spain, France decided to attack Cartagena. In March 1689 France sent Admiral Jean-Bernard Desjean (Baron de Pointis; 1645–1707) to Saint Domingue to lead a full-scale naval expedition on the city. De Pointis commanded a squadron of ten warships. He was joined by Governor du Casse, who commanded another squadron of colonial ships. A fleet of seven buccaneer ships escorted the two naval squadrons. The entire expedition had a crew of about sixty-five-hundred men. Not surprisingly, the arrogant admiral and the rowdy buccaneers instantly disliked each other, and it was up to du Casse to bring about agreement on essentials, such as the ship's articles and the division of the booty.

The fortresses at Cartagena were strong but also old; they had been designed for earlier forms of warfare. As it happened, at the time of the French attack Spain did not have sufficient forces there. The Spanish governor was quickly forced to surrender Cartagena to the huge French fleet. In exchange for about half the city's wealth, de Pointis promised not to destroy the city or harm its inhabitants. The buccaneers were stunned by this decision. They were ready for a thorough plundering of the city, and they were not satisfied with their share of the booty.

The French naval forces withdrew from Cartagena, but the buccaneers lingered. When the French fleet was out of sight, they went on a rampage, looting Cartagena and torturing residents to find every last valuable in the city. When at last they had loaded their treasure and were on their way back to Saint Domingue, a convoy of English warships apprehended them. The English seized their booty and hung many of the buccaneers as pirates. De Pointis, on the other hand, delivered the original Cartagena prize to the French king. As his reward, he received a significant portion of the proceeds and became a very wealthy man.

Cartagena was one of the last buccaneer raids. Piracy from Port Royal ceased completely on June 7, 1692, when an earthquake toppled most of the town into the sea. In 1697 the major powers in Europe made peace. With no legitimate commissions for privateers, many colonial governments began to actively hunt down pirates. Sea raiders would seek, and find, new havens in the Caribbean, but the era of the buccaneers of the New World had ended.

For More Information

BOOKS

Cordingly, David. "Buccaneer Explorers." In *Pirates: Terror on the High Seas from the Caribbean to the South China Sea.* Edited by David Cordingly. East Bridgewater, MA: World Publications, 1998, 2007.

————. *Under the Black Flag: The Romance and the Reality of Life Among the Pirates.* New York: Random House, 2006, p. 40.

Exquemelin, Alexander. *The Buccaneers of America.* Translated by Alexis Brown. Introduction by Jack Beeching. Mineola, NY: Dover Publications, 2000, pp. 11, 80, 100, 106–7, 117.

Lane, Kris E. *Pillaging an Empire: Piracy in the Americas, 1500–1750.* New York: M.E. Sharpe, 1998.

Latimer, Jon. *Buccaneers of the Caribbean: How Piracy Forged an Empire.* Cambridge, MA: Harvard University Press, 2009.

Marx, Jenifer. "Brethren of the Coast." In *Pirates: Terror on the High Seas from the Caribbean to the South China Sea.* Edited by David Cordingly. East Bridgewater, MA: World Publications, 1998, 2007, p. 50.

PERIODICALS

Pyle, Howard. "Jamaica, New and Old." *Harper's* 80, no. 477/35 (December 1889 to May 1890): 378–96.

WEB SITES

Hamilton, Donny L. "The Port Royal Project: History of Port Royal." *Nautical Archaeology at Texas A&M University.* http://nautarch.tamu.edu/portroyal/PRhist.htm (accessed on January 3, 2011).

"Pirates, Buccaneers and Privateers." *Rochedale State School.* www.rochedalss.eq.edu.au/pirates/pirate1.htm (accessed on January 3, 2011).

The Golden Age of Piracy

Most of the images of piracy in popular culture have origins in a short era known as the golden age of piracy, which began at the end of the seventeenth century and spanned the first three decades of the eighteenth century. During the golden age, some very colorful pirates gained control over areas of the Caribbean Sea and the east coast of North America, and severely damaged European trade routes to Africa and Asia.

Although the pirates of the golden age were probably not very different from the pirates of other times, a few features distinguish them. First, most golden-age pirates had little or no remorse about attacking their own nations' ships. Although many started out as privateers (private owners commissioned by a state or government to attack the merchant ships of an enemy nation), during the golden age a large number of them decided to "go on the account," or become a pirate. They raided ships of any nationality, and their plundering (robbing of goods by force) was strictly for their own profit.

A second difference was that golden-age pirates operated in a large geographic area. Based mainly in the Caribbean, they spread out to Africa, the Middle East, Asia, and along the east coast of North America. This was largely because Great Britain's empire was rapidly growing. In remote regions of Africa and Asia, where British trade was beginning to flourish, there was a window of time in which enormous wealth was being transported by sea without sufficient protection. Pirates pounced on this opportunity. In the Americas, naval power was inadequate to protect the rapidly growing trade of the British colonies, and governmental authority onshore was weak or altogether lacking. For a short time pirates were able to move into the ungoverned areas and use them as bases for their highly successful raids of merchant ships.

One of the distinguishing factors of the golden age is the work of a writer who chronicled the era under the name of Captain Charles Johnson. Johnson's *A General History of the Robberies and Murders of the Most Notorious Pirates*, published in 1724, provides vivid details of

WORDS TO KNOW

booty: Goods stolen from ships or coastal villages during pirate raids or attacks on enemies in time of war.

convoy: A collection of merchant ships traveling together for protection, often escorted by warships.

cutlass: A short, heavy, single-edged sword.

flota: A Spanish treasure fleet that transported goods and riches from the New World to Spain every year.

grapeshot: A cluster of small iron balls usually shot from a cannon.

letter of marque: A document licensing a private ship owner to the seize ships or goods of an enemy nation.

monopoly: Exclusive control or possession of something.

musket: A muzzle-loading shoulder gun with a long barrel.

mutiny: An open rebellion by seamen against their ship's officers.

piragua: A dugout canoe.

pirate base: A place where pirates lived under their own rule and maintained their own defense system.

pirate haven: A safe place for pirates to harbor and repair their ships, resupply, and organize raiding parties.

privateer: A private ship or ship owner commissioned by a state or government to attack the merchant ships of a hostile power.

---

sensational pirate crimes and personalities. It is not known whether Johnson based his tales on first-hand observations or on news reports and trial records. However, historians have determined that Johnson is accurate with his facts, although he may have added a his own embellishments to some tales. Johnson's book brought the golden-age pirates to life for readers of all ages.

The origins of the Pirate Round

In the last two decades of the seventeenth century, sea raiding in the Caribbean was temporarily on the decline for a number of reasons. Thousands of sailors, privateers, and pirates, the majority of whom were English, still sought opportunities to find their fortunes at sea. In the 1690s some of these seamen found their way to the coasts of Africa and Asia. There they preyed on slave traders and merchant ships transporting valuable Asian goods from the shores of India and the Middle East back to Europe.

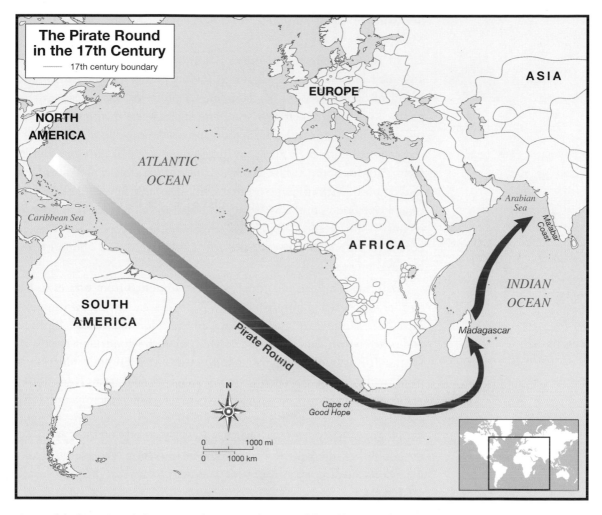

A map of the Pirate Round, the seventeenth-century sailing route followed by pirates from the western Atlantic, traveling around the southern tip of Africa, stopping at Madagascar, then on to targets in the Arabian Sea and Malabar Coast. MAP BY XNR PRODUCTIONS INC./CENGAGE LEARNING.

These pirates followed a course known as the Pirate Round. Starting in the Caribbean Islands or the shores of the Americas, they sailed around the Cape of Good Hope at the southern tip of Africa and then north to the island of Madagascar in the Indian Ocean. At Madagascar the pirates were able to repair their ships in the island's hidden and defendable harbors and get much needed food, drink, and rest. From there the pirates sailed north along the eastern coasts of Africa to carry out raids in the Arabian Sea and along India's Malabar Coast.

In 1685 a pirate named Adam Baldridge left Jamaica for Africa. By 1691 he had established a prosperous trading post and pirate base on the Island of Saint Mary off Madagascar. (A pirate base is a place where pirates lived under their own rule and maintained their own defense system.) There he provided fresh food and drink to the pirates. Baldridge charged the pirates high prices for his goods; a bottle of rum that sold in New York for about twelve cents cost nearly ten dollars at Baldridge's trading post. With his large profits, Baldridge built himself a castle and several warehouses on Saint Mary and began to call himself the "king of pirates." Other traders established similar trading posts at Madagascar ports. According to one estimate, by 1700 there were about fifteen hundred pirates based there.

Baldridge shipped the pirate goods he obtained from pirates to his partner, Frederick Philipse (1626–1702), a wealthy and prominent New York landowner. Although the pirate trade was illegal, Philipse and other North American traders welcomed the goods and paid well for them. Trade in the English colonies was restricted under the provisions of the Navigation Acts, a series of acts dating from 1651 under which the colonists were permitted to trade only with England. The colonists resented England's monopoly, or exclusive control, on trade with them. Without competition, England was able to set high prices on the goods the colonists needed. Merchants in Boston, Philadelphia, and New York sought the exotic products and fair prices that the pirate trade offered.

Thomas Tew

Thomas Tew (d. 1695), a seaman from Rhode Island, was a pioneer of the Pirate Round. In 1690 a group of investors in the English colony of Bermuda backed Tew in a privateering mission to raid a French slave trading post on Africa's Guinea Coast. At that time, England, France, Holland (present-day Netherlands), and Spain were fighting each other in the Nine Years' War (1688–97). The governor of Bermuda issued Tew a letter of marque, a document licensing a private ship owner to seize the ships or goods of an enemy nation. Once Tew's ship was at sea, however, he changed his plans. Doubting that a raid on the trading post would be profitable, Tew proposed to his crew that they should forsake the terms of their privateer license and become pirates in search of more profitable prey. The crew heartily agreed, and in 1692 the ship headed to the Indian Ocean.

Tew sailed his ship around the Horn of Africa (the easternmost projection of Africa) and stopped to rest in Madagascar. Then he sailed up into the Red Sea. There he encountered a large and richly laden ship, probably a treasure ship of the Mughal emperor. (The Mughal Empire ruled all of South Asia, including present-day Bangladesh, Bhutan, India, Nepal, and Pakistan.) Although the Indian ship was well armed and defended by three hundred soldiers, it did not expect an English ship to attack. Tew and his crew easily seized the ship. The booty, chests full of gems, ivory, pearls, spices, silk, and gunpowder, had a value of £100,000, and each pirate's share was about £3,000. (Booty is the goods stolen from ships or coastal villages during pirate raids or attacks on enemies in time of war.) The average wage for a sailor at that time was between £11 and £15 per year, so this was an enormous fortune. When he returned to Rhode Island, Tew was welcomed by colonial business-men and officials, despite having violated the terms of his letter of marque. News of his raid inspired many sailors to sign on for expedi-tions on the Pirate Round.

Henry Every

The most famous raider of the Pirate Round was English seaman Henry Every (also spelled Avery; c. 1653–1699). In 1694 Every was serving as first mate on a ship hired by the Spanish to raid French forts and ships in the Caribbean. When the Spanish failed to pay the crew, Every and some of his shipmates executed a bloodless mutiny, or open rebellion against the ship's officers. They seized one of the Spanish ships, renam-ing it the *Fancy*. The crew elected Every as its captain and set sail for Africa. Every quickly gained the loyalty of his crew. He commanded his ship justly and gave all members of the crew a vote in important decisions.

In August 1695 near the mouth of the Red Sea, the *Fancy* encoun-tered the treasure fleet of the Mughal emperor. Every attacked two ships from the fleet, one of which was the well-armed *Ganj-i-sawai*, the emperor's ship. When the crew of the Indian ship prepared to defend themselves, a cannon exploded on deck, killing everyone around it. During the confusion, Every's men boarded the treasure ship and it was soon under their control. The pirates tortured the ship's passengers to force them to reveal where their valuables were stored. Every and his crew repeatedly raped female passengers. Some of the women jumped overboard to their deaths to escape the horror.

The *Ganj-i-sawai* was packed with treasures. Its gold, silver, ivory, and precious gems were valued at about £150,000. Each pirate on Every's ship received a share of £1,000 from the booty. Not surprisingly, the Mughal emperor complained to the English government. By the time the pirates reached the Caribbean, England had offered a reward for their capture. Every tried to find a colonial governor that would give him a pardon, but none dared. He and his crew fled in different directions. Some of the shipmates were found, and a few were hanged. Every disappeared, never to be heard from again.

Although Every had disappeared, his legend grew. According to stories circulating in England and its colonies, Every had gone on to become the king of a mythical pirate nation located on Madagascar. Every's kingdom was said to be a paradise where everyone was equal, and pirates were rich and free to do whatever they pleased. According to popular belief, during his raid on the *Ganj-i-sawai*, Every had fallen in love with the Great Moghul's daughter, a passenger on the ship, and had married her. These stories could not have been further from the violent truth, but the legends continued. In 1709 a book about Every's Madagascar kingdom enchanted English readers with a romanticized, and purely fictional, view of the pirate king. In 1713 one of London's popular theaters staged a play about Every called *The Successful Pyrate*. These fictional portraits had a powerful effect, as Colin Woodard notes in *The Republic of Pirates: Being the True and Surprising Story of the Caribbean Pirates and the Man Who Brought Them Down*: "To abused young sailors and cabin boys, [Every] had become a hero. He was one of their own, a man who stuck up for his fellow sailors and led them to a promised land, a sailor's heaven on earth."

William Kidd

As the Pirate Round grew ever more prosperous, it sparked conflicting reactions in England and the colonies. Many businessmen wanted a share of the wealth. They invested in privateering missions in Africa and the Indian Ocean, and they expected the captains of these expeditions to plunder ships and ports well beyond the terms laid out in their letters of marque. On the other hand, by the last decade of the seventeenth century, piracy on the Pirate Round had begun to damage the business of the East India Company, England's huge joint stock company that had gained a monopoly on Indian trade. The company demanded that England secure its trade routes against pirates. Aside from these commercial interests, some segments of English society also called for a stop to piracy when news of the raiders' violence appeared in newspapers.

Scottish privateer William Kidd (c.1645–1701) got caught in the middle of these conflicting views. In 1695 Richard Coote (Earl of Bellamont; 1636–1701), the governor of Massachusetts, sought a way to profit from the Pirate Round. He assembled a group of merchants to invest in a privateering expedition in the Indian Ocean and appointed Kidd as its commander. The investors secured a letter of marque for Kidd, authorizing him to attack French ships and hunt down pirate ships. It was a "no prey, no pay" commission, meaning that Kidd and his crew would only be paid if they successfully plundered ships; they would then receive a percentage of the prize.

Kidd departed for the Indian Ocean in 1696. He started with a small crew and picked up more sailors on his journey. Some of the new recruits were experienced pirates and Kidd had difficulty maintaining control of the unruly men. Once, when Kidd stopped an English ship and had just begun to interview its captain, some of his men began to torture the crew—without Kidd's permission—to find out where the ship's treasures were stashed. In another incident, when Kidd's ship anchored off some islands in the Arabian Sea, his crew brutalized the native inhabitants, raping the women and beating the men. Later still, Kidd's gunner, William Moore, complained about the captain's decision not to attack a Dutch ship. (England and the Netherlands were allies, so such an attack would be piracy.) In a rage, Kidd threw a metal bucket at Moore, fracturing his skull. The gunner died one day later.

By January 1698 Kidd's crew was threatening mutiny. Kidd knew the only way to maintain control was to lead them in a successful raid. He was therefore relieved to encounter a potential target: a 400-ton (363-metric-ton) Armenian merchant ship called the *Quedah Merchant*. There was a problem, though. He was only commissioned to raid French ships. According to Captain Johnson, Kidd shrewdly raised a French flag over his own ship. He knew that most merchant vessels carried shipping passes from several different nations. If the captain of the merchant ship thought Kidd's ship was French, he would almost certainly present a French pass, hoping to avoid a privateer raid. The scheme worked. The ship's English captain

William Kidd swinging a bucket at a crewman, William Moore, fracturing his skull.
© BETTMANN/CORBIS.

presented Kidd with French papers. This made a raid more or less legal, and Kidd's men seized and plundered the ship. They collected a fortune in booty and went on to raid several more ships before heading home.

When he returned to the Americas, Kidd was surprised to learn that an arrest warrant had been issued for him on the charge of piracy. Because of the turn in public opinion, Governor Coote feared any association with Kidd, although he desperately wanted the booty from Kidd's raids. Kidd was arrested and sent to England for trial, where he was convicted of piracy and murder and sentenced to death. He protested his innocence, saying that he had simply done what his investors had hired him to do and what privateers had been doing for centuries. In 1701 thousands gathered at Execution Dock on the Thames River in London to witness Kidd's hanging. Afterward his dead body was coated with tar and placed in a metal case. It hung over the Thames for several years as a warning to all pirates.

Before his arrest, Kidd buried much of his booty on Gardiners Island, near New York City. After his arrest, Coote recovered a portion of the booty, but he was convinced there was more and spent years looking for it. If there was any buried treasure beyond what Coote uncovered, it was never found. Although buried treasures are associated with pirates in popular culture, few pirates were known to have buried treasure.

War, peace, and privateers

In 1700 the Spanish king died without children. He left his kingdom to one of the heirs to the French throne. The rest of Europe was threatened by the idea of a combined French and Spanish power, because it would have the power to dominate the other countries. Within a year the continent was engulfed in the War of Spanish Succession, which lasted until 1714. In this war, as in so many others, the European powers used privateers to harass their enemies, and the Caribbean became the scene of constant raids.

Because privateering was a vital part of the British war effort and the British government wanted an ever larger force of privateers during the War of the Spanish Succession, in 1708 Parliament legislated that privateers no longer had to give up a portion of their booty to the government; it was all theirs to keep. More sailors became privateers. Then, in 1714, a treaty among European nations restored peace. Thousands of privateers in the Caribbean suddenly found themselves without employment. Some former privateers decided to continue raiding Spanish ships, even though it was no longer legal. Among these pirates were Benjamin Hornigold (d. 1719), his first mate Edward Teach, better known as Blackbeard (c. 1680–1718), and Charles Vane (c.1680–1721).

Nassau

Hornigold began by moving with a large group of privateers to the ruined town of Nassau on New Providence Island in the Bahamas. During the war, the British colony on New Providence had been repeatedly stormed by Spanish and French forces; the town of Nassau had been burned to the ground. Few settlers and virtually no government remained on the island. Nassau featured a perfect harbor for pirates. It was too shallow for the large warships that pursued pirates, and it had many hiding places for pirate vessels.

Situated between Cuba and Florida on the Florida Straits, New Providence Island was ideally located in the middle of Spanish shipping lanes. With large canoes called *piraguas* and light weapons, such as cutlasses (short, heavy, single-edged swords) and muskets (muzzle-loading shoulder guns with a long barrel), Hornigold and his band of pirates successfully raided Spanish merchant ships from their new base. Their success drew other pirates to Nassau, and the port quickly became a pirate haven, a safe place for pirates to harbor and repair their ships, resupply, and organize raiding parties.

An act of nature sealed Nassau's fate as the central pirate haven of the golden age. For centuries Spain had shipped the treasures it was taking from the New World back to Spain in an annual flota (treasure fleet), which sailed as a convoy, or a collection of merchant ships sailing together for protection, often escorted by warships. In July 1715 a fleet of ten treasure ships left Havana, Cuba, headed for Spain. They carried an exceptionally large load of gold, silver, pearls, exotic Asian wares, and other valuables. Off the coast of Florida, the flota was struck by a fierce hurricane, and all ten ships sank. Spain rapidly sent rescue teams to retrieve the valuable cargo, but they could not recover all that had been lost in the sea.

Pirates and privateers throughout the Americas flocked to the Florida shores with hopes of finding the sunken treasure. British privateer Henry Jennings (d. 1745) headed a group of about three hundred seamen that arrived soon after the wreck. They raided the Spanish rescue camp, taking what treasure had been recovered. This group found Nassau a convenient base of operations, and Jennings settled there as one of the pirate haven's leaders. Both Hornigold and Jennings, the two main leaders at Nassau at this time, considered themselves privateers, not pirates. They would only attack French and Spanish prey. At the time, however, Britain was not at war, and they had no legal authority to raid any ships.

The pirate population in Nassau grew rapidly. Markets for trading pirate booty were established on nearby islands, and necessary supplies were imported. The pirates drawn to Nassau, a diverse lot of impoverished sailors, adventurers, and criminals, were, for the time being, too strong for any local authorities to control.

Samuel Bellamy

One of the first pirates in Nassau was Samuel "Black Sam" Bellamy (c. 1689–1717), who arrived at the scene of the Florida shipwrecks in 1715, hoping to find a fortune. By the time he arrived, though, the Spanish treasures had already been plundered. Not wanting to go home empty-handed, he sailed to Nassau, where he joined Hornigold's pirate crew. Bellamy quickly proved himself an able pirate, and raiding Spanish and French ships brought him wealth and prestige among the pirates.

By 1716 Hornigold had fallen out of favor with the crew of his ship, because he continually refused to raid English ships. To most of the pirates, peace had rendered privateering a thing of the past, and Hornigold's scruples about raiding English ships cut into their profits. Hornigold's crew decided to exercise the democratic practices that governed most pirate ships, by voting Hornigold out and electing Bellamy to be their new captain. Over the next year Bellamy and his crew raided more than fifty ships in the Caribbean and along the Atlantic coast of North America. They raided strictly as pirates, attacking any ship regardless of nationality, and they amassed a great fortune.

In a very short period of time, Bellamy had raised himself from poverty to become the commander of a highly successful pirate fleet. His reputation grew, not only for his successes, but also for his outspoken views about pirate life. Like many other pirates, Bellamy had experienced the indignities of life on merchant and navy vessels when he was a young sailor. He believed that piracy freed men from oppression and made everyone equal. Despite his life of crime, Bellamy viewed himself as a leader among men. He enjoyed making grand speeches about piracy, and his speeches seemed to capture the spirit of the era.

In February 1717 Bellamy seized a 300-ton (272-metric-ton) English slave ship, the *Whydah*, which was on its way back to England after selling its cargo. Bellamy kept the ship and refitted it for piracy. He then sailed up the east coast of North America. The *Whydah* encountered a furious

Sam Bellamy: A Free Prince

Pirate captain Samuel "Black Sam" Bellamy (c. 1689–1717) was fond of speaking his mind. His speeches to his crews often reflected the golden-age pirates' anger at the upper classes of English society, particularly ship owners and captains. In 1717 Bellamy seized the ship of a Captain Beer. While his men were looting Beer's vessel, Bellamy had time to share his views with the captain, who wrote down his captor's words soon after being released. The portion of the speech quoted below took place after the pirate crew had voted to burn Beer's sloop. Bellamy apologized to the captain for this but then seemed to recollect past grievances with ships' captains and began to rant, as quoted by Colin Woodard in *The Republic of Pirates: Being the True and Surprising Story of the Caribbean Pirates and the Man Who Brought Them Down*:

> Damn ye, you are a sneaking puppy, and so are all those who will submit to be governed by laws which rich men have made for their own security, for the cowardly whelps [puppies] have not the courage otherwise to defend what they get by their knavery.... They vilify [say bad things about] us, the scoundrels do, when there is only this difference [between rich men who are not pirates and pirates]: they rob the poor under the cover of law ... and we plunder the rich under cover of our own courage.

In parting, Bellamy said, "I am a free Prince, and I have as much authority to make war on the whole world as he who has a hundred ships at sea and an army of 100,000 men in the field."

storm just as it approached Cape Cod, Massachusetts. The ship was wrecked, and Bellamy and all but two of his crew were killed.

More than 250 years later, in 1984, underwater explorer Barry Clifford (1945–), discovered the *Whydah* off Cape Cod. Hundreds of thousands of relics that were recovered from the sunken ship can be viewed today at the Whydah Museum in Provincetown, Massachusetts.

Hornigold and Blackbeard

When Bellamy and his shipmates removed Hornigold as their captain, Hornigold's first mate, Blackbeard, remained loyal. Blackbeard had begun sailing with Hornigold around 1715. After Bellamy took over Hornigold's ship and crew, Blackbeard and Hornigold continued to raid ships from Nassau. One of their prizes was a large slave ship, which they refitted as a forty-gun pirate ship. Hornigold gave the ship to Blackbeard to command. Blackbeard renamed it the *Queen Anne's Revenge*. Together, Hornigold and Blackbeard, with a small fleet, proceeded to raid French and Spanish ships up and down the Atlantic coast of North America. Blackbeard and Hornigold parted ways in 1717.

As a pirate captain, Blackbeard was highly successful, and he soon established fame as the most frightening of all pirates. In truth, by pirate standards, he was not exceptionally violent or cruel. He was a natural leader, exceedingly brave, and wise enough to know that a pirate's success lay in his ability to terrify. He crafted a frightening image, as described by Captain Charles Johnson in *A General History of the Robberies and Murders of the Most Notorious Pirates*:

This beard was black, which he suffered to grow of an extravagant length; as to breadth it came up to his eyes. He was accustomed to

Blackbeard crafted a frightful appearance to terrify his foes in battle. PRIVATE COLLECTION/ PETER NEWARK IIISTORICAL PICTURES/THE BRIDGEMAN ART LIBRARY INTERNATIONAL.

twist it with ribbons, in small tails ... and turn them about his ears. In time of action, he wore a sling over his shoulders with three brace of pistols hanging in holsters like bandaliers, and stuck lighted matches under his hat, which, appearing on each side of his face, his eyes naturally looking fierce and wild, made him altogether such a figure, that imagination cannot form an idea of a fury, from hell, to look more frightful.

Woodes Rogers and the antipiracy campaign

In 1718 Britain sent naval forces and a new governor to the Bahamas to establish a legitimate government on New Providence. The new governor,

Woodes Rogers (c. 1679–1732), was also tasked with eradicating piracy in the Caribbean. An ex-privateer and slave trader, Rogers had once launched an expedition from Britain to the Pacific coast of South America. He had proved an able commander at sea. Rogers set out for Nassau in January 1718 with a fleet of seven vessels.

Rogers had a plan to rid the colonies of piracy. He brought to Nassau a pardon from the king. All pirates who turned themselves in before September 5, 1718, and promised to stop their criminal activities would be pardoned for previous crimes and could keep whatever booty they had amassed. After September 5, Rogers was authorized to use all his forces to hunt down and prosecute pirates.

The commodore of the pirates

Hornigold and Blackbeard reacted in different ways to the news of Rogers's approach. Hornigold decided to accept the king's pardon and returned to Nassau. Blackbeard sailed on, seeking a new base of operations. He chose Ocracoke Island, off North Carolina. By 1718 he was in command of a pirate fleet of heavily armed ships, with a crew of about four hundred men. There were, as yet, no British naval warships available to stop him. Calling himself the commodore of pirates, he achieved virtual control of the east coast of North America.

In May 1718 Blackbeard accomplished one of his most notorious feats. He anchored his fleet in the harbor of Charles Town (present-day Charleston), South Carolina, and stopped all traffic going in and out of the harbor. He quickly captured eight or nine vessels in the harbor, holding some of the passengers hostage. The terrified residents of Charles Town watched as one of Blackbeard's boats rowed ashore, and the pirates made their ransom demands. As it happened, all Blackbeard wanted from the city was a chest of medical supplies. If he did not receive the supplies within three days, however, he vowed to behead his hostages and burn the seized ships. Charles Town handed over the supplies, and Blackbeard released his hostages and left the port.

The end of pirate havens

When Hornigold returned to Nassau, there were between one thousand and fifteen hundred pirates there. The pirates were divided about accepting the king's pardon. Some, like Hornigold, wanted to turn themselves in, while others intended to continue as pirates. Few wanted to fight the new governor and his massive forces, but Charles Vane, a Nassau-based pirate known for his cruelty and dishonesty, decided he would rather go out in a blaze of glory than to sit idly while Nassau was taken over.

On July 24, 1718, Woodes Rogers's powerful fleet approached the Nassau harbor. In the night, Vane unloaded one of his ships and doused it with pitch and tar. Two of his pirates sailed the ship directly at Rogers's fleet and set their vessel on fire. The heat from the fire set off the ship's cannons and guns, and it nearly destroyed the two warships escorting Rogers's fleet. While the fire ship drew the attention of Rogers's crew, Vane stealthily sailed out of the harbor. Rogers moved his forces onto the island without further trouble.

Leaving Nassau to its new governor, Vane sailed up the Atlantic coast to Ocracoke Island. There he and Blackbeard and their pirate crews engaged in a week-long party. Reports of the wild festivities reached the fiercely antipirate Virginia governor, Alexander Spotswood (c. 1676–1740). Fearing that Blackbeard would make the entire eastern seaboard into a pirate haven, Spotswood put a plan into action. In November 1718, two ships commanded by Robert Maynard (1684–1751) set out from Hampton, Virginia, to capture Blackbeard.

Maynard arrived at Ocracoke Island on November 21. As he approached Blackbeard's ship, it fired on him. When the pirates boarded Maynard's ship, the troops were ready for them and fierce hand-to-hand combat followed. Blackbeard was wounded by a gunshot on boarding, but he immediately engaged in a sword fight with Maynard. There are several versions of Blackbeard's end. According to Captain Johnson, after a long and heated fight, the naval commander's blade broke. When Blackbeard lunged to strike him, one of Maynard's men drew his cutlass and slashed the pirate's neck and throat in a fatal blow. Bleeding profusely from the neck, Blackbeard continued to fight but soon collapsed and died. Maynard had Blackbeard's head removed and hung it from the front of his ship.

Meanwhile, on New Providence Island, more than six hundred pirates asked for, and received, pardons. Some, including Hornigold, joined Woodes Rogers as pirate hunters. Other pirates who accepted the king's pardon soon returned to their old raiding practices. Rogers was prepared for this and sent out his pirate hunters after them.

Blackbeard and Robert Maynard fighting to the death. PRIVATE COLLECTION/PETER NEWARK HISTORICAL PICTURES/ THE BRIDGEMAN ART LIBRARY INTERNATIONAL.

Bartholomew Roberts

Although Nassau was no longer a safe haven for pirates, the golden age was not over. Some pirates returned to the Pirate Round, since the Caribbean was becoming hostile to pirates. One of these men,

Welsh pirate Bartholomew "Black Bart" Roberts (1682–1722) was just beginning his short, but profitable, career. Roberts had been second mate on a slave ship when it was captured off the west coast of Africa by another Welsh pirate, Howell Davis (c. 1690–1719), in 1719. Davis had forced Roberts to join the pirate ship against his will, but he set to work anyway, using his skills in navigation to aid the captain. Six weeks after Roberts's capture, Davis was killed by Portuguese forces in an ambush off the African island of Principe. Despite his lack of experience as a pirate, the crew elected Roberts as their new captain. According to Johnson, Roberts believed that "since he had dipped his hands in muddy water, and must be a pirate, it was better being a commander than a common man." Roberts's first act as pirate was to return to Principe to avenge his former captain's death by attacking the Portuguese fort there.

Roberts quickly gained the loyalty of his crew. He was a stern, but natural leader who demanded discipline. Roberts differed from most pirates in that he did not drink alcohol. He was tall and handsome and particular about his clothes. Roberts is said to have captured four hundred ships and traveled tens of thousands of miles during his thirty months as a pirate. He and his crew left Africa and began raiding in Brazil in 1719. In 1720 they passed New England and sailed up to Newfoundland, an island off the east coast of present-day Canada, where they raided hundreds of ships. They spent six months successfully raiding the Leeward Islands, a chain of islands in the northeastern Caribbean Sea where it meets the Atlantic Ocean. In 1721 Roberts returned to Africa to raid slave ships. By that time he commanded a fleet of four large and powerful ships with a crew of 508 men. His raids were noted for their sheer daring, and Roberts did not hesitate to use violence and torture.

Colonial forces pursued Roberts for some time, finally catching up with him in Africa. In February 1722 a British warship commanded by Captain Chaloner Ogle (1681–1750) approached Roberts's ship. Roberts dressed for this occasion, as he did for most attacks, putting on an exquisite red waistcoat (a sleeveless and collarless garment worn under an overcoat), a large brimmed hat with an unusual red feather, and a thick gold chain bearing a large diamond cross. Wearing his brace of pistols on a scarlet silk sling suspended from his shoulders, he boldly strode the deck, giving orders. The British ship pulled up and fired grapeshot (a cluster of small iron balls shot from a cannon). One round tore out

Roberts's throat, killing him instantly. Carrying out his earlier request, his crew anchored his body and threw it into the sea so it would not be taken by the British. Ogle captured three of Roberts's ships, arresting more than two hundred pirates.

A month later the pirates from Roberts's fleet were tried at Cape Coast Castle, a slave-trading center in West Africa. It was the largest pirate trial and execution of the golden age. Fifty-four pirates were hanged, and thirty-seven were sentenced to labor camp (where most would die). Seventy-four men were acquitted after claiming that they had been forced to join Roberts's crew. More than seventy African pirates from Roberts's ship were sold into slavery.

The end of an age

After the trial of Roberts's men, piracy steadily decreased. Several factors contributed to the end of the golden age of piracy. For one thing, the governments of the new American colonies got rid of many of the corrupt officials who had been profiting by the crimes of pirates. In 1721 Britain passed the Piracy Act, which punished those who traded with or aided pirates. Britain's Royal Navy was another factor. By the 1720s it had become the leading maritime power in the world, and it was dedicated to protecting British trade routes and suppressing piracy. Beginning with the efforts of Rogers and Spotswood, the British anti-piracy campaign picked up momentum, with warships chasing down and prosecuting pirates throughout the Caribbean, North American, and African seas.

Harsh laws and strict enforcement were another key factor. Between 1716 and 1726 more than four hundred men were hanged for piracy. In the year 1723 alone, eighty-two pirates were hanged. Little mercy was shown to pirates by the courts. While it had been the custom in the seventeenth century to hang only the captain and top officers of a pirate ship, in the eighteenth century, entire crews were hung.

Pirate hangings were major social events in eighteenth-century Britain and its colonies. People brought picnic lunches and gathered to watch with their friends and families as convicted pirates were paraded to the execution dock. A prayer was said, and the pirate was allowed to make a speech, if desired. Then he was hung. The body was left hanging over the waters for a day and a half. Afterward, the bodies of the best-known pirates were frequently coated with tar to preserve them and then hoisted over a harbor

The public hanging of a pirate in England in the eighteenth century. Pirate hangings were major social events in eighteenth-century England and its colonies. PRIVATE COLLECTION/PETER NEWARK HISTORICAL PICTURES/THE BRIDGEMAN ART LIBRARY INTERNATIONAL.

for display. The gruesome decomposing bodies were a constant reminder of what lay in store for any who dared to continue raiding ships. By the end of the 1720s the British navy had gained control of its trade routes and its American colonies. The golden age of piracy was over.

For More Information

BOOKS

Cordingly, David. *Under the Black Flag: The Romance and the Reality of Life Among the Pirates.* New York: Random House, 2006.

Johnson, Charles. *A General History of the Robberies and Murders of the Most Notorious Pirates.* Guilford, CT: The Lyons Press, 1998, 2002, pp. 60, 162.

Marx, Jenifer. "The Golden Age of Piracy" and "The Pirate Round." In *Pirates: Terror on the High Seas from the Caribbean to the South China Sea.* Edited by David Cordingly. East Bridgewater, MA: World Publications, 1998, 2007.

Shomette, Donald G. *Pirates on the Chesapeake: Being a True History of Pirates, Picaroons, and Raiders on Chesapeake Bay, 1610–1807*. Centreville, MD: Tidewater Publishers, 1985.

Woodard, Colin. *The Republic of Pirates: Being the True and Surprising Story of the Caribbean Pirates and the Man Who Brought Them Down*. Orlando, FL: Harcourt, 2007, pp. 27 and 173–74.

PERIODICALS

"The Real Pirates of the Caribbean." *USA Today* (January 2009): 42.

WEB SITES

Age of Pirates. http://ageofpirates.com (accessed on January 3, 2011).

"Pirates of the Whydah," *National Geographic*. www.nationalgeographic.com/whydah/main.html (accessed on January 3, 2011).

7

Life Aboard Ship in the Golden Age of Piracy

The golden age of piracy spanned the years 1690 to 1730. During that time, pirates raided and plundered (robbed of goods by force) vessels and ports over a huge area, including the Caribbean Islands, the east coast of North America, Africa, and the Indian Ocean. Unlike the privateers of earlier times, who were authorized to raid enemy ships and ports by their governments during wartime, most golden-age pirates raided strictly for their own profit. By everyone's standards they were criminals, and often violent ones. Some historians contend, though, that many young sailors became pirates in an attempt to escape the injustices and oppression they had experienced as members of the lowest classes in eighteenth century society. Many pirates of the golden age ended all connections to their home countries, swearing allegiance only to their comrades on their pirate ships. Aboard a pirate ship, they formed a very different culture than the one they had left behind.

According to pirate historian Marcus Rediker, during the peak years of the golden age, the decade from 1716 to 1726, there were a total of forty-five hundred to fifty-five hundred pirates, with perhaps about one thousand to twenty-four hundred on the seas at any given time. The pirates hailed from many nations and ethnic groups, although the majority came from the British Isles. An example of this diversity can be seen on the pirate ship *Whydah* under the command of pirate captain Samuel Bellamy (c. 1689–1717). According to Kenneth J. Kinkor, in "Black Men Under the Black Flag," the crew of the *Whydah* "included not only English, Irish, Scottish, Welsh, and British colonials, but also Frenchmen, Dutchmen, Spaniards, Swedes, Native Americans, African-Americans, and Africans." Pirates came almost exclusively from the lowest classes of European and colonial society, and most had served as seamen for merchant or naval ships prior to becoming pirates. All pirates of this age were men, with the exception of only four known women.

WORDS TO KNOW

barnacle: A shell-like marine animal that attaches itself to the underwater portion of a ship's hull.

blunderbuss: A short musket with a flared muzzle.

booty: Goods stolen from ships or coastal villages during pirate raids or attacks on enemies in time of war.

careening: A regular process of cleaning the bottom of a ship.

cat-o'-nine-tails: A whip with nine knotted cords.

cutlass: A short, heavy, single-edged sword.

duel: A prearranged fight with deadly weapons to settle a quarrel under specific rules.

flintlock pistol: A small and comparatively lightweight gun that loads through the front of the barrel.

grapeshot: A cluster of small iron balls usually shot from a cannon.

grenado: An early form of hand grenade comprised of hollow balls made of iron, glass, or wood and filled with gunpowder.

maroon: To strand an individual on a deserted island or shore with few provisions.

impressment: The practice of forcibly recruiting sailors to serve in the navy.

plunder: To rob of goods by force, in a raid or in wartime.

pirate base: A place where pirates lived under their own rule and maintained their own defense system.

privateer: A private ship or ship owner commissioned by a state or government to attack the merchant ships of an enemy nation.

ransom: A sum of money demanded for the release of someone being held captive.

rigging: The system of ropes, chains, and other gear used to support and control the masts and sails of a sailing vessel.

scurvy: A disease caused by a lack of vitamin C, characterized by spongy and bleeding gums, bruising, and extreme weakness.

ship's articles: The written sets of rules and conditions under which pirates operated on any given expedition.

Golden-age pirates left few written accounts behind. Historians like Rediker and Kinkor, though, have used existing evidence to piece together what their lives were like, what motivated them, and how they interacted with one another and with the rest of the world. Pirate historians today are greatly aided by *A General History of the Robberies and Murders of the Most Notorious Pirates*, a contemporary history of the golden age written under the name of Captain Charles Johnson and first published in 1724. Johnson's book provides a wealth of details about the lives and deeds of the pirates that might otherwise have been lost.

The life of an English sailor

The vast majority of golden-age pirates came from the ranks of ordinary eighteenth-century seamen. The wretched conditions experienced onboard naval or merchant vessels profoundly influenced them in their later careers. For an English sailor at that time, everyday work aboard ship was hard and extremely dangerous. Crew members were killed or maimed handling heavy cargo and climbing up masts in rough weather. Heavy rigging frequently fell from the masts, crushing sailors below. (Rigging is the system of ropes, chains, and other gear used to support and control the masts and sails of a sailing vessel.) In winter the seamen worked in freezing, windy weather in wet clothing. If the risky work did not kill the sailors, illness often did. The ships were full of rats, cockroaches, and other vermin (small insects or animals that cause harm and annoyance) that spread infectious diseases, such as dysentery, which caused severe diarrhea, and typhus, which caused high fever, rash, and delirium.

Food onboard an eighteenth-century vessel was meager and often rotten. The main foods, salted beef and pork and dry biscuits, were stored in barrels. After a few weeks at sea the dried meats began to rot, and the biscuits became infested with maggots (the larvae of flies). The water supply became foul and spread disease. To avoid illness, most sailors drank alcohol instead of water. A major killer of sailors was scurvy, a deadly disease caused by a diet lacking in vitamin C, which is found in fresh fruit and vegetables. Sailors with scurvy developed spongy, bleeding gums. They bruised easily and grew weak. Eventually their bones broke, their teeth fell out, and their sores stopped healing. Historians believe that scurvy killed more sailors than any other factor of life at sea.

Sailors were generally treated poorly by their employers. Once they signed on to a ship, they were under the control of the ship's captain, and discipline was harsh. A common punishment for unruly sailors was flogging with a cat-o'-nine-tails, a whip with nine knotted cords. Some ship captains physically abused their crews. David Cordingly writes in *Under the Black Flag: The Romance and the Reality of Life Among the Pirates* that a ship "could be turned into a torture chamber by a sadistic captain [one who derived pleasure from inflicting pain on others].... The records of the High Court of Admiralty are filled with horror stories of the brutality inflicted on seamen." Sailors' wages for their work were pitifully low and greedy ship masters cheated many seamen out of what little they had earned. The laws of eighteenth-century England did not protect the seamen but rather empowered ship captains and ship owners.

IMPRESSMENT OF BOSTONIANS BY KNOWLES.

Sailors being pressed into service in the English Navy. © NORTH WIND PICTURE ARCHIVES/ALAMY.

The conditions of an English seaman's life were so awful that physician and author Samuel Johnson (1709–1784) once remarked, as quoted by Marcus Rediker in *Between the Devil and the Deep Blue Sea: Merchant Seamen, Pirates and the Anglo-American Maritime World, 1700–1750*, "No man will be a sailor who has contrivance [cleverness in planning] enough to get himself into jail: for being in a ship is being in jail with the chance of being drowned. . . . A man in jail has more room, better food, and commonly better company."

Not surprisingly, not enough men voluntarily signed up to go to sea for the merchant or navy forces to function. England therefore authorized the Royal Navy to forcibly recruit sailors, a practice known as impressment. Press gangs, groups of men armed with clubs and led by a naval officer, were dispatched to harbors and cities where they rounded up sailors on streets, in their homes, at the tavern, and even some who were just returning to port from another voyage. The sailors pressed into service had no choice but to go to sea, sometimes for more than one year at a time. Merchant ships often resorted to trickery to entice seamen, either by getting them thoroughly drunk and then signing them on or by lying about the terms of their service.

When pirates raided a merchant ship, they often gathered all its sailors on the deck and asked who among the crew wished join them as pirates. In most cases, quite a few sailors instantly stepped forward. Notorious pirate Bartholomew Roberts (1682–1722), as quoted by Johnson, summed up why they chose piracy: "In an honest service [as a sailor] there is thin commons [little food], low wages, and hard labour; in this [piracy], [there is] plenty and satiety, pleasure and ease, liberty and power. . . . No, a merry life and a short one, shall be my motto."

Pirate democracy

Sailors who joined pirate ships signed on as equal members of the crew. Almost all pirate ships practiced a rough form of democracy, following customs of social organization in which every shipmate had a say in important decisions. There were no social classes onboard, and the power that the ship's captain held over the crew was very limited.

Ship's articles, the written sets of rules and conditions under which pirates operated on any given expedition, were the foundation of pirate democracy. Ship's articles had developed during the seventeenth century with the buccaneers of the New World. (For more information see **The Buccaneers of the New World**.) All pirate expeditions began with every member of the crew signing the articles. Although they differed in a few details, the articles of most pirate ships were remarkably similar.

A good example of ship's articles were those of Bartholomew Roberts. Roberts's articles ensured equality for members of his ship. They stated that every pirate onboard had a vote in important decisions. Everyone was equally entitled to whatever food and liquor was aboard. Division of the booty was nearly equal, though those who took the greatest risks got a slightly larger reward. (Booty is the goods stolen from ships or coastal villages during pirate raids or attacks on enemies in time of war.) The captain and quartermaster of the ship were entitled to two shares of the booty; the master, boatswain, and gunner received a share and a half; other officers received a share and a quarter; and all other crew members were entitled to one share.

What Pirates Ate

Golden-age pirates experienced cycles of feast and famine while they were at sea. When they set out on an expedition, they packed their vessels with fresh foods, such as meats, eggs, cheeses, and vegetables, as well as longer-lasting foods, such as dry beans, pickled vegetables, salted beef and pork, and hardtack biscuits (hard crackers made of flour and water). The pirates brought along some livestock to kill for later meals and kept poultry in cages to provide eggs. During the first couple of weeks at sea, pirates feasted. After that, the remaining fresh food began to rot. The animals were killed and eaten.

A few weeks into the voyage, the food stored in the hold came out. Even the dried foods eventually went bad. Ship's cooks used heavy spices to cover up the taste of rot. Pirates were known to eat only in darkened rooms, so they would not have to see the maggots (fly larvae) in their biscuits and dried meats. Water went bad on the pirate ship, too, and pirates generally only drank rum and ale. Alcoholism was a major problem among seamen and pirates. Some pirates died from alcohol abuse; others died performing dangerous tasks while their judgment was impaired by alcohol.

A pirate vessel quickly went from famine to feast when the pirates raided a ship full of fresh stores or stopped at a port where they could steal or purchase new supplies. Temporary satisfaction came when the pirates were able to catch sea turtles and fish. When possible, the ship's cook prepared the favorite pirate meal, salamagundi, a salad or stew consisting of any ingredients available, usually some combination of chopped meat, fish, turtle, garlic, wine, boiled eggs, onions, cabbage, olives, oil, and lots of spices.

The articles also contained provisions for medical care and disability. For anyone who was injured during a pirate raid, there was money to provide for him. If a pirate lost a limb or was otherwise crippled, he would receive eight hundred dollars; other injuries would be paid in proportion to how serious they were. There were also rules of conduct to keep order. There was no fighting allowed onboard the ship. Quarrels between two men were to be taken ashore and handled by a duel, or a prearranged fight with deadly weapons, conducted under specified rules. Deserting the ship was punished by death or marooning (stranding an individual on a deserted island or shore with few provisions). Everyone was to keep their weapons clean and in good order. No boys or women were allowed on the ship. Roberts's ship's articles had special rules about drinking at night and forbade gambling for money on his ship. Some ship's articles forbade the pirates to harm women on the vessels they raided.

Roles of captain and crew

There were three levels of authority on a pirate ship: the captain, the quartermaster, and the pirate council. The captain and quartermaster were elected by the ship's crew. During a pirate raid, the captain had complete authority over the crew, and his orders were to be obeyed without question. At any other time, however, a captain could be voted out of office by his crew if they were not satisfied with his performance. One of many instances of a pirate captain being removed by his crew occurred in 1718, when Captain Charles Vane (c. 1680–1721) decided to retreat when his fleet encountered a French warship. His crew, headed by English pirate John "Calico Jack" Rackham (1682–1720), felt Vane had acted in a cowardly manner. They voted him out of office, elected Rackham as captain, and took over the fleet, sending Vane off in a small, unarmed vessel. Captains of pirate ships received very few special privileges. They did not have their own sleeping quarters aboard ship, and they ate with the crew. Seamen did not join the pirates to be controlled by a new set of authority figures.

The quartermaster was almost the equal of the captain. His role was to represent the interests of the crew. Along with handling any disputes, the quartermaster made sure that everyone received equal treatment, equal food and drink, and equal shares of the booty. The most important decisions made on a pirate ship, though, were not made by the captain or quartermaster, but by the pirate council, which was made up of every crew member. On many pirate vessels, the pirate council voted on every decision.

A ship's crew was made up of seamen who had joined willingly and seamen who had been forced by the pirates to join when their ships were captured in a raid. Many seamen who did not initially want to join the pirates became willing participants after being forced to join. Others escaped at the first opportunity. Pirates were usually particular about the sailors they recruited. They needed people with specialties, such as surgeons, musicians, carpenters, and navigators. They preferred unmarried men who had no ties outside the pirate ship, and they admired courage above all things.

Pirate vessels

Pirates stole whatever types of vessels came closest to suiting their purposes. In the eighteenth century the word *ship* was more specific than it is today, meaning a large sailing vessel with three or more masts with square-rigged sails. Warships and large merchant vessels were ships. Pirate captains, such as Edward Teach, better known as Blackbeard (c. 1680–1718), and Bartholomew Roberts, sailed in huge square-rigged ships, using them to head fleets of smaller pirate vessels. (Square-rigged ships had masts set at right angles to the ship's hull.) Most pirates sailed in smaller vessels, usually sloops or schooners, that could escape from law enforcement authorities by darting in and out of coves and shallow inlets.

In the eighteenth century, pirates had a variety of ships to choose from. Some of the most common vessels are described below, listed from smallest to largest:

A sailor is recruited for service on a pirate ship. Pirates were usually particular about the sailors they recruited because they needed men with special skills. PRIVATE COLLECTION/PETER NEWARK HISTORICAL PICTURES/THE BRIDGEMAN ART LIBRARY INTERNATIONAL.

Sloop: The most popular pirate vessel. An eighteenth-century sloop was a fast vessel with a single fore-and-aft rigged mast, meaning that the mast was positioned for sails set lengthwise along the ship. Sloops had narrow bows (fronts) and were fast and maneuverable. They weighed about 100 tons (91 metric tons) and varied in length from 30 to 70 feet (9 to 21 meters). Sloops could carry up to seventy-five pirates and were often armed with four to twelve guns in the upper deck. Some of the best sloops in the eighteenth century were built by shipbuilders in Jamaica and Bermuda.

Schooner: A two-masted vessel, similar in size to a sloop, weighing 100 tons (91 metric tons), and carrying about seventy-five pirates. Schooners had narrow hulls, making them very fast, and a large bowsprit, a pole extending forward from the front of the vessel.

They were usually built in North America; those built in Baltimore, Maryland, were renowned.

Brigantine: A two-masted vessel with two sails rigged to each mast. This variety of vessel included brigs and snows. Brigantines were about 80 feet (24 meters) long, weighed about 150 tons (136 metric tons), carried about one hundred pirates, and were armed with about ten cannons. With their two masts, brigantines could be rigged with many combinations of square-rigged or fore-and-aft sails. They were heavier than sloops and were better suited to raiding and combat than hit-and-run attacks.

Frigate: A three-masted, medium-sized warship. The sizes ranged greatly, from 250 to 500 tons (227 to 454 metric tons), and they could carry two hundred men or more. Frigates were more seaworthy, but slower, than sloops and brigantines. They had a raised quarterdeck and forecastle, where their twenty-four to forty guns were carried. They had good storage space and, with large stores of food and water, they could remain at sea for long periods.

Pirates altered the vessels they stole to fit their needs. They removed the cabins and the structures on the upper decks to make more room for guns and crew. Pirates almost always added more cannons to the vessels to gain the advantage during their raids. Using all the fire power of a pirate ship required a large crew, and pirate ships were always crowded.

Eighteenth-century vessels were made of wood, and the tropical seas teemed with shipworms, wormlike mollusks that could bore holes in the wooden hull (frame) of the vessel. If the shipworms were left to their work, the vessels began to leak. Careening, a regular process of cleaning the bottom of a ship, was required, preferably once every three months. Careening involved beaching (landing on a beach) the vessel during a high tide and then heaving it over onto one side on the beach. The pirates then cleaned the exposed side, removing barnacles and weeds. (A barnacle is a shell-like marine animal that attaches itself to the underwater portion of a ship's hull.) They replaced damaged planks and then coated the hull with tar, sulfur, and tallow (animal fat commonly used in candles). Careening was a particular problem for pirates. With their vessels out of commission, their defense systems were down as well. If the pirates were unable to find a harbor where they would be safely hidden while they cleaned the vessel's bottom, they delayed careening. This caused the vessel to become riddled with leaks, slowing it down and sometimes severely damaging it.

The Jolly Roger pirate flags of famous pirates, including (from left to right) Walter Kennedy, Christopher Moody, Edward England, Henry Every, Christopher Condent, John Rackham, Bartholomew Roberts, Edward Low, and Blackbeard. PRIVATE COLLECTION/PETER NEWARK HISTORICAL PICTURES/THE BRIDGEMAN ART LIBRARY INTERNATIONAL.

The Jolly Roger

The Jolly Roger, the flag of a pirate ship, originated among the buccaneers of the New World in the seventeenth century. The buccaneers usually used solid red flags, and the French term *jolie rouge,* or "pretty red," may have been the basis of the term *Jolly Roger.* The red flag signaled to ships under attack that "no quarter would be given," meaning the pirates would grant no mercy if they met with resistance. In the eighteenth century, most pirates began to use black backgrounds for their flags, although red flags were still used. Each pirate captain designed his own flag, but they all carried the same basic images of death. Many had an image of a grinning skull with crossed bones, or crossed swords, beneath it. Others displayed an image of a dancing skeleton. Blackbeard designed a flag with a skeleton holding an hourglass in one hand (meaning that time was running out), while the other hand stabbed at a bleeding heart. The images were designed to induce fear.

Pirates used other flags besides the Jolly Roger when it was convenient. By flying a British, Dutch, French, or other national flag, a pirate ship might pass for a merchant ship and avoid pursuit by naval forces or pirate hunters. Pirates frequently tried to fool the ships they wished to attack into submission by displaying a friendly country's flag. Unlike privateers in earlier eras, though, pirates generally did not claim one nationality over another. Their flag was the Jolly Roger, and their ship was their nation.

Pirate attack methods and weapons

When pirates spotted a merchant ship they wished to attack, they usually began by raising the Jolly Roger. Merchant vessels, even the large ships, tended to have small crews of only about ten to eighteen men. The crews were not well armed or trained to fight. Pirate vessels, on the other hand, were likely to have seventy or more heavily armed pirates aboard. Most merchant ships surrendered without resistance when they saw a Jolly Roger raised.

Some merchant ships did resist pirate attacks, and for good reason. Certain pirate captains were known for their violence and gruesome torture techniques. There was no guarantee; even if a ship surrendered to the pirates without fighting, it still might suffer a terrible fate. Therefore, some merchant ships, when they could not escape from pirates, prepared to fight. Battle began when the merchant ship fired its cannons at the pirate vessel, which usually caused the pirates to counterattack with full force. They tried to do as little damage to the ship as possible, since it would soon be in their possession and might be of value to them. They were not always as careful with the lives of the merchant ship's crew.

To start their attack pirates often threw grenados, an early form of hand grenade, onto the enemy's deck. Grenados were small hollow balls made of iron, glass, or wood. They were filled with gunpowder and had fuses that were lit before they were tossed. When they exploded on the merchant ship's deck, they killed and injured the people within close range. The pirates also loaded their cannons with grapeshot and fired it across the decks of the merchant vessel. Grapeshot is a cluster of small iron balls (looking like a bunch of grapes) that are loosely packed in a canvas bag. When fired, the iron balls spread out from a cannon's muzzle at high speed and sprayed a large area with deadly missiles. If the merchant ship continued to resist after grenados and grapeshot were fired, the pirates resorted to using the big guns. Sometimes they fired on the main section of an enemy ship with cannons. At other times, they used their cannons to shoot down the enemy's mast, thereby disabling the ship and creating chaos on the deck.

To board, pirates frequently approached the merchant ship in small vessels. They used grappling hooks and boarding axes to climb the sides of the ship. The axes also served as deadly weapons once onboard. The pirates carried many other weapons on their bodies as well. They had firearms, such as the flintlock pistol, a small and comparatively lightweight gun that loaded through the front of the barrel. A pistol only fired a single shot, so most pirates carried several pistols, often in sashes strapped over their shoulders. Pirates also carried the much larger blunderbuss, a short musket with a flared muzzle. Pirates usually had the upper hand in close fighting. They were experts with small knives known as daggers and with swords known as cutlasses, the most popular of pirate weapons. With their 2-foot (0.6-meter) blades and single curved edge, cutlasses were skillfully wielded to cut down the last resisting sailors.

Violence and torture

When a ship had surrendered and the crew was subdued, some pirate crews interrogated the sailors to find out how their captain treated them. Many pirates, having been employed as sailors in earlier life, had bitter feelings about ship captains. If the crew reported that their captain abused them, he was at great risk of being tortured or killed. One pirate, Philip Lyne, confessed after his arrest that during his pirate career he had killed thirty-seven ship commanders. In *Between the Devil and the Deep Blue Sea*, Rediker describes the last words of another pirate, William Fly (d. 1726), who had killed a ship master. Fly announced from the gallows before his hanging that "all Masters of Vessels might take Warning by the Fate of the Captain that he [Fly] had murder'd, and to pay Sailors their Wages when due, and to treat them better; saying, that their Barbarity to them made so many turn Pyrates." While abusive captains had cause for fear, the pirates' interrogations of their crews could work in a captain's favor if his crew spoke highly of him.

Revenge was behind many acts of pirate violence. Bartholomew Roberts, for example, swore revenge on all ships from the Caribbean colonies of Barbados and Martinique, because the governors of those two islands had tried to capture him. When he caught ships off Martinique, he cruelly tortured and killed their crews, whipping some to death, cutting off the noses and ears of others, and using some for target practice. Resisting a pirate attack was the most common way of infuriating pirates, particularly if any pirates were injured or killed in the struggle. At times, pirates slaughtered the whole crew of a resisting ship.

In their attitudes toward violence, pirates differed greatly. Many historians believe that, despite his fearsome image, Blackbeard consistently avoided killing or hurting his captives. The majority of pirates used violence and torture, or the threat of it, for a specific purpose: to find the ship's treasures. A few exceptionally sadistic pirate captains of the golden age stand out. Charles Vane, for example, was known for cruelty. In a raid in 1718 Vane grabbed a seaman from a ship he had attacked and had his crew bind the man's hands and feet to a pole. They placed a loaded musket into his mouth and then forced lit matches under his eyelids to force him to talk.

The two most infamously cruel pirates of the golden age were George Lowther (d. 1723) and Edward Low (c. 1690–c. 1724). When these two pirates met in the Cayman Islands, Lowther's Jolly Roger already inspired terror in seamen far and wide. He was known for his unique methods of torture, one of which was putting slow-burning matches between his victim's fingers and letting them burn through the flesh and into the bone if his victim failed to reveal where the ship's valuables were.

Low, a mean-spirited bully and thief, served in Lowther's crew before setting out with a pirate ship of his own. Low practiced unspeakable cruelties on his captives. In one incident, he got a small taste of his own medicine. Near the African island of Madagascar, a vessel resisted his attack. Low's gang of pirates boarded and, according to Johnson, "cut and mangled them [the ship's crew] in a barbarous manner." When one of the pirates swung his cutlass at a sailor, however, he missed his mark and cut deeply into Low's lower jaw, cutting away the flesh to expose his teeth. After that incident, Low was as physically disfigured as he was emotionally unbalanced. In a later incident off the coast of Brazil, a captain of a ship Low had attacked threw the ship's treasures overboard rather than give it to the pirates. According to Johnson, Low "raved like a fury, swore a thousand oaths, and ordered the captain's lips to be cut off; which he broiled before his face, and afterwards murdered him and all the crew, being thirty-two persons."

Pirates of the golden age had very short careers as pirates. Most of the well-known pirate captains and a significant number of the rank-and-file pirates were dead by the early 1720s. Pirates were killed during attacks, caught by authorities and executed, or stricken down by ship-board diseases. For pirates of the golden age, the ideal was to live life to the fullest for the short time allotted to them and then to face their inevitable death bravely when the time came. With their tough attitude about their

How Pirates Dressed

The majority of pirates began their careers at sea as common sailors. Most continued to wear sailors' clothing as pirates, particularly while onboard their ship. Sailors' clothes were rough, and usually the clothes they were wearing when they signed up for an expedition. When these clothes wore out, the sailors often made clothes from worn-out canvas sails and blankets. Most of this clothing was coated with tar to make it waterproof. For pirates busy working on a ship, these simple clothes were practical.

In cold weather pirates wore a short, heavy coat called a fearnought or a canvas jacket. In warmer weather they wore a white-linen or cotton shirt, or went without a shirt. Their breeches, or pants, were wide and loose, usually reaching to midcalf in length and made of canvas or wool. Pirates usually went barefoot on the ship. Some pirates wore a small knitted cap called a Monmouth cap. Others wore a kerchief tied around their head. Many wore the popular tricorn hat, a three-cornered hat usually made from felt or leather, with a turned-up brim that provided protection from the harsh tropical sun and also kept rain out of their faces. Clothing worn in raids was often coated with tar, which was thought to slow down a sword thrust. Leather doublets, or tight-fitting buttoned jackets, were worn for the same reason.

Unlike common sailors, most pirates had a store of clothing and adornments they had stolen during their raids. Pirates tended to dress up for attacking ships and for their trips to shore. From the exotic textiles, jewels, feathers, and other ornaments they had acquired, they put together wildly colorful costumes. Some donned bright silk scarves, ribbons, gold hoop earrings, chains, and pendants before loading up with weapons for a raid. On shore, pirates often made a spectacle. In "The Golden Age of Piracy" Jenifer Marx writes, "They minced along in silver-buckled high heels, tricorn hats under their arms, clad in plundered combinations of rich-hued and often mismatched garments of embroidered silks and satins, velvets and lace, which often verged on the ludicrous."

Pirate captains usually dressed in a more gentlemanly manner than the crew. This was partly because they sometimes needed to pass for merchant ship captains to avoid pursuit or to trick a targeted ship into submission. Many pirate captains wore wigs, which was the fashion at the time. Pirate captains Bartholomew Roberts and John "Calico Jack" Rackham were well-known for their fashionable and elegant clothes. But pirate crews and their captains were regarded as equals, and many captains, like Blackbeard, opted for the practical attire their crews wore onboard.

own pain and death, pirates rarely showed remorse about the terrible pain and suffering they caused others.

Libertalia

Despite the disturbing elements of piracy, some observers saw the promise of a bold new world in the pirate form of democracy. In the second edition of *A General History of Pirates*, Johnson describes a pirate utopia (an ideal country) called Libertalia (also spelled Libertatia), located on Madagascar.

Legends of a pirate paradise on the island had been around for a long time, but most historians agree that Libertalia never actually existed.

According to Johnson, Libertalia was founded by French pirate James Misson in the late seventeenth century. Misson despised the European social world, where the rich had all the power and the poor were forced to serve as laborers with few rights and little opportunity to improve their situation. On Madagascar Misson established a pirate nation based on the equality of all its residents. Libertalia was a socialist society; all property was divided equally, so there were no rich and poor classes. Its government was democratic, with everyone having an equal vote. Justice and rights extended to all, and freedom was a natural right.

The reality in Madagascar was far from this vision. By 1711 the scattered pirate bases that had arisen on the island a decade earlier had dissolved. (A pirate base is a place where pirates lived under their own rule and maintained their own defense system.) The pirates on Madagascar had fought among themselves and with the native people of the island. Their once thriving bases had turned into filthy camps lacking even the most basic necessities. In his travels privateer and pirate hunter Woodes Rogers (c. 1679–1732) spoke with seamen who had recently spent time on Madagascar. Rogers, as quoted by Cordingly, said, "They told me that those miserable wretches [pirates still living on Madagascar], who had made such a noise in the world, were now dwindled to between 60 or 70, most of them very poor and despicable, even to the natives."

Slavery and black pirates

Johnson's description of Libertalia contains a speech by Misson in which he bans slavery from Libertalia, saying, as quoted by Kinkor, that "no Man had Power of the Liberty of another." After going to so much trouble to assert his own liberty, Misson had no intention of enslaving other people. About people of African descent he said, "That however these Men were distinguished from the Europeans by their Colour, Customs, or Religious Rites, they were the Work of the same Omnipotent Being, and endued with equal Reason." Since there is little solid evidence that golden-age pirates in general held anti-slavery attitudes, most historians agree that the speech probably reflects the views of Johnson more than those of the pirate population, but there are some reasons to believe that golden-age pirates differed from the mainstream on this issue.

Records show that a significant number of golden-age pirates were black men. According to Kinkor, of the approximately 1,000 pirates who were active between 1715 and 1726, about 25 to 30 percent were black. For example, in 1717 Samuel Bellamy had a crew of 180 men, of which 153 were white and 27, or 15 percent, were black. In 1724 George Lowther had a crew of 23, of which 16 were white and 9, or 39 percent, were black. In an estimate of Bartholomew Roberts's crew of 267 men in 1721, 197 were white and 70, or 28 percent, were black. These are all far higher percentages of black men than would have been found on merchant ships or in the British Royal Navy.

When pirates raided a slave ship, they generally did not treat all slaves equally. Those slaves who had recently been captured from Africa and spoke a language unknown to the pirates were of little use to them. Some pirates released these unwanted slaves ashore or left them on the vessels they had looted; other pirates left the slaves with the slave traders or sold them. In 1721 Roberts showed complete disregard for the lives of hundreds of slaves. When the captain of a slave ship refused to pay the ransom he demanded, Roberts burned the entire ship, including all the slaves who were shackled inside. (A ransom is a sum of money demanded for the release of someone being held captive.)

Men of African descent who spoke English, usually those who had escaped slavery in the colonies, were often recruited as pirates. Those with knowledge of the sea were particularly desirable. There is little historic evidence about how these crew members of African descent were treated aboard pirate ships. While some historians contend that they generally served as laborers or servants, others argue that black men experienced the same liberty aboard pirate ships as everyone else. According to Kinkor, no rules forbidding people of African descent from carrying weapons exist in any surviving ship's articles. Thus, it is likely that black pirates were fully armed. They were probably enthusiastic fighters, especially since pirates of African descent were almost always sold into slavery or returned to former slave owners when pirate ships were captured by authorities. Kincor argues that "the deck of a pirate ship was the most empowering place for blacks within the eighteenth-century white man's world."

Women pirates

While men of various races and ethnic backgrounds were common on pirate ships, women were not. Many ship's articles strictly forbade bringing

Female pirates Anne Bonny and Mary Read. © LEBRECHT MUSIC AND ARTS PHOTO LIBRARY/ALAMY.

women onto ships. Only four women are known to have ever joined the ships of the golden-age pirates. The names of two of them, Mary Harley and Mary Cricket, appear in pirate trial records of 1726, but their stories are not known. The stories of Anne Bonny (1700–c. 1782) and Mary Read (c. 1690–1721), however, were made famous by Johnson's book.

In 1720 John "Calico Jack" Rackham (so named because of his fancy manner of dressing) was on his ship, the *William*, recovering from a drunken spree with his crew off the coast of western Jamaica. A sloop commissioned to track down the pirates pulled up nearby, and shots were exchanged. As the pirate hunters began boarding the *William*, the male pirates remained below in the hold, where they had been drinking. Only two pirates staged a resistance, the heavily armed Bonny and Read. A disgusted Read called down into the hold, telling the rest of the crew to get back on deck to fight. When they would not budge, she shot her pistol into the dark, killing one of the crew.

Rackham and his entire crew were captured and taken to Jamaica to stand trial for piracy. They were convicted and sentenced to hang. Before his death, Rackham asked to see Bonny. According to Johnson, "all the comfort she gave him, was, that she was sorry to see him there, but if he had fought like a man, he need not have been hanged like a dog."

Bonny and Read were tried separately, and their trials were public sensations. Victims of their attacks testified that both women were willing pirates and very able ones. They dressed like men when they were attacking ships, but dressed as women the rest of the time. Bonny and Read were both convicted of piracy and sentenced to death, but after their sentences were read, both informed the court that they were pregnant. The laws of Great Britain prohibited pregnant women from being executed. They were spared hanging, but Read developed a fever and died shortly afterward. No one knows what happened to Bonny.

The pirate life disappears

By 1720 most pirates still raiding the seas were being hotly pursued by pirate hunters and naval expeditions. In their travels the last pirates of the era could not help but see the decomposing bodies of the renowned pirate captains that had been hoisted over harbors worldwide as a warning to others. Eventually the remaining pirates heeded the warning and began new lives doing something else.

For More Information

BOOKS

Cordingly, David. *Under the Black Flag: The Romance and the Reality of Life Among the Pirates.* New York: Random House, 2006, p. 133.

Eastman, Tamara J., and Constance Bond. *The Pirate Trial of Anne Bonny and Mary Read.* Cambria, CA: Fern Canyon Press, 2000.

Johnson, Captain Charles. *A General History of the Robberies and Murders of the Most Notorious Pirates.* Guilford, CT: The Lyon's Press, 1998, 2002, pp. 213, 297–98.

Kinkor, Kenneth J. "Black Men Under the Black Flag." In *Bandits at Sea: A Pirate Reader.* Edited by C.R. Pennell. New York: New York University Press, 2001, pp. 198, 201.

Marx, Jenifer. "The Pirate Round." In *Pirates: Terror on the High Seas from the Caribbean to the South China Sea.* Edited by David Cordingly. East Bridgewater, MA: World Publications, 1998, 2007, p. 109.

Rediker, Marcus. *Between the Devil and the Deep Blue Sea: Merchant Seamen, Pirates and the Anglo-American Maritime World, 1700–1750.* New York: Cambridge University Press, 1987, pp. 258, 273.

———. "Libertalia: The Pirate's Utopia." In *Pirates: Terror on the High Seas from the Caribbean to the South China Sea.* Edited by David Cordingly. East Bridgewater, MA: World Publications, 1998, 2007.

WEB SITES

Foxe, Ed. "Pirate Life." *Pirate Mythtory.* www.bonaventure.org.uk/ed/ pmlife.htm (accessed on January 3, 2011).

"Pirates, Brethren of the Seas: Ships." *Thinkquest.* http://library.thinkquest.org/ J0110360/ships.htm (accessed on January 3, 2011).

8

The United States and Privateers

In the 1770s when the thirteen British colonies in North America—Virginia, Massachusetts, New Hampshire, Maryland, Connecticut, Rhode Island, Delaware, North Carolina, South Carolina, New Jersey, New York, Pennsylvania, and Georgia—decided to fight for independence, they faced a formidable challenge. Great Britain's military forces were powerful and well established, while the individual colonies had only a few small groups of untrained volunteer forces. The prospects at sea were even worse. England possessed the world's most powerful naval force, and the colonies had no navy at all. When the American Revolution (1775–83) began, the colonies hastily started building a small navy, but it was evident that the Continental Navy would not be able to stand against the British Royal Navy.

Within the first months of the Revolution, the united colonial government decided to license private ships to raid British merchant ships. A large force of privateers from every colony formed as a result. (A privateer is a ship or ship owner commissioned by a state or government to attack the merchant ships of an enemy nation.) The American privateers actually captured many more ships and played a greater role in harassing the enemy and boosting morale during the Revolution than the Continental navy. After the war ended, there were mixed feelings about privateers in the new nation, but they continued to play a significant role in all U.S. conflicts at sea for many more decades.

The American Revolution begins

In 1774, amid a storm of protests in the thirteen colonies against Great Britain's taxation and trade policies, the First Continental Congress met in Philadelphia, Pennsylvania, with delegates from twelve of the thirteen colonies. It was a chance for the normally independent colonies to try to work together to find ways to protest against Britain's colonial policies. At

WORDS TO KNOW

admiralty court: A court that administers laws and regulations pertaining to the sea.

bond: A type of insurance in which one party gives money to another party as a guarantee that certain requirements will be followed. If these requirements are not followed, the party that issued the bond keeps the money permanently.

commerce raiding: Also *guerre de course*; a naval strategy in which a weaker naval power attacks its stronger opponent's commercial shipping.

convoy: A collection of merchant ships traveling together for protection, often escorted by warships.

frigate: A three-masted, medium-sized warship.

impressment: The practice of forcibly recruiting sailors to serve in the navy.

letter of marque: A document licensing a private ship owner to the seize ships or goods of an enemy nation.

line of battle combat: A form of combat in which enemies form opposing columns of ships and fire cannons and other large guns at one another.

maritime: Relating to the sea.

militia: A volunteer military force made up of ordinary citizens.

prize: The goods, human captives, and ships won in pirate raids.

ship of the line: A large, heavy warship designed for line of battle combat.

ship's articles: The written sets of rules and conditions under which pirates operated on any given expedition.

war of attrition: A conflict in which a nation tries to wear down its opponent in small ways, hoping to gradually weaken the enemy's forces.

---

that time, most of the delegates had no desire to break away from Great Britain. Circumstances soon changed drastically. When the Second Continental Congress met in Philadelphia on May 10, 1775, the colonies were already at war. Less than three weeks earlier the British had attempted to seize colonial weapons and ammunition at Concord, Massachusetts, initiating the Battle of Concord and the Battle of Lexington, the first military battles of the American Revolution. The Second Continental Congress was faced with the monumental task of managing the war. One of its first moves was to create the Continental Army; Virginia statesman and militia officer George Washington (1732–1799), was appointed its commander.

The challenge ahead was enormous. The American colonies had no central government, treasury, or standing army or navy. The colonial militias, small military forces made up of ordinary citizens, had little training, few weapons, and an extreme shortage of gunpowder. The colonies had never before acted together as one nation. Washington believed the best option was to wage a war of attrition, a conflict in which the colonists would try to wear down their opponent in small ways, hoping to gradually weaken the much stronger British forces. He hoped that in the meantime, the colonists could persuade other European nations to join them and help defeat the British. Although the focus was mainly on battles on land, a sea policy was also necessary. The colonies desperately needed all kinds of supplies. They depended on sea trade and were vulnerable to Britain's naval powers.

Building naval forces and a strategy

American leaders had many misgivings about creating a naval force, considering the size and reputation of the British navy. In 1775 the Royal Navy had at least 270 vessels, including 130 ships of the line. Ships of the line are huge, three-masted battleships. They varied in size from 120 to 200 feet (37 to 61 meters) long and 30 to 60 feet (9 to 18 meters) wide, weighing between 1,200 and 2,000 tons (1,089 and 1,814 metric tons). They carried from six hundred to eight hundred men and had 40 to 110 cannons and other large guns mounted along their decks. Ships of the line were designed for a form of naval combat known as *guerre d'escadre,* or line battle, in which enemy fleets formed opposing columns of ships and fired cannons and other large guns at one another. In this form of battle, the bigger ships almost always won.

The Americans did not have the time or the funds to construct ships of the line or to train a professional navy for line battle. Therefore, they built smaller, faster vessels. The largest were frigates, three-masted warships carrying between twenty-eight and forty-four guns. There were also brigs, vessels with two square-rigged masts (masts with sails set at right angles to the ship's hull); schooners, vessels with two fore-and-aft masts (masts positioned for sails set lengthwise along the ship); and sloops, single-masted vessels. The American vessels were not designed for line battles; they were designed for *guerre de course,* or commerce raiding. The ships cruised by themselves or with one other ship. They avoided British warships, and instead harassed smaller British merchant and naval vessels and protected American merchant ships. Their function was to disrupt British trade, keep American coastal trade open, transport troops, and gather military and other supplies.

Throughout the war, fifty to sixty American warships put to sea, but there were never more than thirty-four in use at any one time. The separate

A British ship of the line battleship. In line battle, these large ships almost always won. © HISTORICAL PICTURE ARCHIVE/ CORBIS.

colonies quickly established their own navies, but it was clear that these small naval forces were insufficient. One by one, the colonies passed legislation authorizing privateering raids against the British. In March 1776 the Continental Congress reluctantly joined the colonies in passing legislation allowing privateers to raid British warships and merchant ships. The sea strategy for the first years of the Revolution was set. Three forces, the Continental navy, the states' navies, and privateers, would all find ways to harass British vessels for the purpose of disrupting trade and forcing Britain to concentrate on defense rather than on attacking or blockading the colonies. The privateers quickly became the largest and most effective of these forces.

Using privateers

In many ways the use of privateers was a natural outgrowth of the thirteen colonies' maritime history. The colonies were all located near the ocean. Before good roads could be built to connect the vast territories, almost all travel, and all trade, was conducted by sea. Traders in the port cities, such as Boston, Massachusetts; Newport, Rhode Island; Philadelphia, Pennsylvania; and Charleston, South Carolina; had made their fortunes by putting together complex and risky maritime expeditions.

Americans were also experienced in sea raiding. Because of wars in Europe, privateering raids had been nearly constant in American waters throughout the eighteenth century. French and Spanish privateers had been drawn by the abundant and profitable British colonial trade flowing from the ports of North America and the Caribbean islands. France, especially, resorted to privateering raids on British merchant ships to harass its enemy, since it could not hope to win a maritime battle against the powerful Royal Navy. To protect its trade, Britain issued its own letters of marque against France and Spain. (A letter of marque is a document licensing a private ship owner to the seize ships or goods of an enemy nation.) Many private raiders from the colonies had gained maritime (sea) battle experience and grown rich raiding French ships during the French and Indian War (1754–63; a war fought in North America between England and France involving some Native Americans as allies of the French).

Privateers greatly expanded the naval powers of the colonies. They were uniquely equipped to advance the war effort with their raiding, and they were available immediately. With business in the colonies thoroughly disrupted by the war, privateers provided employment and brought in much-needed supplies and products. The colonists also hoped that, if the privateers did enough damage to British commerce through their raiding, the British public might pressure its government into ending the war.

There were many arguments against using privateers. Many Americans feared that the Continental Congress was, in effect, licensing a force of outlaws that would soon run out of control. An immediate problem was that recruitment for privateer expeditions cut deeply into the available supply of men for the Continental Navy. Privateer ships were far more attractive to most sailors than navy ships. They had less harsh discipline, potentially better pay, and, because they limited their raiding to merchant ships, they avoided the dangers involved in attacking warships. With most sailors opting for privateer expeditions, the Continental Navy had persistent problems finding enough men to sail its ships.

Regulating privateers

Without resources to train or oversee the forces of privateers it licensed, the Continental Congress attempted to maintain some control through regulations. It created uniform letters of marque that licensed private vessels of the "United Colonies" to seize sea vessels belonging only to inhabitants of Great Britain. A privateer could not obtain letters of marque without first posting a bond of five thousand to ten thousand dollars. (A bond is a type of insurance in which one party gives money to another party as a guarantee that certain requirements will be followed. If these requirements are not followed, the party that issued the bond keeps the money permanently.) Privateers were also required to recruit one-third of the crew from landsmen, men who did not have skills in sailing. This was to ensure that the Continental Navy did not lose too many recruits to the privateers. The Continental Congress required that privateers take all prizes (goods, human captives, and ships captured in pirate raids) to an admiralty court, a court that administers laws and regulations pertaining to the sea. The court had the sole authority to approve the prize. After obtaining approval from the courts, the privateer could sell the ship and its cargo and the proceeds could be divided among the investors and the crew. Privateers were prohibited from using unnecessary violence against the crew of a captured ship.

Like pirate ships of earlier times, each privateer ship had its own set of ship's articles, the written sets of rules and conditions under which the privateers operated on any given expedition. Every member of the crew signed the articles, which set out the the duties of the crewmen and how prizes would be divided.

The first American privateers

The first raid on a British ship by private citizens occurred in June 1775, well before laws governing privateering had been enacted. In the tiny, remote town of Machias Bay in present-day Maine, colonists learned about the battles at Concord and Lexington that had occurred eight weeks earlier. The majority of the townspeople were firmly on the rebels' side. To show their support, they erected a "liberty pole," a pine tree bearing only its top branches, which became a symbol of the Revolutionary movement. At the time, the town was awaiting the arrival of a British ship delivering necessary supplies. The town expected to exchange lumber, which they had already cut and prepared, for the arriving goods. To their dismay, the people of Machias Bay learned that the British planned to use the lumber to build barracks for the British troops who were then occupying Boston.

When the 100-ton (91-metric-ton) British schooner, the *Margaretta*, arrived at Machias Bay, its commander, James Moore, demanded that the colonists take down the liberty pole and threatened to fire his cannons on the town if they refused. The townspeople angrily took down the pole, but later an enraged gang of townsmen decided to go after the *Margaretta*. Armed with pitchforks, axes, and hunting guns, the townsmen captured one of Moore's sloops, the *Unity*, and elected Jeremiah O'Brien as its captain. After fortifying the *Unity*'s sides with planks to protect themselves from the larger ship's cannons, the group of colonists sailed after the *Margaretta*. After a chase, they overtook the ship and boldly rammed into it. As the raiders began to board his ship, Moore fired upon them, killing one man instantly. Even with Moore's crew tossing grenades on their sloop's deck, the colonists continued boarding and were instantly engaged in hand-to-hand combat with the crew on the ship's deck. During the fight, the colonists shot Moore and killed or wounded several of his men. Once Moore had fallen, the crew of the *Margaretta* surrendered the ship. Moore died the next day.

The Massachusetts Provincial Congress awarded Jeremiah O'Brien with the British sloop. Fortifying it with guns from the badly damaged *Margaretta*, he set off to capture more British ships. Eventually his raids brought in enough money for him to post bond as a privateer for the state of Massachusetts. Other raiders from Machias Bay continued to harass the Royal Navy throughout the war.

Another success among the early privateers occurred in November 1775. A large British ship, the *Nancy*, was heading for Boston, Massachusetts, when it was hit by a storm. It arrived in the coastal waters off Massachusetts in need of help. Seeing a ship it assumed to be with the Royal Navy, the *Nancy* flagged it down. The other ship was actually the *Lee*, an American privateer authorized to raid British ships. The *Nancy* surrendered to the American crew without resistance. The *Nancy* was carrying two thousand muskets, two thousand bayonets, three thousand rounds of shot for 12-inch (30-centimeter) cannons, and hundreds of pounds of gunpowder. The cargo was vital to America's early war effort, since the colonies were sorely lacking in weapons and ammunition.

An American privateer capturing a British ship.
PRIVATE COLLECTION/THE BRIDGEMAN ART LIBRARY INTERNATIONAL.

Success in the first years of the American Revolution

In the first year of the American Revolution about 136 privateer vessels were licensed to raid British ships. These first privateer vessels varied greatly in size and shape, having been hastily converted from fishing and whaling boats and merchant vessels. As the war progressed, more and more privateer vessels were built for their purpose. Most of these later vessels were either two-masted schooners, weighing about 100 tons (91 metric tons) and able to carry up to about seventy-five crew members, or brigantines, heavier two-masted vessels with two sails rigged to each mast, weighing about 150 tons (136 metric tons) and able to carry up to about one hundred crew members.

Privateers with smaller vessels and those from New England tended to do their raiding in the northern Atlantic Ocean off Newfoundland (in present-day Canada), where they preyed upon British traders and fishermen. Privateers with larger vessels and those from southern ports often sailed south to the Caribbean Sea, where large merchant ships laden with expensive cargoes traded. They also raided along the shores of the colonies. Between November 1775 and April 1776, the American privateers had captured thirty-one British ships off Boston, which at that time was occupied by British forces. The raids played a role in the British withdrawal from Boston in March 1776.

As the first privateers began their attacks, British merchant ships sailing alone were unprepared, and many were seized. After reports of the raids reached Britain, the merchant ships formed convoys (groups of merchant ships traveling together for protection) before sailing from England. The convoys were large, usually consisting of about one hundred ships with Royal Navy warships as escorts, and they were slow. Despite the dangers, many merchants opted to travel alone, using smaller and faster vessels and arming their crews to fight the privateers.

Before long, Britain began to commission its own privateers. British privateers took their prizes to admiralty courts set up in the Caribbean and in Nova Scotia, in present-day Canada. According to some estimates, Britain had as many privateers as the colonies. The American seas became infested with raiders. Robert H. Patton describes the scene in his article, "The Unlikely Role of Patriot Pirates: Privateers Plundered British Ships and Made Fortunes to Boot." He writes:

> Waters from Trinidad [a Caribbean island] to Canada teemed with warships and transports under opposing flags chasing or fleeing one another. Captured British prizes were sailed to Massachusetts for trial, American prizes to Antigua [a Caribbean island and British colony] and Halifax [Nova Scotia]. On the way, all were vulnerable to recapture and redirection to an enemy port; and all, quite commonly given the great distances involved, might be recaptured yet again.

Risks and rewards

No matter how much patriotism a privateer might feel, privateering was first and foremost a business. Privateer expeditions usually originated when investors joined together to pay for them. It was an expensive undertaking, involving purchasing the ship, outfitting it for raiding, buying weapons and ammunition, hiring a captain and officers, and equipping and feeding its crew for long periods at sea.

The profits of privateering could be enormous. Some of the larger privateers raided dozens of ships, and the total prize was valued at hundreds of thousands of dollars and more. When the prizes were large, the investors made a huge profit, and crew members made more money than a sailor could hope to earn in a lifetime. Port cities shared in the bounty, gaining new income and goods. Thriving new businesses arose based on the maintenance of the ships and the booty of the privateers.

On the other hand, many privateer vessels were captured or destroyed by the British or wrecked by storms. Investors usually put their money in several expeditions in order to be able to cover the costs of lost missions with the profits from successful missions. The members of privateer crews faced great personal danger. The risk of death and injury on a ship in wartime was always great, whether by enemy fire, disease, or shipwreck.

Privateers also risked capture by the enemy. Because Britain did not accept the United Colonies (as the name appeared on letters of marque) as a sovereign nation, it refused to acknowledge American letters of marque. Britain not only viewed privateers as pirates, but also members of the Continental Navy, since a non-nation could not form a navy. Until 1778 no American seamen received prisoner-of-war status, which provided for the right to a trial and for prisoner exchanges between warring nations. The British did not go so far as to hang their captives as pirates, but they treated them more harshly than prisoners of war. Some were put on prison ships, such as the *Jersey*, anchored off Brooklyn, New York. Others went to prisons in England. Conditions in the prisons were so terrible that many prisoners died of disease and starvation.

Benjamin Franklin, the French, and privateers

Imprisoned American seamen had a friend in American statesman Benjamin Franklin (1706–1790), who served as a representative of the thirteen colonies in Paris, France. Franklin went to France on a mission to persuade the French to join the colonies in their fight against the British. On

February 6, 1778, after he had spent nearly two years negotiating with the French, the Franco-American Treaty of Alliance was signed. France promised to support the Americans against the British. This was a long-awaited turning point. The war now became a major European conflict. Britain was now forced to defend its own waters as well as the colonial seas. Spain joined the fight against Britain in 1779, as did the Dutch in 1780.

In 1778 Britain agreed to treat captured American privateers and navy men as prisoners of war. This provided Franklin with the opportunity to secure the release of American prisoners by exchanging British prisoners for them. But first he needed British prisoners to trade, and by 1779 Franklin had begun working with privateers to obtain them. In Dunkirk, France, he met with American investors who sought a privateering commission for their ship, the *Black Prince*. Franklin issued them a letter of marque, asking only that the *Black Prince* capture British prisoners to exchange for Americans. In four expeditions in the Irish Sea and the English Channel, the *Black Prince* captured many British ships and eventually took fifty-two prisoners to France for exchange. Franklin issued letters of marque to several other privateers in France. Whether or not they were effective in getting prisoners for exchange, Franklin's privateers still sorely aggravated the British near their home port.

Continental Navy heroes

With the French alliance, privateers and Continental Navy ships gained the use of French ports from which to base their operations. This was a crucial step in bringing the war to British waters. The Continental Navy finally achieved some significant successes. For example, Irish American naval officer Gustavus Conyngham (c. 1744–1819), commander of the Continental Navy cutter, the *Revenge*, managed to capture more than sixty British prizes in only eighteen months in the English Channel.

The most famous naval hero of the American Revolution, Scottish captain John Paul Jones (1747–1792), had been a seaman since he was twelve. He had received a post in the Continental Navy as a lieutenant in 1775 and was promoted to captain the next year. In his raids along the coast of North America, he took more than twenty-five prizes in 1776. In 1777 he sailed to France, where he worked with Franklin in his plan to obtain British prisoners to exchange for the American seamen held by the British. In 1778 Jones raided British vessels in the Irish Sea and assaulted the port of Whitehaven, England.

John Paul Jones attacks the British warship Serapis. MARY EVANS PICTURE LIBRARY/EVERETT COLLECTION.

In 1779 Jones took command of a worn-out vessel armed with forty-two guns, which he renamed *Bon Homme Richard* in honor of Franklin. (Franklin's yearly publication, *Poor Richard's Almanac*, had been published in France as *Les Maximes de Bonhomme Richard*.) Jones set sail from France with a small fleet of navy vessels and two French privateers.

Jones led his fleet around the coasts of Ireland and Scotland, taking several prizes. On September 23, 1779, he sighted two British warships escorting a convoy of ships off the coast of Flamborough Head, Yorkshire. Jones brought his ship alongside one of the warships, the *Serapis*. The two enemy ships opened fire on each other with their cannons. Jones managed to lash his ship to the *Serapis*, and he and his crew boarded in a rain of musket and grenade fire, driving the enemy from the deck. At that moment, however, two large guns that had been stored on the lower deck of the *Bon Homme Richard* exploded, killing and wounding the men around them. Although the Americans had lost men and their mounted guns, and their ship was leaking badly, Jones and his men fought on.

After an hour of fierce fighting with both ships on fire, the British captain asked Jones if he was ready to surrender. Jones replied, "I have not yet begun to fight," and these words became one of the famous quotes of the Revolution. The battle raged for two more hours before the British captain lost his nerve and surrendered. Jones abandoned the sinking *Bon Homme Richard* and took over the severely damaged British warship. He took the surviving British crew as prisoners to exchange for American prisoners. The French and Americans celebrated Jones as a war hero. To the British he was a traitor and a pirate.

A privateer hero

Although less reported, the privateers had their share of spectacular naval victories. In 1780 American privateer Jonathan Haraden (1744–1803), who had been successful in capturing British vessels in Caribbean and American waters, commanded a small, fourteen-cannon privateer, the *General Pickering* with a crew of about forty-five men. His mission was to deliver American sugar to trade in Bilbao, Spain. While sailing to Spain, the *General Pickering* successfully defended itself against an attack by a more heavily armed British ship. On the return voyage Haraden was feeling confident from the earlier success.

One night the *General Pickering* approached the *Golden Eagle*, a large British schooner with twenty-two guns. Haraden, seeing that his ship had not been observed, ordered his crew to quietly pull alongside the British vessel. Calling out into the darkness, he warned the British commander to surrender, boldly claiming that his ship was an American frigate of the largest class. Haraden's bluff worked. The *Golden Eagle* surrendered without a fight.

A few days later, Haraden was heading for Bilboa with the *Golden Eagle* in tow. Suddenly, a massive, forty-two-gun British privateer, the *Achilles*, appeared and advanced quickly. Haraden held his course, and a fight ensued. By sunset the *Achilles* had recaptured the *Golden Eagle*, but the fight was not over.

The two embattled ships stayed close to the Spanish shore during the night. By morning a crowd of people had gathered on the beach to watch the battle. In the darkness, Haraden had managed to position the *General Pickering* in such a way that when the British ship approached, it was in his direct line of fire. After a difficult three-hour battle, the *Achilles* was forced to retreat, and Haraden recaptured the *Golden Eagle*.

The effect of privateers on the American Revolution

Historical records of privateers in the American Revolution are incomplete, and the estimates of how many privateers were active during the war vary greatly. Over the course of the war, about seventeen hundred letters of marque were issued. According to one estimate, approximately three thousand American privateer vessels put to sea, although many estimates are significantly lower. The privateers captured an estimated six hundred British vessels and between twelve thousand and sixteen thousand British seamen during the war. (In comparison, the Continental Navy captured 196 British ships.) The American privateers cost Britain about eighteen million pounds (the equivalent of about $302 million today). They severely damaged British trade and caused insurance rates for British shipping to rise from 30 to 50 percent. Well-publicized raids such as Haraden's crushed British morale and resulted in increasing calls for an end to the war. The privateers did not have a direct effect on the American victory, but they played an important role in the nearly impossible fight at sea.

The new U.S. government quickly moved to abolish privateering once the war was over. Despite his support of privateers, Franklin argued for a clause in the peace treaty with Britain that would prohibit privateering in future conflicts. Only a few years after the war, however, the United States gradually became involved in hostilities between Britain and France. In 1796 French forces were attacking U.S. merchant vessels in the Caribbean, and French privateers were raiding off the East Coast of the United States. The United States had dissolved its navy, and the states were prohibited by the Constitution from forming their own navies. Once again, as the United States began to build a navy from scratch, a force of privateers was licensed to raid enemy ships. However, the United States's part in the conflict was over fairly quickly and the foreign privateers dispersed.

Privateers in the War of 1812

American privateers played an important role in the War of 1812 (1812–15) between the United States and Great Britain. The United States had two motives for going to war: to force Great Britain to repeal its unfair regulation of American trade with Europe and to stop its practice of impressment, or forcibly recruiting sailors to serve in the navy. Under this practice, British forces removed seamen from U.S. merchant vessels and forced them to serve in the Royal Navy.

When the War of 1812 began, the U.S. Navy had only sixteen vessels. The need for a privateering force to oppose the Royal Navy was clear, and few Americans worried whether the privateers were motivated by profit or patriotism. Merchant and fishing vessels of all types were quickly outfitted for raids against the British ships. In the early days of the war, privateers in small, hastily rigged vessels succeeded in their raids against unsuspecting British merchant ships. But it was not long before the British focused their efforts on the privateers and captured or destroyed the smaller vessels.

As the war advanced, larger and better-armed American privateers engaged the British. A few were remarkably successful. For example, the 350-ton (318-metric-ton) privateer, the *America*, with twenty guns and a crew of 120, brought in prizes valued at six hundred thousand dollars over the course of the war. The 168-ton (152-metric-ton) *Yankee* with eighteen guns and 120 men took prizes worth nearly three million dollars. During the entire war, American privateers captured at least 1,345 British ships.

As the war continued, it became more difficult for privateers to leave their ports. Britain imposed an ever-tightening naval blockade along most of the East Coast. The British also set up convoys for their shipping, which were effective against American privateer raids. Even the port cities were hit hard by British naval strength. When the British learned that privateer vessels were being built in the port city of Essex, Connecticut, for example, it attacked the city and burned twenty-eight ships. It was one of the greatest financial losses of the war for the Americans.

After two years, both sides had wearied of the conflict, and the United States and Great Britain signed a peace treaty on December 24, 1814. News of peace did not reach the generals on either side right away, and on January 8, 1815, a massive force of British soldiers rushed the American troops in

Thomas Jefferson's Call for Privateers

When the United States declared war on Great Britain in the War of 1812, its navy was comprised of only sixteen vessels. Calls for privateers were widespread throughout the country, and there was little controversy connected to it. Statesman and former U.S. president Thomas Jefferson (1743–1826; president 1801–9) reflected a popular viewpoint when he encouraged the nation to embrace the privateering tradition. He said, as quoted by Benson J. Lossing in *Harper's Popular Cyclopedia of United States History from the Aboriginal Period to 1876*:

> [War] is simply a contest between nations of trying which can do the other the most harm....What difference to the sufferer is it if his property is taken by a national or a private armed vessel?... In the United States every possible encouragement should be given to privateering in time of war with a commercial nation.... By licensing private armed vessels, the whole naval force of the nation is truly brought to bear on the foe; and while it lasts, that it may have the speedier termination, let every individual contribute his mite [sic] in the best way he can to distress and harass the enemy and compel him to peace.

New Orleans, Louisiana, under General Andrew Jackson (1767–1845). The Americans had received advance word of the attack and were well prepared to defend the city. After several hours, a U.S. victory was clear. With only six dead and seven wounded, the U.S. troops had caused twenty-five hundred deaths and injuries among the attackers, including their commander. This was one of the few clear American victories in the war. In his defense of New Orleans, Jackson was aided by a pirate, smuggler, and privateer named Jean Lafitte (c. 1776–c. 1823).

Jean Lafitte

Sometime around 1811, Jean Lafitte set up a trading business near New Orleans in Barataria Bay, where he and a large gang of privateers were based. Lafitte had earlier been a privateer, but found it more profitable to trade the booty of other privateers. He also bought and sold slaves. Most U.S. authorities considered Lafitte to be a criminal because he traded in illegally seized goods.

In 1814, at the height of the War of 1812, British agents approached Lafitte. They offered him a position in their forces as well as a large sum of money if he would aid them in their attack on New Orleans. Lafitte refused the offer, and quickly reported the British plans to Louisiana's governor. Governor William Claibourne (1775–1817) did not trust Lafitte and assumed his report was just a trick. Despite Lafitte's attempt to help his nation, in September 1814 a U.S. naval force attacked his base at Barataria Bay, capturing his ships and goods, and arresting eighty of his men on charges of piracy.

Lafitte again offered his services to help ward off the British; this time he made his offer to the U.S. Army. By this time, Jackson had received reports confirming Lafitte's account of the British plans to invade New Orleans, and authorities welcomed Lafitte's offer. Lafitte and three dozen of his comrades agreed to serve in the U.S. Army in exchange for a pardon. Lafitte provided useful maps and information about the Barataria area, and he and his gang of raiders fought bravely alongside the other soldiers during the Battle of New Orleans. In the years following the war, however, Lafitte returned to his pirate ways.

Containment of privateers

Lafitte's character, a mixture of courage, spirit, greed, and a general disrespect for law and authority, was not uncommon among privateers

Jean Lafitte served as an American privateer during the War of 1812. PRIVATE COLLECTION/PETER NEWARK AMERICAN PICTURES/THE BRIDGEMAN ART LIBRARY INTERNATIONAL.

or pirates. The potential for lawlessness among privateers became apparent after the War of 1812, when thousands of privateers from several countries suddenly found themselves without work. Some sailed to Central and South America, where Spain, greatly weakened by the

European wars, was losing control of its colonies. Between 1808 and 1825, the nations of Latin America fought successful wars of liberation. American and European privateers frequently participated in these wars. When the battles were over, though, many of the privateers continued their raiding. They had no license to raid and, without war, there were no enemy ships. As pirates, they raided ships belonging to any nation. The surge in piracy in Latin America was often violent, and it damaged U.S. trade. For twenty-five years, the growing U.S. Navy struggled to fight Latin American piracy.

In 1856 the leading European powers adopted the Declaration of Paris, which prohibited privateering. Privateers were to be regarded as pirates. They could be captured by the ships of any of the nations that signed the treaty and tried in those nations' courts. The United States did not sign the declaration. It still did not have a modern navy that could stand up to the larger powers, so it wanted to keep the use of privateers as an option.

Privateers in the American Civil War

After the War of 1812, privateering only occurred one more time in the United States, during the American Civil War (1861–65). When the war began, the Confederate States of America (the Southern states that had seceded from the Union in 1861) were in a position similar to that of the thirteen colonies at the beginning of the American Revolution. The Confederacy had no navy and not enough time or resources to construct warships or to train professional naval forces. The Confederate government opted to use privateers. The Confederates intended for privateers to disrupt commerce and scatter the naval forces of the Union.

In the first year of the Civil War, Confederate privateers raided scores of Union ships. News of the Confederate privateers' accomplishments disturbed President Abraham Lincoln (1809–1865; served 1861–65) enough that he offered to belatedly sign the Declaration of Paris prohibiting privateering, but only if its provisions were applied to the Confederacy. This would enable him to legally try the Confederate privateers as pirates. European powers, such as Britain and France, rejected the offer.

Throughout the course of the war, Confederate privateers seized about two hundred U.S. merchant vessels. When the United States captured one of the most successful of the Confederate privateers, the *Savannah*, the crew members were charged with piracy and faced trial in a

Union court. This approach to privateers soon proved unmanageable. While the crew of the *Savannah* awaited trial, the Confederacy selected a similar number of Union officers from among the prisoners of war being held in the South. The Confederacy sent word that this group would face the same punishment that befell the Confederate privateers. The jury did not find the crew of the *Savannah* guilty of the piracy charges, and the Union decided to drop the charges. All later privateers captured by the Union were treated as prisoners of war, not as pirates.

After the first year of the war, a Confederate Navy emerged and privateering declined. After the Civil War, the United States abided by the terms of the Declaration of Paris, although it never signed the treaty. With the development of a sophisticated and powerful navy, the United States never again enlisted the services of privateers.

For More Information

BOOKS

Bradford, James C. "French and American Privateers." In *Pirates: Terror on the High Seas from the Caribbean to the South China Sea.* Edited by David Cordingly. East Bridgwater, MA: World Publications, 1998, 2007, p. 179.

Konstam, Angus. *Privateers & Pirates: 1730–1830.* Oxford, UK: Osprey, 2001.

Lossing, Benson J. *Harper's Popular Cyclopedia of United States History from the Aboriginal Period to 1876,* vol. 2. New York: Harper & Brothers, 1881, p. 1148.

Patton, Robert H. *Patriot Pirates: The Privateer War for Freedom and Fortune in the American Revolution.* New York: Pantheon, 2008, p. 40.

Shomette, Donald G. *Shipwrecks, Sea Raiders, and Maritime Disasters Along the Delmarva Coast, 1632–2004.* Baltimore, MD: Johns Hopkins University Press, 2007, p. 67.

Wilbur, C. Keith. *Pirates and Patriots of the Revolution: An Illustrated Encyclopedia of Colonial Seamanship.* Guilford, CT: Globe Pequot, 1984.

PERIODICALS

Patton, Robert H. "The Unlikely Role of Patriot Pirates: Privateers Plundered British Ships and Made Fortunes To Boot," *U.S. News & World Report* (June 27, 2008). Available online at http://politics.usnews.com/news/national/articles/2008/06/27/the-unlikely-role-of-patriot-pirates/photos/?PageNr=2 (accessed on January 3, 2011).

WEB SITES

"A Naval History of the American Revolution." *AmericanRevolution.org.* www.americanrevolution.org/navy/nav1.html (accessed on January 3, 2011).

9

Piracy in Asia

Piracy in Asia dates back as far as records extend. The early pirates who went out in small groups and robbed from local traders and fisherman will probably remain forever hidden in the shadows of history. In later eras, though, pirate groups became large and organized enough to inflict heavy damage on governments and international trade. From the sixteenth to the eighteenth centuries, China experienced a golden age of piracy that was much longer and much larger than the golden age of piracy in the Caribbean Sea, which lasted from 1690 to 1730. (For more information, see **The Golden Age of Piracy**.) At the height of China's golden age of piracy, there were an estimated seventy thousand pirates off the coasts of China, compared to about fifty-five hundred pirates in the Caribbean at the peak of its golden age. In India and Southeast Asia pirates took part in resisting the domination of the European powers that were scrambling to create trade monopolies and establish colonies in their midst. (A monopoly is exclusive control or possession of something, in this case, trade.) Like the pirates of Europe and the Americas, the Asian pirate groups became strong forces of history in their own right.

Chinese piracy at sea

Written records of piracy in China date back nearly two thousand years. The majority of the piracy occurred in the South China Sea, an area of the Pacific Ocean that is surrounded by southeast China, Indochina, the Malay Peninsula, Borneo, the Philippines, and Taiwan. Since early times, small-time piracy was common along the Chinese coasts. It was almost always the result of poverty. Poor fishermen needed a means of survival during the off-season, so each year when the fishing season ended, many sailed up the coast to plunder (rob of goods by force) distant villages. These part-time pirates worked in gangs, usually made up of family

WORDS TO KNOW

blunderbuss: A short musket with a flared muzzle.

booty: Goods stolen from ships or coastal villages during pirate raids or attacks on enemies in time of war.

dynasty: A succession of rulers from the same family line.

extortion: The use of authority to unlawfully take money.

junk: A Chinese form of sailboat.

matchlock: A musket in which gun powder is ignited by lighting it with a match.

monopoly: Exclusive control or possession of something.

pirate base: A place where pirates lived under their own rule and maintained their own defense system.

plunder: To rob of goods by force, in a raid or in wartime.

prahu: A swift, light, seagoing vessel propelled by oars and used by the pirates of Southeast Asia.

ransom: A sum of money demanded for the release of someone being held captive.

smuggling: Illegally importing and exporting goods.

members. Generally all members returned to fishing when the off-season was over. Sailors, who also came from the poorest segments of Chinese society, often ended up in piracy when they signed up for ship duty. As long as they were paid, they did not care whether the vessel they joined was legitimate or run by pirates. Most of these small-time pirates at sea were only trying to supplement, or add to, their income with piracy. They were not professional raiders.

From the sixteenth to the eighteenth century, the pirate gangs that raided China's seacoasts grew larger and became organized, working together in a tight structure with strong leadership and planning. They built huge, efficient pirate empires that had a powerful impact on China's economy and security. One of the earliest major pirate organizations to strike China was the Wokou (which means "Japanese bandits"), a group of pirates that originated in Japan in the thirteenth century. The Wokou focused its attacks on the coasts of Korea and China. It attacked in large ships holding up to three hundred pirates each. Dressed in uniform—red coats with yellow caps—and armed with a sword in each hand, the Japanese pirates raided villages, often taking stores of grain and capturing people to sell as slaves.

South China Sea, 17th Century

- Dutch possession
- Spanish possession
- 17th century boundary

QING EMPIRE

BURMA

CHIENGMAI

TRAN NINH

LAOS

SIAM

CAMBODIA

ANNAM

Gulf of Tonkin HAINAN

South China Sea

Gulf of Thailand

FORMOSA

Philippine Sea

Babuyan Islands

PHILIPPINE ISLANDS

Sulu Sea

Sulu Arch.

SULU

Celebes Sea

MALAY STATES

Strait of Malacca

ATJEH

SUMATRA

MALAY STATES

Natuna Islands

BRUNEI

MAMPAVA

BORNEO

A map of the South China Sea in the seventeenth century. MAP BY XNR PRODUCTIONS INC./ CENGAGE LEARNING.

The Ming dynasty and China's early mastery of the sea

As the Wokou raided China's coasts, a new set of rulers took control of the country. The Ming dynasty of China was founded in 1368. (A dynasty is a succession of rulers from the same family.) The new government reigned over a vast area, stretching more than 3,000 miles (4,828 kilometers) across the eastern part of the continent. The seas under its rule extended from the coasts of Korea in the north down to Vietnam in the south. The Ming greatly restructured China, establishing a strong military and an agricultural economy. Fiercely proud of China's ancient culture, the Ming scorned foreign influences and trading.

Pirates Through the Ages: Almanac

A painting of Zheng He and his junks. © CHRIS HELLIER/CORBIS.

Before the Ming dynasty, China had enjoyed a profitable trade with Japan and Southeast Asia and had developed the most advanced shipbuilding and navigation technology of its time. In its early years, between 1405 and 1433, the Ming dynasty sponsored a series of international naval expeditions that displayed China's mastery at sea. The expeditions had an enormous fleet of ships with an estimated twenty-seven thousand crew members under the command of Zheng He (1371–1435). They sailed to the South Pacific, the Indian Ocean, the Persian Gulf, and parts of Africa, setting many new milestones in exploration and navigation.

Zheng He's ships, called junks, were huge sailboats ranging up to 400 feet (122 meters) long and 170 feet (52 meters) wide. The junks could carry five hundred men and had nine masts with sails. Junks were more flexible than the Western square-rigged ships. Their sails could be moved inward, toward the center of the vessel, allowing the junk to sail into the wind, making them very fast.

Isolationism

Zheng He's expeditions were remarkably successful, but ended abruptly in 1433 when the Ming rulers closed China's ports and canceled the international tours. Although they did not offer a reason for their unexpected shift in policy, it was clear that they wanted to isolate (keep apart) China from the influence of the foreign traders that were starting to appear with more frequency at Chinese ports. The Ming restricted shipbuilding—only small ships were allowed to be built—and China's navy began to shrink quickly.

The worst blow to many of the Chinese people was a ruling that only the Chinese government could legally trade with foreigners. This was devastating to merchants and other businesspeople whose lives depended on foreign trade. In the early fifteenth century, silver, gold, and copper had been discovered in Japan. Chinese businesses needed these metals, and Chinese merchants had silk and other textiles that were desired in Japan. Trade between the two countries was natural, though illegal. Smuggling, or illegally importing and exporting goods, soon became an economic reality. Merchants set up smuggling bases on islands off China's coast, and the businesses thrived. Thousands of people became dependent on illegal foreign trade for survival.

An opportunity for the Wokou

In the sixteenth century, the Wokou, already equipped with junks and familiar with illegal activities at sea, forced their way into smuggling operations in the islands off China. Although the organization had originated in Japan and still had some bases there, by this time the members of the Wokou were mostly Chinese and presented an odd mix of seasoned pirates, impoverished sailors, and former merchants forced into smuggling by the ban on foreign trade. Some of these merchants carried on legitimate businesses part of the time, smuggled part of the time, and occasionally went out on raiding expeditions in which they plundered coastal towns and other merchants' ships at sea.

By the mid–sixteenth century, the Wokou were well organized and living in bases mainly on islands off the coasts of China and Japan. A wealthy businessman named Wang Zhi commanded a large force of Wokou pirate fleets, comprised of hundreds of junks. The fleets raided local treasuries and grain storehouses along the shores of the east coast province of Zhejiang. Wang Zhi's raiders took control of a few coastal towns and used them as bases for inland raiding. By some estimates, Wang Zhi's forces in Zhejiang amounted to twenty thousand men.

Alarmed, the Ming government dispatched its armies to deal with the pirate forces in 1553 and 1554, but Wang Zhi's forces easily defeated them. Oddly, after his victory over the Chinese troops, Wang Zhi unexpectedly offered his surrender to the Ming, asking for a pardon. Like many other traders who had become pirates, Wang Zhi hoped to return to legal status in China and tried to negotiate with the government to end the prohibition on foreign trade. Not ready to give in to the demands of the pirates, Ming officials executed Wang Zhi.

The Ming continued to send national and local troops to fight the pirates. Other steps they took were equally important in disbanding the Wokou. First, in 1557, the Ming granted permission to Portuguese traders to establish Portugal's first permanent settlement on the island of Macao off China's coast. Historians believe the Ming government made a deal with the Portuguese—the Portuguese could settle on the island if they helped the Ming armies fight the Wokou. Second, in 1567, the Ming government reversed its trading ban and allowed China's private merchants to engage in foreign trade once again. Many Wokou quietly returned to their former trades, glad to leave the life of piracy behind. By 1567 the Wokou were on the decline and trade between Japan and China was thriving, aided by the increasing presence of Portuguese traders. This flourishing trade, though, would lead to a new surge in piracy in the seventeenth century.

Ching-Chi-Ling's pirate empire

Sometime in the early seventeenth century, Ching-Chi-Ling (also written as Cheng Chih Lung or Zheng Zhilong; d. 1661), a young man from a poor but respected family in the Fujian province on the southeast coast of China, made his way to Macao to seek work in a Portuguese factory. While living in Macao, he converted to Catholicism and became an interpreter for the English East India Company, a company established for pursuing trade with Southeast Asia. Ching-Chi-Ling made a fortune in Macao. In 1620 he went to Japan to visit an uncle. There he met and married a Japanese woman, with whom he had one son, Kuo Hsing Yeh (also known as Koxinga and Zheng Chenggong; 1624–1662).

Ching-Chi-Ling's uncle was involved in piracy and showed his nephew how to be a pirate. Impressed, Ching-Chi-Ling invested his fortune in a fleet of junks and began sea raiding. By 1627 he had a fleet of four hundred junks, mostly trading junks that had been captured and converted to pirate uses. They ranged in size from 45 feet (14 meters) to 100 feet (30 meters) long, and they were built to be fast. Pirate junks could carry about two hundred pirates, and they were usually well armed. They were equipped with a large storage space for booty. (Booty is the goods stolen from ships or coastal villages during pirate raids or attacks on enemies in time of war.) They also had living quarters for the captain and his family at the stern (rear) and tiny berths for other crew members in the main hold.

As Ching-Chi-Ling's pirate fleets continued to expand, the pirate chief obtained extensive control over the seas off southeast China. He developed a monopoly on China's burgeoning textile trade. Meanwhile, his pirate crews freely raided ships along China's coasts and forced merchants to pay protection money in order not to be raided by the pirates. By the early 1630s, Ching-Chi-Ling controlled several huge pirate bases. (A pirate base is a place where pirates lived under their own rule and maintained their own defense system.) He had a base at Amoy (present-day Xiamen), a coastal city in the southeast; another on the coast of the southeastern province of Fujian; and a third on the island of Formosa (present-day Taiwan).

Ching-Chi-Ling's rise to power over the coastal regions came as the Ming dynasty was failing. The Manchus, a people native to Manchuria (a vast region in northeast China), had taken control of several areas of China. Because the Ming no longer had the power to stop the Manchus, they offered Ching-Chi-Ling, with his vast powers at sea, a high post in the navy. Ching accepted the position. He gave up piracy but kept his pirate fleets to help defend the beleaguered Ming. In 1629 he was placed in charge of the Ming's defense of Amoy.

In 1644 the Manchus overthrew the capital city of Beijing and established the Qing dynasty, which would rule China until 1912. Ching-Chi-Ling defended the Ming dynasty for two more years. Then, in 1646 he tried to negotiate for a position in the Qing dynasty.

Kho Hsing Yeh

Chi-Chi-Ling's son, Kho Hsing Yeh, remained loyal to the scattered remnants of the Ming dynasty even after his father joined the Qing. Kho Hsing Yeh raised armies and established posts for Ming defense

A statue of Kuo Hsing Yeh (also known as Koxinga), who was celebrated as a national hero in Taiwan for freeing the island from the Dutch. © YANNICK LUTHY/ALAMY.

throughout southern China. For years, Kho Hsing Yeh's forces raided the coasts of China, destroying towns and defeating the Qing in battle.

In 1661 Kho Hsing Yeh attacked Formosa, which had been a Dutch colony since 1624. He attacked the island with a fleet of nine hundred junks and twenty-five thousand troops, pushing the Dutch military off the island. Kho Hsing Yeh then created his own base on the island. He died the next year, but his sons held onto the pirate kingdom on Formosa for twenty more years. They continued to raid China's southeast coast and maintained the massive trading and piracy empire that Kho Hsing Yeh had established. Today Kho Hsing Yeh is still celebrated as a national hero in Taiwan for freeing the island from the Dutch.

Chinese pirates and Vietnam's Tay Son Rebellion

The Qing dynasty recovered control of Formosa in 1683 and relative calm settled on the waters off China. Toward the end of the eighteenth century, however, turmoil in neighboring Vietnam provided the small-time pirates of China a golden opportunity to organize.

For nearly a century, rule of Vietnam under the Lê dynasty had been divided between two families, one ruling in the north and the other in the south. Beginning in the 1760s, three brothers from the town of Tay Son led a rebellion against the governments of local villages of the south, which then spread throughout the countryside. The Tay Son Rebellion's cry was "take the property of the rich and give it to the poor," and the movement, which sought control of all of Vietnam, quickly acquired a large following.

The Tay Son rebels actively recruited Chinese pirates to help fight their battles against the Lê dynasty's military forces. It was a wise move. The Chinese pirates proved highly useful in a 1785 battle, during which the Tay Son rebels captured the city of Saigon and most of southern Vietnam. In response to the Tay Son victories, China's military forces entered the war on behalf of the Vietnamese emperor. In 1788, with the aid of a Chinese pirate army, the Tay Son forces overpowered the Chinese army force. China was forced to acknowledge the Tay Son leaders as the rulers of a united Vietnam.

The new Tay Son emperor lacked the funds to run the huge empire he had fought to control. In 1792 he sent his navy to the Chinese coast to recruit pirates from the Kwangtung, Chekiang, and Fukien provinces. He offered to provide them with junks and weapons and authorized them to freely raid Chinese coasts. In return the pirates would bring him their booty. The Chinese raiders were very successful and their rich cargoes from China helped fund the new Vietnamese empire. For the pirates, the arrangement with Vietnam provided a safe place to organize and hone their skills. By the end of the eighteenth century, the Kwangtung and Fukien coastlines of China were beset by this new breed of well-funded and well-organized pirates sponsored by Vietnam.

The Tay Son emperor died in 1792 without a strong successor. His young son was easily defeated by one of the former ruling families in 1802. The new rulers sent the severed heads of several Chinese pirates to the Qing to show that it would not permit piracy. Chinese pirates who had been stationed in Vietnam returned to China in great numbers. There they were forced to compete with each other in the pirate-infested China seas.

Cheng I makes order among pirates

Among the many pirates returning to China from Vietnam was Cheng I (1765–1807), who came from a long family line of successful pirate chiefs. On his return to China in 1801 he was in command of a small fleet of pirate junks. He married a prostitute, who was known after the marriage as Cheng I Sao (which means "wife of Cheng I"; 1775–1844). The two of them sailed to Kwangtung province, where they focused their extraordinary skills on organizing China's pirates.

Under Cheng I and Cheng I Sao, the major pirate chiefs in the province of Kwangtung organized their small pirate bands into a large confederation with strict regulations. The pirates were divided into six fleets, each with its own flag: the Red, Green, Black, White, Blue, and Yellow fleets. Cheng I took command of the Red Flag fleet. Each of the pirate fleets had its own base of operations and a territory over which it had the exclusive right to raid and demand protection money. The fleet sizes ranged from about seventy to three hundred junks. The junks varied in size, but the large, armed, oceangoing junks were big enough to carry from three to four hundred pirates and twenty to thirty cannons. Other weapons included several forms of mounted swivel guns or blunderbusses (short muskets with flared muzzles) and matchlocks (muskets in which gun powder is ignited by a match). But guns were used mainly for back-up. Chinese pirates excelled in hand-to-hand combat. Along with knives and swords, they usually carried bamboo pikes. Long bamboo pikes would be thrown at their target and short ones with sharp blades were used for close fighting.

Cheng I's Red Flag fleet started out with about two hundred junks with an estimated twenty thousand men and women in 1805. By 1807 it had grown to more than six hundred junks and around forty thousand pirates. Although Cheng I was in command of the entire confederation, he gave the commanders of the other five fleets room to operate as they saw fit. The confederation rules sought to prevent fighting among pirates, attaching heavy penalties to any who fought, betrayed, cheated, or failed to follow the rules.

Although bold, Cheng I was careful. Under his command, the confederacy attacked Chinese and some foreign ships, but not the well-armed and powerful European ships that were appearing with growing frequency along the China seas. The confederation grew strong and efficient. When China sent out antipiracy naval campaigns against one pirate fleet, the other pirate fleets would soon arrive to support it. Together they could always defeat the Chinese navy. The pirate chiefs had created a huge network of suppliers throughout their territory to provide the food and equipment they needed. They planned out their raids ahead of time, using accurate information from informers. The pirate confederation became a source of jobs and income not only for the tens of thousands of pirates, but also for thousands of businesses and services ashore that supplied or traded with them.

By 1805 Cheng I's pirate confederacy had developed a profitable system of collecting protection fees from trading vessels. Virtually every ship in the seas around China was forced to pay. Once the ship had paid what was demanded, it was issued a certificate guaranteeing that the pirates of the confederation would not attack it. This guarantee was honored by all the pirate fleets. Most of the fees were taken annually, so the confederation, much like a large modern corporation, could rely on regular funds coming in to cover its expenses. This extortion, or use of authority to unlawfully take money, gave the confederation supreme control over China's seas.

Chinese Women Pirates

One way that Chinese pirate junks differed from other pirate vessels was that they had women onboard on a regular basis. The captain and a few of the high-ranking crew members usually brought their families on raiding expeditions with them, and captains often had several wives. Women aboard worked side by side with men in the difficult physical labor entailed in running a pirate ship. They were an accepted part of ship life and did not have to hide their gender, as women pirates in the Western world did. According to Dian H. Murray in *Bandits at Sea: A Pirates Reader*, this was a reflection of the customs of many of China's coastal populations. Murray writes:

> In the cramped conditions aboard vessels that housed entire families, women often did as much work as men. Most of the propelling and sculling [rowing] of the small lighters [flat-bottom boats] used for so much of the transport throughout the South China Sea was regarded as women's work, and since most commerce was coastal and did not necessitate long voyages to distant waters, there was no concept of the maritime [sea] world as an exclusively male preserve. The presence of women aboard pirate ships in China should therefore come as less of a surprise than in the West. Indeed, the evidence suggests that women participated in pirate communities as something other than cooks and bottle washers; that they sometimes held rank and commanded ships; and that in certain instances they took part in combat.

Cheng I Sao and Chang Pao lead the confederacy

Cheng I's highly efficient operation had become the largest pirate confederation ever known by 1807. That year, though, Cheng I died. Sources differ on the cause, but many believe he drowned during a storm. Cheng I Sao took over as commander of the huge pirate empire.

Cheng I Sao's rise to command the pirate empire was far beyond the accomplishments of any female pirates before or after her. Perhaps because of this, she chose to bring in a trusted partner, Chang Pao (also known as Chang Po Tsai; died 1822). The relationship between Cheng I Sao and Chang Pao was complicated. Cheng I had kidnapped Chang Pao when he was fifteen years old and the Chengs adopted the boy. Chang Pao quickly became a commander in his own right. After Cheng I's death, Cheng I Sao named Chang Pao commander of the Red Flag fleet. Within a few years, they were married.

Cheng I Sao was a very able pirate chief. Fearless, she authorized raids on the well-armed British, Dutch, and Portuguese ships that Cheng I had avoided. Cheng I Sao demanded discipline and obedience from the pirates under her command. She and Chang Pao developed a set of regulations addressing issues such as the distribution of booty, desertion, disobeying a superior, stealing, and rape. Disobedience, raping a female captive, and stealing from the pirate treasury were among the violations punishable by death. Other crimes resulted in flogging, being shackled, or having one's ear cut off.

Being disciplined did not make the Chinese pirates humane during their raids. Like all pirates, their aim was to arouse as much fear in their prey as possible. Before their raids, according to Tim Travers in *Pirates: A History*, "the pirates stimulated themselves with drinks of wine and gunpowder, which produced red faces and glowing eyes, or ate the hearts of earlier victims to gain courage." Once they were prepared, hundreds of pirates would sweep into a town. With pirates behind them on the junk shooting at the shore, the attackers stormed in with their knives drawn, ready to slash and kill. There was good reason to fear them. One captive, quoted by Travers, describes the pirates' cruel treatment of members of the Chinese navy they had captured: "I saw one man … nailed to the deck through his feet with large nails, then beaten with four rattans twisted together, till he vomited blood, and after remaining some time in this state, he was taken ashore and cut to pieces."

Chinese pirates attacking a European merchant ship in the 1800s. © NORTH WIND PICTURE ARCHIVES/ALAMY.

The end of the pirate confederacy

China reeled under the pirates' attacks. Pirate fleets had damaged China's trade, defeated its antipiracy forces, and destroyed nearly half of Kwangtung's naval fleet. In 1809 the pirate fleets threatened to invade Canton. Unable to forcibly disband the confederation, the Chinese government offered pardons and promised positions in its military to those pirates who surrendered.

Some pirate leaders decided to accept pardons. As the first leaders left the confederation, rivalries among remaining leaders tore the organization apart. Knowing her empire was dissolving, Cheng I Sao negotiated terms with the Qing for a general pardon for all members of her confederation. In 1810 she and Chang Pao accepted pardons and left piracy behind them. The huge pirate empire was no more.

Shap-'ng-tsai and Chui Apoo

European traders in China played a role in defeating one last pirate empire in the 1840s. In the early nineteenth century, British consumers demanded China's tea, silk, and other products. However, trading was a problem because the English East India Company did not have products China wanted. What it did have was an excess of an addictive drug called opium that it had obtained in trade with India. The company started selling opium in China, even though the sale of the drug was illegal there. By the 1830s segments of the Chinese population suffered from drug addiction, and the emperor took steps to stop the trade. The British were willing to fight to maintain their profitable trade, and the First Opium War (1839–42) ensued. The British soundly defeated China. In the terms of peace that followed, the island of Hong Kong, which had long been a pirate base, became a British colony, and other Chinese ports were opened to the British. East India Company sales of opium continued unabated.

About 180 miles (290 kilometers) west of Hong Kong, pirate chief Shap-'ng-Tsai kept a fleet of about seventy junks. He and his lieutenant, Chui Apoo (d. 1851), led a successful enterprise, raiding ships and obtaining protection money from Chinese, American, and British ships passing through the waters off Hong Kong and Vietnam. Other pirates, both European and Chinese, dared to attack the foreign ships off the shores of China, but Shap-'ng-Tsai and Chui Apoo were the most successful. In one expedition in 1849, their fleet captured three British ships carrying opium for trade in China.

The British were not about to allow pirates to interfere with their opium trade after they had fought a war to maintain it. They destroyed Chui Apoo's fleet, which was headquartered at Bias Bay near Hong Kong, in 1849. Next they went after Shap-'ng-Tsai's fleet with a squadron of naval warships. In 1859, after several unsuccessful attempts, the British Royal Navy chased Shap-'ng-Tsai's fleet to some islands off Vietnam near the gulf of the Tonkin River. The British forces, which included two steam warships and a large fleet of Chinese junks, surrounded the pirates and engaged them in a fierce two-day battle. An estimated eighteen hundred pirates were killed and fifty-eight pirate junks were destroyed. Shap-'ng-Tsai escaped with a small force, but he soon surrendered to the Chinese government. He was awarded a pardon and a position in the Chinese navy.

The destruction of Chui Apoo's pirate fleet at Bias Bay in 1849. © ANCIENT ART & ARCHITECTURE/DANITADELIMONT.COM.

The British established a permanent naval presence in the northern part of the South China Sea. Piracy never stopped in the region, but the days of the large, organized Chinese pirate confederations were over.

Kanhoji Angria: India's pirate king

The increasing influence of European traders and colonizers was being felt throughout Asia in the early eighteenth century. In India a European quest to monopolize trade there was accompanied by nationwide turmoil. The Mughal Empire, which ruled all of South Asia (present-day Bangladesh, Bhutan, India, Nepal, and Pakistan), was falling apart. Wars and conflicts erupted among the regions. Adding to the turmoil, the rich trade routes from Asia to Europe had attracted pirates from Europe and the Caribbean to India's west coast, known as the Malabar Coast.

One of the most powerful among the groups that rebelled against the Mughal emperor was the Marathas, who had established their own Hindu empire in central India. In the late seventeenth century, Kanhoji Angria (also spelled Conajee Angria or Kanhoji Angre; c. 1669–1729) became a commander in the Maratha navy. According to Angus Konstam in *Pirates: Predators of the Seas*, the Maratha navy was, "no more than an organization of pirates who controlled the 240-mile stretch of India's western seaboard."

Angria's forces demanded that all ships passing through their coastal region pay for a *dastak*, or pass, to ensure protection from pirates. Those who did not pay had their ships seized by Angria's men. By 1703 Angria had built up his fleet to sixty well-armed ships. He was determined that European traders, and particularly the English East India Company, should pay for his dastak like everyone else. Since his boats were no match for the large European ships, he devised a strategy for raiding, using his smallest and most maneuverable vessels to initiate the attack and then following up with his larger ships and cannons. This allowed his fighters to board the European vessels. In hand-to-hand fighting they far outmatched the Europeans.

The East India Company complained bitterly to the Maratha ruler about Angria's raiding of their ships, but the Maratha commander stubbornly refused to stop. In 1710 Angria captured the company's island headquarters off Bombay in what may have been the most daring of all his raids. There, to the company's dismay, he set up a well-fortified pirate base within view of one of the region's major commercial centers.

In 1712 Angria raided an East India Company vessel, taking hostages. As part of the ransom he agreed to quit raiding East India Company ships for four years. (A ransom is the sum of money demanded for the release of someone being held captive.) He honored the agreement, but before the four years were up, the British company's naval forces began a series of attacks on his bases. Angria's small but strong navy repulsed all of the attacks. Many of the East India Company's leaders were sent back to England in shame.

Angria died in 1729 without having suffered a single defeat to the East India Company. His fleet, commanded by his sons, continued to harass the company's ships until the 1750s. According to many sources, Angria was a strong and thoughtful leader, fond of learning and deeply religious. He had remained in the service of the Maratha Empire throughout his life. The East India Company, which had good reason to fear

The English East India Company

The English East India Company (EIC) was formed by charter (a document endorsed by the queen) in 1600 to pursue trade in the East, particularly for procuring pepper and other spices that were in high demand in Europe at that time. Although Portugal dominated the sea routes between the South China Sea and Europe in the sixteenth century, the EIC began business in India as early as 1608, setting up a system of fortified trading/military posts in the coastal cities of Bombay, Surat, Calcutta, and Madras. By the end of the seventeenth century, the EIC had formed a monopoly on trade with India while its major rival, the Dutch East India Company, had a near-monopoly on Indonesian trade.

Around the end of the seventeenth century, the English government gave the EIC immense powers, like those of a state, in India. The EIC was granted the right to raise military forces, establish its own legal system with the power to try criminals, mint its own money, and declare war. Throughout the seventeenth century, the EIC struggled to maintain its monopoly over Indian trade, constantly challenged by independent English traders and by the French and Dutch East India trading companies. The English company prevailed.

In the eighteenth century, the Mughal Empire, which had ruled the entire Indian subcontinent (comprised of the present-day Bangladesh, Bhutan, India, Nepal, and Pakistan) since the mid–sixteenth century, was failing. Some of the local rulers who opposed the EIC found themselves in a position to try to obstruct English trade. The EIC began to interfere in local politics, and by all accounts, its officers handled this badly. In fact, many of the company's officers were accused of corruption and sent home. The English government stepped in to oversee the company's Indian operations by the end of the eighteenth century. As the English government took more control of India, it ended the company's monopoly on trade in India. England assumed full control of India in 1857–1858, and the failing EIC was dissolved.

Angria, attached the label of "pirate" to him. To the people of his empire who resented the intrusion of the foreign colonizers, he was a hero.

Piracy in the Strait of Malacca

From the seventeenth century onward, the arrival of European traders increased and greatly altered pirate activities in Asia. These changes were dramatic in the Strait of Malacca, a 550-mile (885-kilometer) channel in Southeast Asia separating the Indonesian Island of Sumatra from the Malay Peninsula. The strait became a busy trading route in the eighteenth century, when first the Portuguese and then the Dutch developed monopolies in the spice trade and shipped large quantities of spices from the surrounding islands back to European customers.

The channel and the surrounding seas of the Malay Archipelago (the largest island group in the world, including Borneo, Sulawesi, Java, Luzon, Mindanao, New Guinea, and Sumatra) had been ideal for sea raiders long before the foreigners arrived. Thousands of tiny islands dot the seas, providing inlets and rivers where boats can hide and wait for their prey. Coastal people in these islands developed a way of life that depended on shallow canoes called prahus, which they refined over the years. The Ilanun, who were based near Mindanao island in the Philippines, had the largest and swiftest prahus. Although there is evidence that the Ilanun did not begin their sea raiding until the mid–eighteenth century, once started, they seem to have taken to it with a vengeance. The Balinini were based primarily on the island of Jolo in the Sulu Sea between Borneo and Mindanao. Like the Ilanun, they raided the sea traffic around the Philippines. Dyak and Malay sea raiders lived throughout Southeast Asia and usually limited their raiding to local fishermen and traders. All of these groups except the Dyak were out to capture slaves. The Dyak, traditionally headhunters, killed and beheaded their victims.

Among these and other island people, sea raids had for centuries been an accepted means of livelihood and a common way of resolving disputes and hostilities among the various coastal communities. The sultan of Johore, a kingdom in the southern part of the Malay Peninsula, said, as quoted by John Falconer in *Pirates: Terror on the High Seas from the Caribbean to the South China Sea*, "Piracy is our birthright and so brings no disgrace."

The Europeans initially showed little concern about pirates, whose victims were usually local people or Chinese or Indochinese seamen. This changed in the nineteenth century, when the English statesman Thomas Stamford Raffles (1721–1826) decided to challenge the Dutch trade monopoly by establishing a British-held port on the Strait of Malacca. He founded Singapore in 1819, and it quickly developed into a major trading port. Conflicts between the Dutch and British over trade were resolved under the Anglo-Dutch Treaty of 1824, in which the Malay Archipelago was divided, with the area north of the Strait of Malacca, including Singapore, under Britain's control and the area to the south under Dutch control. In the treaty the British and Dutch mutually agreed to oppose piracy in the region.

Although most of the pirate raids in the region were directed at local villages and traders, pirates did attack European ships. In time the accounts of pirate raids frightened traders, damaging European trade. One frequently told story was that of English captain James Ross, whose ship was captured by pirates in the strait. Convinced there was treasure hidden somewhere onboard, the pirates tortured Ross to make him reveal its location, though apparently he did not have the information they wanted. First they tied his son to an anchor and forced the captain to watch as his son drowned. Next, they slowly cut off each of Ross's fingers, joint by joint. Tales such as this one, of torture and murder, circulated increasingly among the British seamen.

European trading companies and settlers increasingly interfered with local rulers in an attempt to stop the raiding. Many historians contend that the British traders and settlers used tales of piracy as an excuse to increase their forces and gain more power in the region. Whatever the motivations, negotiations with local people were frequently mishandled, leading to distrust between the newcomers and the locals. As hostilities increased, some local pirates increased their attacks on European ships.

In the 1830s a combined force of British Royal Navy and English East India Company ships set up an antipiracy base in Singapore. For the next thirty years, these forces fought a long series of fierce battles with the region's pirates, finally destroying them. Piracy never completely disappeared from the Strait of Malacca, however, and in the twentieth century it would plague maritime traders once again.

For More Information

BOOKS

Falconer, John. "The Eastern Seas." In *Pirates: Terror on the High Seas from the Caribbean to the South China Sea*. Edited by David Cordingly. East Bridgewater, MA: World Publications Group, 1998, 2007.

Gosse, Philip. *The History of Piracy*. New York: Tudor, 1932, 1995.

Konstam, Angus, with Roger Michael Kean. *Pirates: Predators of the Seas*. New York: Skyhorse, 2007, p. 148.

Murray, Dian H. "Cheng I Sao in Fact and Fiction." In *Bandits at Sea: A Pirates Reader*. Edited by C.R. Pennell. New York: New York University Press, 2001, p. 256.

———. "Chinese Pirates." In *Pirates: Terror on the High Seas from the Caribbean to the South China Sea*. Edited by David Cordingly. East Bridgewater, MA: World Publications Group, 1998, 2007.

———. *Pirates of the South China Coast, 1790–1810*. California: Stanford University Press, 1987.

Travers, Tim. *Pirates: A History*. Stroud, Gloucestershire, UK: Tempus, 2007, pp. 214 and 243.

Warren, James Frances. *Iranun and Balangingi: Globalization, Maritime Raiding and the Birth of Ethnicity.* Honolulu: University of Hawaii Press, 2002.

PERIODICALS

Antony, Robert. "Piracy in Early Modern China." *International Institute for Asian Studies (IIAS) Newsletter* no. 36 (March 2005): 7. Available online at www.iias.nl/nl/36/IIAS_NL36_07.pdf (accessed on January 3, 2011).

Gwin, Peter. "Dangerous Straits." *National Geographic* (October 2007). Available online at http://ngm.nationalgeographic.com/2007/10/malacca-strait-pirates/pirates-text.html (accessed on January 3, 2011).

WEB SITES

Koerth, Maggie. "Most Successful Pirate Was Beautiful and Tough." *CNN.com.* http://edition.cnn.com/2007/LIVING/worklife/08/27/woman.pirate (accessed January 3, 2011).

Warren, James Frances. "A Tale of Two Centuries: The Globalisation of Maritime Raiding and Piracy in Southeast Asia at the End of the Eighteenth and Twentieth Centuries." *Asia Research Institute.* www.ari.nus.edu.sg/docs/wps/wps03_002.pdf (accessed on January 3, 2011).

Modern Piracy

Throughout the eighteenth century and the first half of the nineteenth century, the major world governments waged forceful, and ultimately successful, campaigns against large pirate groups around the world. Piracy never ceased altogether, but the large surges in organized piracy, such as those of the Barbary corsairs and the Knights of Malta in the Mediterranean Sea and the Chinese pirate empires in the South China Sea, were so thoroughly crushed that by the twentieth century, piracy came to be seen as a practice of the past. Then, starting in the 1980s, waves of piracy began to emerge in hot spots around the world, one region at a time.

In many ways, piracy has not changed greatly over the centuries, although there are a few notable differences. Modern pirates almost always target vessels at sea; they do not conduct raids on coastal communities like pirates of the past did. Readily available technology, including cell phones and global positioning systems (GPS), have given pirates a new edge in coordinating attacks. Modern pirates frequently use automatic weapons and speedboats in their raids. To carry out high-profile thefts, they have formulated painstakingly precise strategies involving large networks of specialists and suppliers. Although some of the equipment is more advanced, modern pirates are basically just following in the footsteps of the pirates who came before them. The notable pirate feats of earlier eras also utilized intricate strategies and advanced equipment for the times. Twenty-first-century pirates have simply adapted the ancient criminal tradition of robbing at sea to modern circumstances.

Pirates and the Vietnamese boat people

The earliest wave of piracy in the modern age occurred in the waters off Southeast Asia in the years after the Vietnam War (1954–75; a war in which Communist North Vietnam successfully took over South Vietnam). Circumstances in postwar Vietnam led hundreds of thousands of people to try

WORDS TO KNOW

barge: A large, flat-bottomed boat used to transport cargo, usually over inland waterways.

failed state: A state without a functioning government above the local level.

high seas: The open waters of the ocean that are outside the limits of any country's territorial authority.

hijack: To take over by force.

intellectual property: A product of someone's intellect and creativity that has commercial value.

jurisdiction: The sole right and power to interpret and apply the law in a certain area.

mangrove: A tropical tree or shrub characterized by an extensive, impenetrable system of roots.

nautical mile: A unit of distance used for sea navigation. One nautical mile equals 6,080 feet (1.9 kilometers). One mile across land equals 5,280 feet (1.6 kilometers).

organized crime syndicate: A group of enterprises run by criminals to carry out illegal activities.

patent: A government grant that gives the creator of an invention the sole right to make, use, and sell that invention for a set period of time.

pirate haven: A safe place for pirates to harbor and repair their ships, resupply, and organize raiding parties.

prize: The goods, human captives, and ships captured in pirate raids.

ransom: A sum of money demanded for the release of someone being held captive.

tanker: A ship constructed to carry a large load of liquids, such as oil.

territorial waters: Waters surrounding a nation over which that nation exercises sole authority.

trawler: A fishing boat that uses open-mouthed fishing nets drawn along the sea bottom.

vigilante: Someone who takes the law into his or her own hands without the authority to do so.

---

to leave that country. In the late 1970s and early 1980s, many gathered what little money they had, crowded into rickety old boats with other refugees, and set out on the seas in search of a new home. Besides being dangerously overcrowded and leaky, the old boats made easy targets. Poor fishermen who had turned to piracy lurked in the Gulf of Thailand. The Thai pirates boarded the Vietnamese boats and robbed the defenseless passengers of what little they had. They also brutally raped hundreds of women and young girls, often murdering them and throwing them overboard. Those who survived the savage assaults were sometimes kept as captives or sold into prostitution in Thailand. Many of the other passengers were murdered during the raids or died when the pirates sank their boats and left them to drown.

Horrifying reports of the violence soon reached other parts of the world. In 1981 the Office of the United Nations (UN) High Commissioner for

Vietnamese boat people in 1982. These refugees were easy targets for pirates. MICHEL SETBOUM/GETTY IMAGES NEWS/ GETTY IMAGES.

Refugees, as quoted in a November 9, 1981, *Time* magazine article, reported the dismal statistics: "Women on 81% of the boats reaching Thailand in the first nine months of 1981 were raped, most of them many times over. A total of 552 were attacked in front of their relatives; another 200 were carried off to other fishing vessels." Efforts to stop the violence were slow, but the UN and the United States finally stepped in to help Thailand put an end to the attacks. Although the number of attacks eventually decreased, the attacks on Vietnamese boat people continued into the early 1990s, including many more murders and rapes.

Piracy hot spots of the 1990s

By the end of the 1980s, an increase in raids at sea in other parts of the world was noted, but there was little interest in these crimes outside of their immediate victims. According to some reports, pirates attacked forty-eight ships in 1989. (Reports vary and are usually estimates since many attacks do not get reported.) Most of these attacks were on commercial ships, although fishing boats were also targeted.

A few of these early attacks were surprisingly well-organized ones in which fully loaded cargo ships and tankers (ships constructed to carry large loads of liquid, such as oil) were hijacked, or taken over by force. Southeast Asia was the site of several pirate attacks on large ships. In 1990, for example, the *Marta* was traveling from Bangkok, Thailand, to Busan, Republic of Korea, carrying about two million dollars worth of tin plate as cargo. Four heavily armed pirates boarded the ship. They overpowered the crew and locked them up, and then changed the ship's course. The pirates sailed for two days to a site at sea where they were met by accomplices with a barge. (A barge is a large, flat-bottomed boat used to transport cargo, usually over inland waterways.) After unloading the ship's entire cargo onto the barge, the pirates released the crew and then fled with their enormous prize. (Prizes are the goods, human captives, and ships captured in pirate raids.) The carefully planned robbery was successful due to inside information and a network of helpers. It was thought to be the work of an organized crime syndicate, a group of enterprises run by criminals to carry out illegal activities. There were several similar attacks in Southeast Asia within the next few years.

The South China Sea, the former site of China's large pirate empires, was another hot spot of piracy in the mid–1990s. (For more information on China's pirate empires, see **Piracy in Asia**.) Cargo vessels there were stopped by what appeared to be Chinese coastal authorities, people dressed in uniforms and arriving in boats with official markings. These "officials" took over the ships and sailed them into Chinese ports, where they unloaded the cargo. They held the crew in the port until receiving payment of a large "fine" from the ship owners. In some cases the ships were renamed, repainted, and sold. It was clear that these incidents were hijackings. China, under pressure from international antipiracy agencies, investigated and found that several of the attacks had been the unauthorized work of some corrupt officials in its Border Patrol Bureau. Other attacks at this time may have been the work of people impersonating Chinese officials. China increased its regulations for security against piracy.

Journalists and other interested parties claimed that China had not done enough to stop the pirates, but at the end of the 1990s, China proved that it would not tolerate piracy at sea. In 1998, a Hong Kong cargo ship, the *Cheung Son*, was hijacked by pirates posing as Chinese customs officials. The pirates beat the twenty-three crew members to death and threw their bodies overboard. Then they sold the ship and cargo for three hundred thousand dollars. Although the ship was never found, police later found photographs of the pirates celebrating their killing spree on the ship's deck. The Chinese government spared no effort in catching the pirates. The suspects were quickly arrested. After a huge trial in a Chinese court, thirteen pirates—twelve Chinese and one Indonesian—were sentenced to death for their part in the attack on the *Cheung Son*; an additional twenty-five people involved in the crime received long prison sentences.

The Philippines was another pirate hot spot in the 1980s and 1990s, particularly around the island of Mindanao, where conflict raged between the government and several insurgent, or rebel, groups. Most of the pirate attacks targeted fishing vessels. Although sometimes very violent, the Filipino pirates were usually not highly organized, and their targets were small. According to some experts, piracy flourished due to poor governmental control of the seas, lack of police, and government corruption in an area in which people lived in extreme poverty and lacked other opportunities for survival.

Piracy also developed in several areas off the coast of South America in the 1990s, particularly off Brazil, Colombia, and Venezuela. In fact, after armed pirate gangs raided ships in the major Brazilian ports of Rio de Janeiro and Santos, the International Shipping Federation ranked the ports as two of the most dangerous in the world. One of the most famous examples of piracy in the seas off Brazil occurred in 2001, when the *Seamaster*, a 118-foot (36-meter) boat on a round-the-world environmental mission, was attacked while at anchor at the Brazilian port of Macapá, on the Amazon River. Seven armed attackers boarded the ship, overpowered the crew, and began stealing the crew's property. During the robbery, the boat's captain, champion yachtsman and former America's Cup winner Sir Peter Blake (1948–2001) of New Zealand, managed to grab a rifle. He fired a shot at one of the pirates, and the pirates shot back, killing Blake. The attack drew publicity because the captain was a well-known public figure. Involving small-time pirates seeking only minor rewards, it was typical of piracy at the time along the coast of Brazil.

Sir Peter Blake stands next to the Seamaster, *in Brazil, just three months before the yacht was attacked by pirates and Blake was killed.* AP IMAGES/ TASSO MARCELO.

Strait of Malacca piracy in the 1990s

Many of the pirate attacks of the early 1990s occurred in the Strait of Malacca, a 550-mile (885-kilometer) channel separating the Indonesian island of Sumatra from the Malay Peninsula. In a 2007 *National Geographic* article on piracy in the strait, Peter Gwin explains that the Strait of Malacca is a "critical choke point in the global economy." Some seventy thousand merchant vessels pass through the strait each year, transporting about one-fifth of the world's seaborne trade, making it the second busiest commercial shipping lane in the world. But the geography of the strait has made it popular with pirates for centuries. According to Gwin, "the strait's geography makes it nearly unsecurable.... Some 250 miles (400 kilometers) wide at its northern mouth, the strait funnels down to about ten miles (16 kilometers) across near its southern end and is dotted with hundreds of uninhabited mangrove islands, offering endless hideouts to all manner of criminals." (Mangroves are tropical trees or shrubs characterized by an extensive, impenetrable system of roots that prevent passage through the waters for all except those familiar with the setting.)

In the 1990s pirates—often poor fishermen trying to find work or supplement their meager income—increasingly boarded ships as they slowed down to pass through the strait. Sometimes the pirates also boarded ships at anchor, usually at night. The pirates stole cash from the crew and grabbed whatever other valuables they could find and then sped off. Their payoff for these crimes was relatively small.

In 1997 Asia experienced a financial crisis that resulted in widespread unemployment and political instability. Indonesia had the greatest unrest, and in 1998 its dictator, Suharto (1921–2008), was forced to resign, resulting in additional political instability. As Indonesia drastically reduced its military and naval forces due to a lack of funds, pirate attacks in the region increased sharply, and there was little or no authority to stop them. In fact, some observers claimed that Indonesian security forces were involved in pirate raids in the region.

Strait of Malacca piracy in the twenty-first century

By the turn of the twenty-first century, the majority of piracy worldwide was occurring in the regions of Southeast Asia surrounding the Strait of Malacca. Pirates there had begun to coordinate their attacks in order to reap larger profits. Raids on ships often involved several speedboats, each carrying a small gang of pirates. The pirates learned to board larger ships using ladders and grappling hooks, and they armed themselves with guns and automatic weapons as well as knives and machetes. The speedboats frequently traveled with a lead ship that coordinated the attacks and carried enough food, ammunition, and fuel to allow the pirate gangs to chase ships farther out at sea. This resulted in a sharp increase in the number of armed attacks on ships in the high seas (the open waters of the ocean that are outside the limits of any country's territorial authority) and on remote territorial waters (the waters surrounding a nation over which that nation exercises sole authority). With careful advance planning and the help of accomplices, the pirates were equipped to carry off entire cargoes, often comprised of huge amounts of goods, such as metals, grains, and oil.

These well-organized pirate gangs soon found that the best profits came from hijacking entire ships, including the cargo and crew. They bargained with ship owners for ransom, or payment to release the ship, cargo, and human captives. Shipping companies often paid the ransom without reporting the incident to authorities in order to avoid the long delays in their shipping schedules that would be brought about by an investigation into the attack. Investigations could take months and cost the companies millions of dollars in lost business. Shipping companies also wished to avoid increases in the cost of their insurance that would result from reporting a pirate attack.

The Other Piracy: Intellectual Property Theft

Intellectual property is a product of someone's intellect and creativity that has commercial value. When ideas or knowledge are expressed in tangible form, such as in a scientific invention or discovery, a book or article, music, a film, a company logo, a manufacturing process, a computer software product, or the design of an athletic shoe, the creators' rights to them are protected by laws. Copyright, patent, and trademark laws grant the creator the exclusive right to distribute, copy, use, or sell their product. Intellectual property (IP) piracy is the unauthorized use, reproduction, and/or distribution of materials that are protected under those laws.

IP piracy has always existed, but it became a much bigger problem with the development of the Internet. In some fields, such as the music industry, the digital age has brought about easy and fast ways of distributing products for free. In 1999, for example, peer-to-peer file sharing emerged, in which individuals can make exact copies and share original computer files of recorded music, which is protected material. Napster, the first known service to facilitate the sharing of files via the Internet through a system

of linked servers and users, claimed more than twenty-six million users in 2001. The music industry and some musicians protested. They were not getting paid for their product and, in their view, the people who copied music files were stealing. The service was eventually shut down in response to the legal action taken against it for its participation in copyright infringement. Even so, by 2010, record sales had fallen by 50 percent since 2000.

Patent infringement occurs when someone violates the terms of a patent, which is a government grant that gives the creator of an invention the sole right to make, use, and sell that invention for a set period of time. Most cases of patent infringement occur when someone tries to sell an invention that is patented under someone else's name.

A trademark is an officially registered symbol that identifies a product's manufacturer or distributor. Trademark infringement occurs when products are manufactured or sold under the trademark of another company without that company's permission. Counterfeit products are copies of products protected under trademarks that are made

Pirate organizations soon grew more sophisticated. Hijacking ships, selling huge loads of goods, kidnapping crews and passengers, and dealing with the shipping companies for ransom required exceptional planning and large networks of people onshore as well as at sea. The pirates were often aided by insiders, members of the crew of the targeted ship who gave them information and helped them take over the ship once they had boarded. The pirates also had suppliers at several ports. They used sophisticated radio, computer, and GPS technology to track ships at sea and to communicate among themselves. Their profits became much larger. The pirates who organized and led these activities were professional criminals, and their with the intent of passing them off as genuine. Manufacturing and selling counterfeit purses, watches, sunglasses, and many other products have become big business in many countries.

According to the U.S. Chamber of Commerce, IP piracy cost the United States an estimated $250 billion a year in the first decade of the twenty-first century. The agency also claims that intellectual property theft is responsible for the loss of over 750,000 American jobs. Many industry analysts dispute these figures, saying there is simply no way to accurately assess the losses. Some commentators point to positive aspects of IP piracy: IP piracy has paved the way for new ways of conducting commerce in the digital age. For instance, after the popularity of Napster became apparent, Apple developed iTunes, a proprietary digital media player application. The iTunes store allows a customer to purchase and download music and many other products via the Internet, providing a lot of the same services that piracy did, while allowing customers to pay for the products.

Fighting against IP piracy is complicated by the fact that it crosses national boundaries, while laws regarding it may differ from country to country. Some observers note that cultural differences have led to some forms of IP piracy. Copying is not considered an offense in some regions, and countries tend to differ on issues of what constitutes an infringement of IP law. In 2010 the U.S. Congressional International Anti-Piracy Caucus drew attention to five countries that are most responsible for the piracy of U.S. products: Russia, China, Canada, Spain, and Mexico. China, considered the leading producer of pirated goods in the world at the turn of the twenty-first century, was producing massive quantities of movies, music, books, electronics, designer jeans, and many other products under phony U.S. trademarks.

Some social analysts dislike the use of the word *piracy* for IP theft. Piracy is, after all, defined as robbery committed at sea. There are, however, a few similarities between these two forms of theft. Both can have a negative impact on international trade. Regulating IP piracy worldwide, particularly in light of the use of the Internet, is as daunting as trying to control the world's oceans and waterways. But piracy at sea entails the use of force, and victims of IP piracy do not face the threats of violence and kidnapping. Despite the terminology, they are very different types of crime.

work was often compared to organized crime on land. Violence in pirate attacks, with resulting deaths and injuries, increased.

Fighting Strait of Malacca piracy

Concerned about growing piracy in the early 1990s, the International Maritime Bureau (IMB), a division of the International Chamber of Commerce (ICC), established the IMB Piracy Reporting Centre, based in Kuala Lumpur, Malaysia. The center tracks pirate attacks around the world and sends out immediate alerts to sea traffic. Since the center opened

A map of the Strait of Malacca showing pirate attacks in 2010.
MAP BY XNR PRODUCTIONS INC./CENGAGE LEARNING.

in 1992, the IMB has issued annual reports of the number of reported piracy attacks worldwide. It reported more than thirty-six hundred attacks between 1998 and 2009.

The number of pirate attacks soared during the 1990s. From an estimated 48 attacks in 1989 and 107 attacks in 1991, the number jumped to 300 in 1999 and then peaked at 469 in 2000. That year, seventy-two people were killed in pirate attacks, and 65 percent of the attacks occurred in Southeast Asia. In 2003 there were 445 attacks. Of these, 189 attacks occurred in the seas of Southeast Asia, 121 in Indonesia, and 35 in or close to the Strait of Malacca.

Attitudes of the nations surrounding the Strait of Malacca—Singapore, Indonesia, and Malaysia—changed significantly after the pirate attacks in their area peaked in 2000. By 2004 they had begun to cooperate with each other in their fight against piracy. Indonesia, by most accounts

Members of a Malaysian police amphibious assault unit participate in a joint antipiracy exercise with Japanese and Thai forces in 2007. Cooperation among the nations surrounding the Strait of Malacca led to a remarkable drop in pirate attacks in the region. AP IMAGES/ANDY WONG.

the weak link in the antipiracy effort, stepped up its efforts and received aid from regional governments to build and equip its maritime police forces. The drop in pirate attacks was swift and remarkable. In 2004 there were thirty-eight attacks in the strait, and in 2008 there were only two—an 87 percent decrease from 2000.

Shift in hot spots: Africa

Unfortunately, as the Strait of Malacca came under control, other pirate hot spots developed. A few long-term hot spots in Africa, primarily Nigeria and Somalia, began to experience a surge in pirate attacks. Nigeria had 28 attacks in 2009. Captain Pottengal Mukundan, director of the IMB, warned that this was an alarming development, because attacks in the waters off Nigeria were often more violent than attacks occurring elsewhere off Africa. He feared that the violence could become a trend among neighboring countries.

Somalia was the most troubling hot spot in terms of sheer numbers. Pirate attacks off Somalia in the twenty-first century began slowly, with only 1 reported attack in 2004, increasing to 31 attacks in 2007, with 154 people taken hostage. In 2008 Somali pirates were responsible for 111 attacks. They hijacked 42 vessels that year with increased use of firearms and knives. In 2009, 271 pirate attacks were attributed to Somali pirates—more than half of the worldwide total of 406. That year, Somali pirates boarded 153 vessels, hijacked 49 vessels, and attempted another 84 attacks. They fired on 120 vessels and took 1,052 crew members hostage. They were responsible for injuring 68 crew members and for killing 8. By that time, Somali pirates were getting international attention on a regular basis with their high-profile attacks.

Early Somali piracy

Somalia experienced violent turmoil after its dictator was ousted from power in 1991, and warring factions have prevented a new central government from forming. As of 2010, Somalia still does not have a formal government. Located on the Horn of Africa (the easternmost projection of Africa), Somalia's eastern coastline lies along the Indian Ocean. Its northern coastline is on the Gulf of Aden, an arm of the Arabian Sea that connects the Red Sea to the Indian Ocean. Each year about twenty-one thousand ships cross the gulf, which is sometimes called "pirate alley." More than 30 percent of the world's oil passes through these waters on its way to consumers worldwide. Somalia is considered an ideal location for piracy at sea. It is a failed state (a state without a functioning government above the local level), its people are impoverished, and it lacks sufficient power to police its own waters, yet it is located on shores passed daily by some of the world's most richly laden merchant ships.

In the 1990s and early 2000s large numbers of foreign commercial trawlers began to fish in the waters off the coast of Somalia. (Trawlers are fishing boats that use open-mouthed fishing nets drawn along the sea bottom.) Local fishermen, who were barely able to eke out a living as it was, resented the foreigners for taking their meager resources. A group of vigilantes (people who take the law into their own hands) began to stop the fishing boats, demanding that they pay to fish there. Confrontations

The Kidnapping of Paul and Rachel Chandler

Private yachts were among the many oceangoing targets of Somali pirates in the first decade of the twenty-first century. On October 22, 2009, British couple Paul and Rachel Chandler were sailing their 38-foot (12-meter) yacht from Seychelles, an island nation in the Indian Ocean, to Tanzania, when a group of Somali pirates kidnapped them. The pirates took the couple to Somalia's Mudug region somewhere between the coastal village of Elhur and the small inland town of Amara. There, they were separated and reportedly held in cages. The pirates demanded seven million dollars in ransom and threatened to kill the couple if they were not paid. Following policy, the United Kingdom Foreign Office refused to pay.

The Chandlers were guarded by pirates armed with assault rifles, and they were reportedly moved every few days. Paul, who was fifty-nine at the time of the kidnapping, and Rachel, who was fifty-five, reported being treated poorly, and Rachel in particular complained of ill health. Their captors did allow a doctor to come in and examine them, and on a couple of occasions journalists were permitted to interview them. In June 2010 the Chandlers' relatives arranged to pay a ransom of $430,000. With the flurry of media activity that accompanied it, though, the pirates decided to demand more money and did not release the couple. A second payment was reportedly made in secret in November, and the

Rachel Chandler, at a location in central Somalia where she was being held after she and her husband, Paul, were kidnapped by pirates. MOHAMED DAHIR/AFP/GETTY IMAGES.

Chandlers were finally free to go home after more than one year in captivity. An estimated three hundred to six hundred other people were being held hostage by the Somali pirates at the time.

ensued, and the vigilantes began to hijack the vessels, forcing shipping companies to pay large ransoms to get their boats and crews back.

Like many pirates before them, the early Somali pirates frequently presented themselves as do-gooders who rob from the rich and give to the poor. They claimed that the commercial fishers had destroyed their local fishing industry and that Western and Asian enterprises had dumped toxic waste into the region's seas. In their view, their sea raids were an effort to protect their families and villages. Desperate poverty and an utter lack of opportunity for other kinds of work also spurred their piracy.

Many Somali pirates had fought in Somalia's civil wars and uprising. They had emerged from the wars armed and trained in the use of automatic weapons and rocket-propelled grenades, or unguided, explosive rockets. They adapted their combat strategies to raiding at sea, attacking their prey in a coordinated wave of speedboats equipped with sophisticated communications systems and navigation devices. Known for their boldness, Somali pirates attacked commercial fishing vessels, merchant vessels, cargo ships chartered by the UN World Food Programme containing food aid meant for Somalis, tankers, and luxury cruise vessels. They typically kidnapped crews and passengers and demanded heavy ransom for the release of cargo, ship, and crew, though in some cases they stole ships, had them refitted, and sold them. At any given time in the period from 2008 to 2010, hundreds of hostages were being held in Somali port towns by the pirates. For example, at least 544 people were taken hostage in the first six months of 2010.

Some high-profile Somali pirate attacks

International attention was drawn to the Somali seas in late 2008, when several high-profile hijackings occurred in a short span of time. On September 23 the Ukrainian merchant vessel *Faina*, a ship loaded with Russian-made tanks, grenade launchers, and ammunition, was hijacked by a group of about fifty Somali pirates. The hijacking caused great international concern that the cargo of powerful weapons might wind up in the hands of pirates, terrorists, or insurgents. The *Faina* and its crew of twenty was held for more than four months before the ship owners paid a ransom of $3.5 million for their release.

On November 15 off the coast of Kenya, Somali pirates hijacked the 1,082-foot (330-meter) Saudi oil tanker *Sirius Star*, the largest ship ever hijacked to that time. The ship was carrying two million barrels of crude oil from Saudi Arabia to the United States, a cargo worth about one hundred million dollars. The pirates took the ship to the Somali harbor of Haradhere and held it there until the ship owners paid a three-million-dollar ransom.

Nothing received quite so much attention, though, as the April 8, 2009, attempted hijacking of the U.S. cargo ship *Maersk Alabama*. Four pirates, led by Abduwali Abdukhadir Muse (c. 1990–), boarded the ship about 240 miles (386 kilometers) off the coast of Somalia as it carried food aid to East Africa. The raid was botched by the pirates from the beginning, when, in the process of boarding the *Maersk Alabama*, they sank their own boat. As they reached the deck, the machine-gun-armed pirates overpowered the ship's captain, Richard Phillips (1963–), and several crew members on deck. Other crew members, however, locked themselves in the engine room. They managed to capture one of the pirates and eventually cut all power in the ship. There was a standoff, which ended when Captain Phillips offered himself to the pirates as a hostage if they would release the ship and its crew. With Phillips as hostage, the pirates fled in the *Maersk Alabama's* lifeboat. Phillips spent one hundred hours in captivity in the small lifeboat, with helicopters hovering overhead and television cameras relaying the scene to millions of viewers worldwide. The captain made an attempt to escape by jumping overboard but gave up when the pirates fired shots at him in the water. In the end, U.S. Navy snipers (skilled shooters) killed three of the pirates in the lifeboat and rescued Phillips. Muse was arrested and later tried in a federal court in New York, where he pled guilty to charges of hijacking, kidnapping, and hostage taking.

Somali pirate havens

Although the number of Somali pirates that board a ship during an attack is usually small (between seven and ten), it takes many other members in the pirate organization to carry out the planning, hijacking, kidnapping, and ransoming. Most of these people are located, along with the pirate fleets, in fishing communities in northeastern and central Somalia. Like pirates throughout history, Somali pirates are based on land and have havens in virtually lawless regions of their country. (Pirate havens are safe place for pirates to harbor and repair their ships, resupply, and organize raiding parties.) In *Pirates: Terror on the High Seas from the Caribbean to the South China Sea* Eric Ellen explains that this is one of the most crucial factors for pirates. He writes, "Most modern pirates are land-based. They need somewhere to operate from, somewhere to hide, and a means of converting their 'treasure' into hard currency. To be successful, they need a degree of cooperation from others, or at least for the local authorities to turn a blind eye."

The Somali pirate havens are mainly found in two regions: the province of Puntland in northeastern Somalia and the Mudug region in north-central Somalia. The Puntland port city of Eyl is considered the primary pirate base in Somalia, but there are other Puntland havens, including Bossaso, Qandala, Caluula, Bargaal, and Garacad. The major pirate base in Mudug is the town of Haradhere.

The larger pirate havens like Eyl and Haradhere bring in more money in ransoms than local governments have in their annual budgets. Thus, the pirates are usually better armed and better equipped than any military or police forces that could be sent after them. The pirate havens have therefore been largely undisturbed by local authorities; there have even been claims that some local government officials are involved in piracy themselves. The pirates serve more or less as rulers of the communities in the areas surrounding their bases. The populations of these villages are mixed in their feelings about the pirates. Some hate the lawlessness the pirates bring to their towns, while others regard the pirates as heroes who bring jobs and income and fight against foreigners who exploit Somalia's resources.

Somali pirates usually operate in large gangs organized around families, or gangs. Each of the pirate havens is thought to be headed by a different pirate family. One of the largest pirate gangs is centered in the small and very poor fishing town of Eyl. Eyl is extremely difficult to reach by land. Before the pirates established their haven there, the village had barely been visited by cars or other modern conveniences. The pirates changed that. In the twenty-first century, pirates anchored the ships they had captured alongside their own speedboats in Eyl's harbor. They also brought their hostages, some of whom would remain in their custody in Eyl for months as their ransoms were negotiated. Militias patrolled the area twenty-four hours a day. Eyl established "restaurants" to feed the hostages being held there. The pirates built large villas for their own use and drove expensive cars through the dirt roads. The people of Eyl, who had few resources in the past, were suddenly employed in such piracy-related jobs as boat builders and repairmen, guards, militiamen, and interpreters. By 2008 piracy had become the economic foundation of the town.

By some estimates, the pirates of Eyl made between thirty and fifty million dollars a year by hijacking ships. The money was divided according to strict rules. The investors who provided cash for the ships and weapons received 30 percent of the prizes. (The investors were often pirates who had recently received ransom money from a successful hijacking.) The hijackers received 50 percent. The remaining 20 percent was distributed throughout the network, to the guards, translators, and cooks, with some going to the poor people in Eyl. The pirates invested some portion of their share of the money in updating their boats and equipment.

Armed Somali pirates prepare a skiff to attack ships in the Gulf of Aden. LEON NEAL/AFP/GETTY IMAGES.

Somali pirates relocate

Somalia has the longest coast in Africa and no navy of its own. Without help from other nations, the fight against piracy could not succeed. Help arrived at the end the first decade of the twenty-first century, with the police efforts of many nations focused on the Gulf of Aden. With that help, the number of pirate attacks in the gulf decreased in 2010. However, the pirates simply began to range farther out to sea in the Indian Ocean. Mukundan warned that they were venturing as far as 1,000 nautical miles (1,853 kilometers) away from the coast to conduct their attacks. (A nautical mile is a unit of distance used for sea navigation. One nautical mile equals 6,080 feet or 1.9 kilometers.) The vastness of the area of attack in the open seas makes policing efforts nearly impossible. In 2010 the pirates also began conducting attacks in the Red Sea.

The cost of piracy

Global commerce increased tremendously in the last quarter of the twentieth century; by the end of the first decade of the twenty-first century, between 80 and 90 percent of international freight was shipped by sea. On any given day there were more than ten million cargo containers filled with goods crowding the oceans. The total worth of the world's trade at sea was estimated at about six trillion dollars. Any disruption in overseas trade impacts many different participants, including the shippers, insurers, investors, industries, and consumers.

The costs of piracy to maritime trade are huge. Although there are some estimates of the annual cost of piracy at sea in the twenty-first century—most ranging between one billion and sixteen billion dollars—many commentators urge against using these rough estimates, since there has been little accurate research in this area. What is important is that global trade would collapse if the world's ships were hindered from transporting the fuel, medicines, foods, and other goods humans depend on. It is vital to keep the seas pirate free.

For More Information

BOOKS

Ellen, Eric. "Piracy Today." In *Pirates: Terror on the High Seas from the Caribbean to the South China Sea.* Edited by David Cordingly. East Bridgewater, MA: World Publications Group, 1998, 2007, p. 237.

Sekulich, Daniel. *Terror on the Seas: True Tales of Present-day Pirates.* New York: St. Martin's, 2009.

PERIODICALS

Baldauf, Scott. "Who Are Somalia's Pirates?" *Christian Science Monitor* (November 20, 2008). Available online at www.csmonitor.com/World/Africa/2008/1120/p25s22-woaf.html (accessed on January 3, 2011).

Gwin, Peter. "Dangerous Straits." *National Geographic* (October 2007). Available online at http://ngm.nationalgeographic.com/2007/10/malacca-strait-pirates/pirates-text.html (accessed on January 3, 2011).

Raffaele, Paul. "The Pirate Hunters." *Smithsonian* (August 2007). Available online at www.smithsonianmag.com/people-places/pirate_main.html?c=y&page=2&#ixzz0udnSdQCn (accessed on January 3, 2011).

"Thailand: Piratical Murders and Rape at Sea." *Time* (November 9, 1981). Available online at www.time.com/time/magazine/article/ 0,9171,922653-1,00.html#ixzz0uWssiIIK (accessed on January 3, 2011).

WEB SITES

Adow, Mohammed. "The Pirate Kings of Puntland." *Aljazeera.* http:// english.aljazeera.net/news/africa/2009/06/2009614125245860630.html (accessed on January 3, 2011).

Fighting Piracy in the Twenty-first Century

Modern piracy has escalated along with the expansion of trade. In the twenty-first century there are more ships transporting the world's goods than ever before, and they make attractive targets for pirates, or robbers at sea. The world's oceans are vast, making up about 71 percent of the earth's surface. For those who wish to stop piracy, patrolling hundreds of thousands of miles of the world's waters in an effort to catch pirates in the act of stealing or hijacking (taking over by force) ships is a nearly impossible task. Nevertheless, by the end of the first decade of the twenty-first century, the fight against piracy brought many of the nations of the world together in a cooperative effort unlike any that had come before.

Throughout history, attempts to eradicate piracy have hinged on several key elements. Most experts agree that the important factors are cooperation among the affected nations, resolution of political problems in the pirates' homelands, and addressing the problem of poverty in the pirates' homelands. Coordinating the efforts of many countries into a unified antipiracy effort has in the past proved a stumbling block. For example, European countries were busy fighting amongst themselves for nearly two hundred years before they finally joined together to eradicate the piracy of the Barbary corsairs. (For more information, see **The Barbary Corsairs**.) More recent efforts to coordinate an international fight against piracy have been aided by the formulation of international laws of the seas. But even with the major nations cooperating in antipiracy naval campaigns, battles against piracy are frequently lost. Failed states (countries that lack a functioning national government) such as Somalia provide pirates safe places to hide after committing their crimes at sea. Broken economies that offer no jobs and extreme poverty lead many young fishermen and seamen to become pirates to make a living.

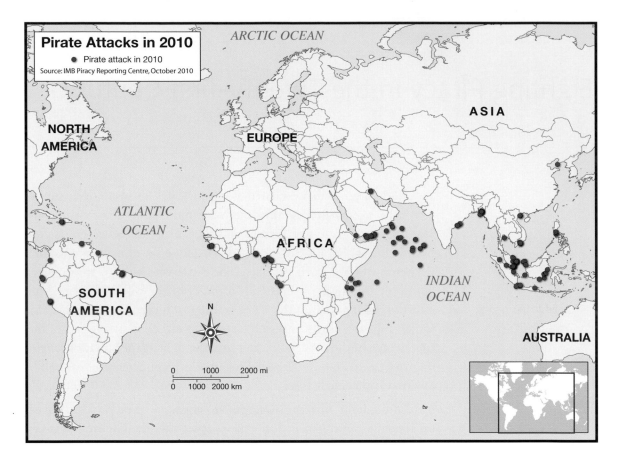

A map of pirate attacks in 2010. MAP BY XNR PRODUCTIONS, INC./CENGAGE LEARNING.

International antipiracy laws

Laws regarding piracy have always challenged lawmakers, primarily because pirates commit their crimes at sea and no one country has jurisdiction over the world's oceans. (Jurisdiction is the sole right and power to interpret and apply the law in a certain area.) Maritime law, the set of regulations that govern navigation and trade on the seas, requires that nations agree about how to treat the many different activities upon the seas, including privateering and piracy. Throughout most of the world's history, there were no international laws regarding piracy, but many countries voluntarily adhered to longstanding international maritime customs.

One maritime custom pertaining to pirates dates back to the ancient Roman notion that pirates are "enemies of the human race," or *hostis humani generis*. In his book, *The Pirate's Pact: The Secret Alliance Between*

WORDS TO KNOW

asylum: Refuge or protection in a foreign country, granted to someone who might be in danger if returned to his or her own country.

coast guard: A government agency responsible for enforcing laws on the seas and navigable waters.

copyright laws: Laws that grant the creator the exclusive right to distribute, copy, use, or sell his or her product.

digital technology: A data technology system that converts sound or signals into numbers, in the form of a binary format of ones and zeros.

failed state: A state that has no functioning government above the local level.

high seas: The open waters of the ocean that are outside the limits of any country's territorial authority.

hijack: To take over by force.

jurisdiction: The sole right and power to interpret and apply the law in a certain area.

maritime: Relating to the sea.

maritime law: The set of regulations that govern navigation and trade on the seas.

nautical mile: A unit of distance used for sea navigation. One nautical mile equals 6,080 feet (1.9 kilometers). One mile across land equals 5,280 feet (1.6 kilometers).

pirate haven: A safe place for pirates to harbor and repair their ships, resupply, and organize raiding parties.

territorial waters: Waters surrounding a nation over which that nation exercises sole authority.

terrorism: The systematic use of violence against civilians in order to attain goals that are political, religious, or ideological.

History's Most Notorious Buccaneers and Colonial America, author Douglas R. Burgess Jr. explains that pirates have long been "a challenge to the very concept of statehood. They divorced themselves from the nation-state, formed extra-territorial enclaves [communities or small states that exist separately from the country surrounding them and act outside of territorial jurisdiction] and made war—as [English writer] Daniel Defoe once wrote—'against the world entire.'" Because pirates are considered enemies of the whole world, they are subject to universal jurisdiction, meaning they can be pursued, tried, and penalized by any nation, regardless of borders or treaties. According to Donald Rothwell in his 2009 article "Maritime Piracy and International Law," the custom of universal jurisdiction "made piracy in effect the first universal crime over which all states had the capacity to arrest and prosecute."

One of the foundations of maritime law, the concept of "freedom of the seas," was accepted by many nations by the seventeenth century.

Under this concept, individual nations had jurisdiction over their territorial waters, that is, those waters extending about 3 nautical miles (5.6 kilometers) out from their shorelines. (A nautical mile is a unit of distance used for sea navigation. One nautical mile equals 6,080 feet or 1.9 kilometers.) Territorial boundaries were later extended to 12 nautical miles (22 kilometers) out from shore. The waters beyond these boundaries, the high seas, are considered international waters. All nations can use them, but none can own or control them. When piracy occurs on the high seas, it is an international rather than a national problem.

UNCLOS, the constitution of the oceans Over the years, maritime customs were set down in treaties between nations. In 1982 the United Nations collected the regulations from existing treaties relating to the world's oceans into a single law, called the United Nations Convention on the Law of the Sea (UNCLOS). The treaty was signed by 158 nations. UNCLOS specifically authorizes official ships of all states to seize known pirate ships. As long as a pirate ship is on the high seas, the authorities of any nation can stop and seize the pirates and their ship, and that nation can punish the pirates under its own laws, regardless of the pirate's nationality.

However, the UNCLOS definition of piracy creates some challenges in maritime law. UNCLOS limits the crime of piracy to those acts that are committed for selfish gain and does not include crimes committed for political reasons. In addition, robbery at sea is only considered piracy if it occurs on the high seas. Crimes that occur in a nation's territorial waters are under the sole jurisdiction of that nation and are not covered by international law. In contrast, the International Maritime Bureau (IMB), a division of the International Chamber of Commerce (ICC) that serves as a watchdog agency over crimes of the sea, created a different definition, describing piracy as "the act of boarding any vessel with an intent to commit theft or any other crime, and with an intent or capacity to use force in furtherance of that act." This definition does not specify whether the crime is done for personal or political reasons or that it occurs on the high seas, and these are areas that have caused some confusion in the fight against piracy.

Antipiracy success in the Strait of Malacca

Around the turn of the twenty-first century, the Strait of Malacca and surrounding waters in the Indonesian archipelago (island group) were the most dangerous waters in the world in terms of pirate attacks. The strait, which lies between Malaysia and the Indonesian island of Sumatra and extends up to Singapore, is one of the world's busiest sea lanes for commercial shipping, with about seventy thousand merchant vessels passing through each year. It is known as a choking point because at some points the strait becomes so narrow the heavy traffic is forced to slow down. This makes boarding the passing ships easier for pirates. By 2004 the strait and the region of Southeast Asia surrounding it were the site of 40 percent of the world's pirate attacks. In 2005 leading insurance specialist Lloyd's Market Association ranked the Strait of Malacca as a war zone because of the pirate attacks, and this rating cost shippers enormous hikes in insurance fees. The navies of the three surrounding nations—Malaysia, Indonesia, and Singapore—each working independently, had been unable to stop the new surge of pirates. As the situation deteriorated, though, they dedicated themselves to a cooperative effort to stop the attacks on ships.

The first major hurdle was to reach an agreement to share intelligence and resources and to coordinate antipiracy missions among the affected Asian countries. In 2004 the Regional Cooperation Agreement on Combating Piracy and Armed Robbery against Ships in Asia (ReCAAP) was finalized in Tokyo, Japan. It was the first government-to-government agreement regarding piracy in Asia, and it included sixteen members in 2010: Bangladesh, Brunei Dar Es Salaam, Cambodia, China, India, Japan, South Korea, Laos, Myanmar, the Netherlands, Norway, the Philippines, Singapore, Sri Lanka, Thailand, and Vietnam. ReCAAP came into force in 2006.

Under ReCAAP, the Malaysian, Indonesian, and Singapore naval forces continued to patrol their own territorial waters around the strait, but by communicating with each other about possible attacks, the patrols became more effective. The three nations also established air patrols over the waters. ReCAAP established the Information Sharing Center in Singapore, and with the help of the IMB Piracy Reporting Centre in Kuala Lumpur, the countries surrounding the Strait of Malacca developed strong intelligence (information) on pirate activities. This information was shared among all interested parties. It was no longer possible for a pirate to raid a ship in the waters of one nation and then disappear into the waters of another. In the first year of joint patrols in Southeast Asia, however, there was only a slight decrease in piracy in the region.

To be truly successful against piracy in the Strait of Malacca, political and economic solutions were also necessary. Piracy experts had determined that the majority of pirates in the strait were from Sumatra. The island had suffered through decades of conflict between a separatist group

To combat piracy in the Strait of Malacca, the surrounding nations began working together. This photo shows a joint training exercise by coast guard officials from Japan, Malaysia, and Thailand in 2007. A "pirate" boat (right) is intercepted by Thailand marine police (center) and a Malaysian marine police speedboat, while a Japanese coast guard helicopter hovers overhead. REUTERS/ ZAINAL ABD HALIM /LANDOV.

and the Indonesian military. Due to the fighting, the Aceh region of Sumatra had become isolated from the rest of the country, and its people were impoverished. Some people took up piracy as a way to survive. This long-term problem was resolved with a peace treaty in 2005. With a strengthened economy and legitimate opportunities to work, many pirates from Aceh decided to leave piracy.

Other factors helped the antipiracy cause. Security companies were hired by shippers to protect ships passing through the strait. Agencies such as the IMB strongly advised against the use of firearms, fearing an escalation of violence in pirate attacks. Still, some of the security forces claimed to have stopped attacks before they happened. When pirates approached a protected ship, the security guards stood in force on the deck, with weapons displayed. The pirates, upon seeing them, turned back.

The combination of naval, political, and economic solutions in south-east Asia was a success, at least for a time. In 2004 there were thirty-eight attacks in the Strait of Malacca, and in 2008 there were only two—an 87 percent decrease in four years. But by that time, Somalia had become the world's piracy hot spot, and that region presented significantly different problems in the fight against piracy.

Somali pirates challenge authorities

Pirate attacks off the Horn of Africa (the easternmost projection of Africa) sharply increased between 2007 and 2008. Early strikes by pirates from Somalia were mainly located in the Gulf of Aden, which lies between Somalia and Yemen and connects the Red Sea with the Indian Ocean. The gulf is one of the most important trade routes in the world.

Conditions in Somalia created an ideal situation for pirates. Since 1991, when Somalia's dictator was ousted, Somalia was considered to be a failed state by most observers. A temporary government, the Transitional Federal Government, has been unable to exercise power over the whole country. Somalia's 1,880-mile (3,026-kilometer) coastline is the longest in Africa, and the country does not have a coast guard, a government agency responsible for enforcing laws on the seas and navigable waters. No foreign forces could legally pursue pirates into Somalia's territorial waters, and Somalia's government did not have the means to pursue them. The Somali economy was also in ruins. Many impoverished young Somali men, some in their teens, turned to piracy for basic survival. Observers note that Somali pirates tend to be fearless because many feel they have nothing to lose.

The world was focused on piracy in the Strait of Malacca when the first large wave of Somali pirate attacks occurred. Little notice was given until 2007, when Somali pirates attacked a UN World Food Programme (WFP) ship that was delivering food aid to people in Somalia who had been displaced by the ongoing civil war there. A guard was killed in the attack. The WFP was forced to suspend its operations to Somalia, where three million people depended on the food shipments to survive. In July 2007 the International Maritime Organization, the UN agency concerned with maritime activities, and the WFP brought Somali piracy to the attention of the UN Security Council. Since about 80 percent of Somalia's humanitarian aid arrives by sea, the WFP wanted protection from the pirates. Several nations responded to the call for help. In November 2007 and again in February 2008, the French navy

Somali boys play soccer on the beach near the pirate haven of Hobyo. Economic conditions in Somalia drive many poor young men, some in their teens, to turn to piracy for survival. MOHAMED DAHIR/AFP/GETTY IMAGES.

accompanied WFP cargo ships as they carried food to Somalia's poor. Denmark, the Netherlands, and Canada also agreed to escort WFP ships.

An international antipiracy campaign

As attention on Somali piracy increased, navies in various parts of the world prepared to mount antipiracy campaigns in east Africa. The legal issues involved in pursuing pirates in territorial waters grew urgent. The waters off Somalia were presumably territorial, but the country had no established national government and no forces of its own to patrol its waters. On June 2, 2008, the UN Security Council addressed the issue when it passed Resolution 1816. The act gave foreign warships the right to enter Somali waters "for the purposes of repressing acts of piracy and armed robbery at sea" by "all necessary means."

Still, issues peculiar to Somalia continued to perplex the naval forces combating piracy. Even with the capacity to seize pirates in Somalia's territorial waters, foreign navies could not stop the pirates from escaping—sometimes with kidnap victims and stolen ships. The pirates could simply return to their pirate havens in remote ports of Somalia. (A pirate haven in as safe place for pirates to harbor and repair their ships, resupply, and organize raiding parties.) No foreign forces could legally pursue them to these havens because crimes that occur within a nation's territory or territorial waters are under the sole jurisdiction of that nation. The Somali transitional government and local forces were not strong enough to intervene. So in December 2008 the UN Security Council passed Resolution 1851, authorizing antipiracy forces of foreign nations to carry out land operations within Somalia. Both Resolution 1816 and Resolution 1851 were passed with the full cooperation of the Somali transitional government.

The UN Security Council also encouraged the establishment of a multinational discussion and coordination group. In January 2009 twenty-four countries formed the Contact Group on Somali Piracy (CGSP). The CGSP divided into specialized groups headed by the different member countries. The United Kingdom led a group focused on naval operations and information-sharing, Denmark led a group that reviewed legal issues, the United States focused on industry awareness and capabilities, and Egypt focused on communications and public information.

In January 2009 the International Maritime Organization held a meeting in Djibouti to discuss the problem of piracy off the coast of Somalia and in the Gulf of Aden. At this meeting, the African and Arab states near the Gulf of Aden agreed to establish the Djibouti Code of Conduct concerning the Repression of Piracy and Armed Robbery against Ships in the Western Indian Ocean and Gulf of Aden. The code became effective January 29, 2009, when it was signed by Djibouti, Ethiopia, Kenya, Somalia, Yemen, Madagascar, Maldives, Seychelles, and Tanzania. By signing the code, countries agreed to ensure that their national legislation criminalizes piracy and armed robbery against ships and provides the framework for them to conduct investigations and prosecute pirates. Inspired by ReCAAP, the Djibouti Code of Conduct was a milestone in regional coordination. The code's signatories agreed to establish piracy information exchange centers in Mombasa, Kenya; Dar es Salaam, Tanzania; and Sana'a, Yemen; and a regional training center for staffs of the information-sharing centers, the coast guard, and other

Smoke rises from a suspected pirate skiff in the Gulf of Aden that was disabled by a U.S. Navy destroyer. The navy vessel is part of the CTF 151 antipiracy task force. MASS COMMUNICATIONS SPECIALIST 1ST CLASS CASSANDRA THOMPSON/U.S. NAVY VIA GETTY IMAGES.

law enforcement personnel was established in Djibouti. The code allowed one signatory country to send armed forces into the territorial waters of the other signatory countries to pursue pirates.

Worldwide forces assemble off Somalia's waters

In 2008 an enormous worldwide antipiracy campaign began. The Combined Task Force 150 (CTF 150) was formed to fight terrorism in the Gulf of Aden, Gulf of Oman, Arabian Sea, Red Sea, and the Indian Ocean. Led by the United States, CTF 150 was a coalition naval task force with more than twenty member nations. As the Somali piracy problem escalated, the CTF 150 contributed some of its ships to patrol for pirates in the Gulf of Aden. In January 2009 the force was replaced by CTF 151, which was dedicated specifically to antipiracy campaigns in the gulf.

CTF 151 worked in cooperation with other forces. The European Union (EU) sent naval forces to the Gulf of Aden under European Union Naval Force Somalia (EUNAVFOR)–Operation Atlanta. This was the European Union's first operational naval deployment outside Europe, and it dedicated up to twelve ships and a number of aircraft to the mission. China sent two destroyers and a supply ship to help in the effort. Initially the ships were deployed to protect China's shipping in the region, but in early 2010 China joined U.S., NATO, and EU forces in a mission called Shared Awareness and Deconfliction (SHADE), which protects a frequently attacked shipping route in the Indian Ocean. Russia, India, Japan, Iran, South Korea, and other countries have sent their own naval forces to join in the antipiracy effort in east Africa.

Near the end of 2008 the North Atlantic Treaty Organization (NATO), an international military alliance, sent its forces to the waters off Somalia under a UN mandate to escort ships carrying food aid and other humanitarian goods, as well as to protect merchant ships and to patrol for pirates. The NATO mission was later named Ocean Shield. The Netherlands contributed a submarine to aid in the NATO patrols. At the end of 2009 the United States contributed unmanned drones, or military surveillance planes, to patrol the Indian Ocean in search of pirates. Stationed on the island nation of Seychelles, the 36-foot-long (11-meter) drones are equipped with infrared, laser, and radar targeting to scout out pirates in large areas and in many conditions.

In July 2009 eleven Arab states united to fight Somali piracy with a newly established Arab Navy Task Force. The force was created to protect the Arab tankers transporting oil and gas that pass through the Gulf of Aden and through the Red Sea to the Suez Canal on the way to the Mediterranean Sea. Initially led by Saudi Arabia, the Arab Navy Task Force included naval forces from Bahrain, Djibouti, Egypt, Jordan, Kuwait, Oman, Qatar, Sudan, the United Arab Emirates, and Yemen.

Other antipiracy measures

Shippers took their own steps to protect their ships from piracy in the east African waters. Despite significant losses in time and money, some shippers decided to divert their vessels to routes passing around South Africa. By some estimates these diversions cost up to one million dollars per ship each trip. Other shipping companies took measures aboard their ships, such as equipping their vessels with pressurized fire hoses to direct

International Organizations Combating Somali Piracy

Beginning in 2008, a massive international effort to stop Somali piracy formed and its members and forces grew rapidly. Though many commentators in 2010 saw little improvement in Somali piracy due to the effort, most appreciated the historic occasion of so many different countries joining forces to protect trade and shipping from the pirates. The major groups involved in the cooperative effort are listed below.

Key Governing Agencies

United Nations Security Council. The permanent peacekeeping organization of the United Nations, with the primary responsibility for maintenance of international peace and security, including the establishment of peacekeeping operations, the establishment of international sanctions, and the authorization of military action. The Security Council is composed of five permanent members (China, France, Russia, the United Kingdom, and the United States) and ten elected members. Its powers are exercised through UN Security Council Resolutions.

International Maritime Organization (IMO). An agency of the United Nations, the IMO regulates all aspects of international shipping, including safety, environmental concerns, legal matters, technical co-operation, and maritime security. Based in the United Kingdom, it has 169 Member States and three Associate Members.

International Maritime Bureau (IMB). A division of the International Chamber Of Commerce (ICC), the IMB is a nonprofit organization established to fight against all types of maritime crime.

UN Contact Group on Somali Piracy (CGSP). An international cooperative group called for in UN Security Council Resolution 1851, the CGSP is responsible for coordinating activities between states and organizations to suppress piracy off the coast of Somalia through increased intelligence, the development of legal frameworks, the education of shippers, enhanced diplomacy, and other means. In 2010 the CGSP included forty-seven member countries and ten international organizations.

at pirates trying to board or using extremely bright lights at night in order to detect pirates well before they attack. Many shippers offered training courses for ship crews, teaching them to evade pirate attacks or how to cope with the pirates once they had boarded.

The IMB recommended that commercial ships remain unarmed. Most of the Somali pirate attacks in 2008 and 2009 did not involve firefights. In fact, for the most part, Somali pirates have used little violence, and they have not harmed their hostages. The IMB feared that if shippers began to use firearms, the pirates were likely to respond by using more force. New nonlethal (not intended to result in death) security products appeared on ships, however, such as a "pain ray" gun that directs an extremely painful energy beam at a target and a sonic gun that blasts

IMO Djibouti Code of Conduct concerning the Repression of Piracy and Armed Robbery against Ships in the Western Indian Ocean and Gulf of Aden. An agreement among certain African and Arab states near the Gulf of Aden under which the signing nations agree to ensure that their national legislation criminalizes piracy and armed robbery against ships and provides the framework for them to conduct investigations and prosecute pirates. Member states in 2010 included Yemen, Saudi Arabia, Oman, Eritrea, Djibouti, Sudan, Kenya, Egypt, Somalia, Tanzania, and Jordan.

Antipiracy Naval Forces

Combined Task Force 151 (CTF 151). U.S.-led coalition naval task force with twenty-five member nations in 2010. CTF151 is dedicated specifically to antipiracy campaigns in the Gulf of Aden and off the eastern coast of Somalia covering an area of approximately 1.1 million square miles.

European Union Naval Force Somalia (EUNAVFOR)–Operation Atlanta. European Union (EU) naval force mission in the Gulf of Aden with a mandate to: protect humanitarian aid vessels and the African Union's shipping; repress acts of piracy and armed robbery; and monitor fishing activities off the coast of Somalia.

Ocean Shield. NATO mission under a UN mandate to use its forces to escort ships carrying food aid and other humanitarian goods, and to protect merchant ships and patrol for pirates.

Arab Navy Task Force. Saudi Arabia-led coalition of Arab naval forces to protect the Arab tankers transporting oil and gas through the Gulf of Aden and the Red Sea.

Shared Awareness and Deconfliction (SHADE). The joined forces of China, the United States, and NATO in a mission to protect frequently attacked shipping routes in the Indian Ocean. SHADE meetings include military representatives from Contact Group (CGSP) nations with military counter-piracy operations in the Horn of Africa.

deafening sound waves. Despite the IMB's warning, some shipping companies hired private security companies, which, for a steep price, provided ships with armed security teams as they passed through dangerous waters.

Prosecuting pirates

When pirates were caught on the high seas by the forces of a state other than Somalia, several factors complicated their arrest, prosecution, and punishment. In any given arrest of a pirate, many different nations are often involved. The pirates might be from one nation, while the ship they attacked might be owned by another nation, and the ship might be sailing under the flag of yet another nation. The kidnapped crew may be a mix of different nationalities, and the naval forces that apprehended the pirates may come from another nation altogether. One of the most basic problems is determining which nation would undertake the time and expense of prosecuting the pirates.

Most nations do not have the resources to hold long, international investigations and trials or to pay for of the expense of imprisoning prosecuted pirates. In addition, some nations are concerned that once they take pirates into custody, the pirates will seek political asylum. (Asylum is refuge or protection in a foreign country, granted to someone who might be in danger if returned to his or her own country.) Because Somalia is so poor, detained pirates are likely to seek legal or illegal residence in a wealthier country once they are within its borders. When they are acquitted of charges or, if convicted, released from prison, pirates may remain in the country where they were detained. Many countries are already overburdened with refugees and immigrants, and most prefer not to allow suspected criminals to enter their borders. Besides, many Somali pirates are juveniles who may not have had many alternatives for survival beyond piracy. Detaining children, who in prison may become the victims of physical and sexual abuse by other prisoners, presents the detaining country with a host of human rights issues.

Most of the foreign forces in the Gulf of Aden, therefore, sought only to disrupt the pirate raids and to protect the ships and their crews, but not to arrest or punish the raiders. For example, in September 2009 a Danish naval antipiracy force captured ten alleged pirates. Danish legal experts questioned whether the pirates could legally be tried in Denmark. However, Denmark, which does not have a death penalty, was unwilling to turn the pirates over to the Somali transitional government for fear that they might be executed. The suspected pirates were therefore released. Russian and Dutch forces, too, have disarmed pirates they captured and then released them. Most naval forces in east African waters tried not to take pirates into custody for the same reason. The United States only prosecuted pirates that had attacked U.S. vessels.

The UN Security Council offered a solution in Resolution 1851, which encourages nations and organizations fighting Somali piracy to make arrangements with the law enforcers of nations in the region. Officials from regional nations, called ship riders, would then ride onboard the foreign naval forces during their antipiracy campaigns. These officials would take charge of arresting the pirates. They were, at

Suspected Somali pirates await trial at the Shimo la Tewa prison in Kenya. AP IMAGES.

least in theory, in a better position to conduct criminal investigations and trials. Initially Kenya was the only regional country to step forward and prosecute Somali pirates detained by foreign forces. Both the United Kingdom and the United States quickly entered agreements with Kenya. But in April 2010 Kenya was forced to suspend the operation, concerned that there were too many cases, and no other nations in the region were helping to carry the load.

However, in June 2010, a new courtroom was built on the grounds of the Shimo la Tewa maximum-security prison ten miles north of Mombasa, Kenya. The court, which will conduct trials of pirates, was built with five million dollars in international donations collected by the United Nations Office on Drugs and Crime (UNODC). By July 1, 2010, Kenya began trying the 105 suspected pirates it was holding. Other nations in the region were expected to begin trying pirates after Kenya had set some standards for the process.

Somali Pirates and Somali Politics

In late August 2010, al-Shabab, a militant Somali Islamist group, stepped up its four-year-old effort to overthrow the Transitional Federal Government (TFG), Somalia's weak, temporary government. Al-Shabab's purpose is to instill an extremely strict form of Islam in Somalia. It claims an association with the terrorist group al-Qaeda and considers the United Nations, the African Union, and most Western countries and nongovernment organizations its enemies. The TFG called on the international community for help against al-Shabab, warning that the billions of dollars being spent on antipiracy programs would be wasted if the government there is overtaken.

During their first few years in action Somali pirates steered clear of Somali politics. They avoided both government authorities and the militant Islamic insurgents, who were strongly opposed to lawlessness and promised to destroy the pirates. This began to change in the spring of 2010. In April al-Shabab attacked the pirate haven of Harardhere in the Mudug region of Somalia. Though initially a raid to stop piracy, al-Shabab quickly realized that the pirates could provide its movement with necessary troops, weapons, and money. The militants joined forces with the pirates at Harardhere. The pirates agreed to split with al-Shabab the ransoms it reaped from raiding international shipping. *New York Times* journalist Jeffrey Gettleman, called this "the West's worst Somali nightmare, with two of the country's biggest growth industries—piracy and Islamic radicalism—joining hands."

Not far from Harardhere, the powerful pirate gang in the haven of Hobyo was using its considerable forces to aid the TFG in its fight against al-Shabab and other insurgents. Local governmental forces in several other regions of Somalia had asked for—and received—help from the pirates. Militias (groups of civilians trained as soldiers but not part of a regular army) were formed based on both government and pirate commands. Gettleman, reporting from Hobyo, noted that local clan leaders foresaw the pirates taking on a more political mission in Somalia. The leaders told Gettleman "that the pirates are getting more ambitious, shrewdly reinvesting their booty in heavy weapons and land-based militias, and now it may be impossible for such a large armed force—the pirates number thousands of men—to stay on the sidelines." It was not clear to observers whether the pirates would come to favor one side or both in the ongoing Somali struggle.

Disappointing results

Despite the unprecedented cooperation and combined forces of the world's naval powers concentrating on the waters in the Somali region, the situation remained bad in 2010. There were one hundred more pirate attacks in 2009 than there had been in 2008, and the largest concentration of them was off the coast of East Africa, where reported incidents had increased seven fold in the four-year period ending in 2009. The number of attacks in the Gulf of Aden was down by 2010, but there were increasing reports of attacks farther out in the Indian Ocean, an area too vast to be patrolled even by the combined forces. Pirates were anticipating the naval patrols' moves and finding ways to avoid detection. Many pirate attacks in 2009 and 2010 were stopped by the various naval forces, but this advantage was offset by the rapidly increasing number of Somali pirate attacks. The supply of willing pirates had increased greatly with the successes of the earlier attacks.

Large ships with multimillion-dollar cargoes continued to fall prey to the pirates. At the turn of the twenty-first century, a raid by Somali pirates brought in, on average, a few thousand dollars, but by 2009, the capture of one ship often brought in a two- to three-million-dollar ransom. By some estimates Somali piracy earned about one hundred million dollars in the course of the year. On the other hand, the costs of the multinational naval forces that patrolled the waters off East Africa were formidable. It cost an estimated one hundred thousand dollars a day to keep just one patrol vessel in those waters, and there were more than forty vessels patrolling at any one time in 2010. Observers agreed that the naval response was an important first step, but not sufficient to stop Somali piracy.

The elusive political solution

Addressing the UN General Assembly on May 14, 2010, UN Secretary-General Ban Ki-moon (1944–) noted, as quoted in the UN report "UN Member States Debate Ways to Fight Piracy off Somalia," that the huge naval efforts of many nations were not enough to cure the Somali piracy problem. He said, "There is simply too much water to patrol, and an almost endless supply of pirates." He added, "There is no doubt that a change in strategy is needed. . . . Stability on land would, undoubtedly, improve the situation at sea." Almost all commentators on Somali piracy agree that the piracy problem is rooted in the failed state of Somalia, which lacks sufficient force to police itself, and the failed economy, which cannot provide jobs or other legitimate means of survival for Somalia's desperately poor people.

Members of the international community made some attempts to help the Somali transitional government and the local provincial governments to crack down on the pirate havens onshore. With outside encouragement and funding from the United Nations, the semiautonomous government of the province of Puntland, one of the main pirate strongholds, agreed to join the fight against piracy. The province of Somaliland also had a functioning government and offered a place to begin to establish jails and court systems that could process arrested pirates. The Somali transitional government, though, faces far too many political and economic problems on land to have any meaningful impact on the piracy at sea.

Most political scholars agree that there will not be a stable government in Somalia in the near future. Nor are any of the nations offering naval forces willing to take the fight against piracy onshore. Americans, in particular, fear becoming involved in the decades-old turmoil there. They remember too well the images of the 1993 Battle of Mogadishu, also known as the "Black Hawk Down" incident due to the book and film that memorialized it, when eighteen soldiers died in a firefight and a mob of Somalis dragged two dead soldiers through the streets of Somalia's capital, Mogadishu. Still, leaders of countries worldwide call for solutions to Somalia's internal problems, knowing that as long as the nation fails to provide law and order and the basic necessities of life, the pirate problem will only increase.

For More Information

BOOKS

Burgess, Douglas R., Jr. *The Pirate's Pact: the Secret Alliance between History's Most Notorious Buccaneers and Colonial America.* New York: McGraw-Hill, 2009, p. xi.

Ellen, Eric. "Piracy Today." In *Pirates: Terror on the High Seas from the Caribbean to the South China Sea.* Edited by David Cordingly. East Bridgewater, MA: World Publications Group, 1998, 2007.

PERIODICALS

Gettleman, Jeffrey. "Pirates Take Sides, Both Sides, in Somalia's War." *New York Times* (September 2, 2010): A1, A10.

Kraska, James, and Brian Wilson. "Fighting Piracy: International Coordination Is Key to Countering present-day Freebooters." *Armed Forces Journal* (February 2009). Available online at www.armedforcesjournal.com/2009/02/3928962 (accessed on January 3, 2011).

Schuman, Michael. "How to Defeat Pirates: Success in the Strait." *Time* (April 22, 2009). Available online at www.time.com/time/world/article/0,8599,1893032,00.html#ixzz0v6OZb6Lt (accessed on January 3, 2011).

WEB SITES

Hagen, Ryan. "The New Anti-Piracy: High Stakes Hijacking on the Open Sea." *GOOD.* www.good.is/post/the-new-anti-piracy-high-stakes-hijacking-on-the-open-sea (accessed on January 3, 2011).

"IMB Piracy Reporting Centre." *ICC Commercial Crime Services.* www.icc-ccs.org/index.php?option=com_content&view=article&id=30&Itemid=12 (accessed January 3, 2011).

Rothwell, Donald R. "Maritime Piracy and International Law." *Crimes of War Project.* www.crimesofwar.org/onnews/news-piracy.html (accessed on January 3, 2011).

United Nations Convention on the Law of the Sea. www.un.org/Depts/los/convention_agreements/texts/unclos/closindx.htm (accessed on January 3, 2011).

United Nations Security Council, Resolution 18 (2008). www.marad.dot.gov/documents/UNSCR_1816-_SIT_IN_SOMALIA.pdf (accessed on January 3, 2011).

"UN Member States Debate Ways to Fight Piracy off Somalia." *UN News Centre.* www.un.org/apps/news/story.asp?NewsID=34703 (accessed on January 3, 2011.

Pirates in Popular Culture

Ask almost anyone to describe a pirate, and he or she is likely to draw from a familiar set of images: an eye patch, a wooden leg, a brightly colored bandana, a parrot, a three-cornered hat, or perhaps actor Johnny Depp (1963–) in the role of Captain Jack Sparrow from the popular *Pirates of the Caribbean* films. If asked, many people are also likely to break into pirate lingo, using terms like "arrr," "matey," and "yo ho ho." The fictional pirates from books, cartoons, movies, video games, and Halloween costumes have become a major part of popular culture. However, they are very different from real pirates, the criminals who steal and commit violence at sea.

According to pirate historians, the popular image of piracy in American and European culture is a blend of history and fiction that has its origins in the eighteenth century golden age of piracy, which lasted from about 1690 to 1730. When the exploits of sea raiders, such as Edward Teach, better known as Blackbeard (c. 1680–1718), William Kidd (c. 1645–1701), and Bartholomew Roberts (1682–1722), were reported in English and colonial newspapers, some people responded with horror, but others began to view pirates as daring adventurers. To some, pirates were bold individuals who had managed to step outside the restrictions of the accepted rules and customs of society to create their own worlds. By the turn of the eighteenth century, some of the golden-age pirates had become legendary heroes in the increasingly romanticized stories that circulated in the port cities of England and its colonies. When the golden age of piracy was over and some time had passed, a sense of nostalgia (a bittersweet longing for something from the past) emerged for the days of pirates and their adventures at sea.

Since real pirates rarely left behind journals or other personal accounts, the details of their lives and personalities are largely unknown. Over the years, stories of pirate exploits, although often based in truth, tended to reflect the attitudes of the storytellers and their eras. Writers,

WORDS TO KNOW

antihero: A leading character or notable figure who does not have the typical hero traits.

Execution Dock: The place in London where pirates were hanged; their bodies were often displayed to discourage others from turning to piracy.

galley: A long, low ship used for war and trading that was mainly powered by oarsmen, but might also use a sail.

harem: The area of a Muslim household historically reserved for wives, concubines, and female relatives.

hypocrisy: Pretending to have qualities or beliefs one does not really have.

impalement: A process of torture and execution by inserting a long stake through the length of the body and then leaving the person to die a slow and painful death.

maroon: To strand an individual on a deserted island or shore with few provisions.

melodrama: A drama, such as a play, film, or television program, characterized by exaggerated emotions, stereotypical characters, and an extravagant plot.

mutiny: An open rebellion by seamen against their ship's officers.

myth: A traditional story that is partly based on a historical event and serves to explain something about a culture.

nostalgia: A bittersweet longing for something from the past.

parody: A spoof, or a work that mocks something else.

pirate haven: A safe place for pirates to harbor and repair their ships, resupply, and organize raiding parties.

sea shanty: A sailor's work song.

swashbuckler: A daring adventurer; also a drama about a swashbuckler.

walk the plank: A form of punishment in which a person is forced to walk off the end of a wooden board extended over the side of a ship and into the sea.

artists, filmmakers, and comedians all made their mark on the original image of the pirate.

Golden age writings

The golden age of piracy was a time when European-based pirates infested large areas of the Caribbean Sea and the east coast of North America, severely damaging European trade routes to Africa and Asia. The pirates' deeds were felt far beyond the ports and merchant ships they raided. In the cities and port towns of England, the names of famous pirates became known in every household. Newspapers did a thriving business selling colorful stories describing pirate raids, the hair-raising efforts of pirate hunters to catch pirates, and grim pirate trials and executions. Pirate stories brought excitement to the lives of ordinary people and were a constant source of discussion for thousands of English sailors. As the stories traveled from person to person, new details were added, and eventually they became myths. (A myth is a traditional story that is partly based on a historical event and serves to explain something about a culture.)

The story of Henry Every English pirate captain Henry Every (also spelled Avery; c. 1653–c. 1699) made his mark early in the golden age when he raided the *Ganj-i-sawii*, a treasure ship belonging to India's emperor, in 1695. The ship was packed with gold and silver, and every man on Every's pirate ship made a fortune from the raid. In the process of looting the ship, the pirates cruelly tortured, murdered, and raped many members of the ship's crew and passengers. India was outraged by the raid, and English traders who were working to establish a profitable trade with India complained bitterly to the king. When Every returned to the Americas, colonial authorities sought him for prosecution under charges of piracy. Every disappeared and was never heard from again. Little is known of his life aside from his short career as a pirate captain, but stories about him flourished anyway.

As soon as Every's raid of the *Ganj-i-sawii* occurred, sailors began to tell the tale. The vast wealth Every had stolen fascinated them. As the story was told and retold, Every turned into a heroic figure. Soon the stories featured Every falling in love with a beautiful woman on the *Ganj-i-sawii*, and many accounts describe her as the emperor's daughter. In some of the stories, Every marries her on the spot and goes on to become the "king of pirates" in Madagascar, an island in Africa. There, it was said, he ruled from a well-defended palace surrounded with tens of thousands of loyal pirates. The facts about Madagascar differed significantly from the stories. Although there was a rough pirate base there, historians have determined that no elaborate pirate kingdom ever existed.

Nevertheless, English writers seized on the legends. In 1709 *The Life and Adventures of Capt. John Avery; the Famous English Pirate (Rais'd from a Cabbin Boy, to a King) Now in Possession of Madagascar*, a sixteen-page biographical pamphlet, was published in London. The pamphlet claims to be based on the journal of a man who had lived in Every's Madagascar kingdom. It built upon the stories that were circulating about Every marrying the emperor's daughter and setting up a government on Madagascar.

Piracy takes to the stage In 1712 a playwright named Charles Johnson (1679–1748) wrote *The Successful Pyrate*, a drama that combines the plot of a 1639 play called *Arviragus and Philicia* with the life of Every as presented in the 1709 pamphlet. The leading character of the play, Arviragus, the king of Madagascar, is a barely disguised version of Every, described as "a sceptered robber at the head of a hundred thousand ... brother thieves ... burning cities, ravaging countries, and depopulating nations," as quoted by Colin Woodard in *The Republic of Pirates: Being the True and Surprising Story of the Caribbean Pirates and the Man Who Brought Them Down*. In this story, Arviragus captures an Indian ship with Zaida, the granddaughter of the Indian emperor, aboard. Zaida, however, is in love with another, who turns out to be Arviragus's long-lost son. Arviragus gives his son and Zaida the Madagascar throne and returns to England a wealthy man.

The Successful Pyrate was considered a terrible play even by contemporary critics, but it was at the forefront of a tradition of popular pirate-themed entertainment. In *Under the Black Flag: The Romance and the Reality of Life Among the Pirates*, David Cordingly describes *The Successful Pyrate* as the first of a "long line of popular melodrama with piratical themes" that were performed in London over the next 150 years. (A melodrama is drama, such as a play, film, or television program, characterized by exaggerated emotions, stereotypical characters, and an extravagant plot.)

In 1879 playwright and lyricist W.S. Gilbert (1836–1911) and lyricist Arthur Sullivan (1842–1900) created a comic opera, *The Pirates of Penzance*, which was a parody (a spoof, or a work, that mocks something) of the earlier pirate plays. The plot of *The Pirates of Penzance* revolves around a silly mistake that occurs when an employer tells a nearly deaf nursemaid to apprentice his son to a "pilot" of a ship. The maid hears "pirate" instead of "pilot" and signs the boy up with a band of sea raiders. The pirates turn out to be harmless and lovable fellows. Even though *The Pirates of Penzance* was not meant to be taken seriously, its lighthearted view had a strong influence on later images of pirates in popular culture.

Daniel Defoe The most notable English writer during the golden age of piracy, Daniel Defoe (1660–1731), wrote about Henry Every in an eighty-three-page pamphlet, *The King of Pirates: Being an Account of the Famous Enterprises of Captain Avery, the Mock King of Madagascar ...* (1720). Defoe wrote the account in Every's voice, as if it were an autobiography. In his preface to the pamphlet, Defoe notes that he wishes

An 1879 songsheet for The Pirates of Penzance. HULTON ARCHIVE/GETTY IMAGES.

to set history straight and undo some of the romantic nonsense that had been written about Every by earlier writers. He writes:

> It has been enough to the writers of this man's life, as they call it, that they could put anything together to make a kind of monstrous unheard-of story as romantic as the reports that have been spread

about of him; and the more those stories appeared monstrous and incredible, the more suitable they seemed to be to what the world would have been made to expect of Captain [Every].

Defoe's version of Every, however, retains many of the legends of the earlier stories. Soon after writing *The King of Pirates*, Defoe wrote a pirate novel, *Captain Singleton* (1720), perhaps realizing that the pirate story he wanted to tell could not be captured in nonfiction in the absence of facts and evidence about Every's life.

Captain Charles Johnson   Four years after Defoe attempted to set down a realistic history of Henry Every, a remarkable chronicle appeared that would shape every pirate history to come. *A General History of the Robberies and Murders of the Most Notorious Pirates* was published under the name of Captain Charles Johnson in 1724. (This is not the same Charles Johnson who wrote *The Successful Pyrate*.) Its first edition contains accounts of twelve well-known pirates, all of whom had recently appeared in the news. The book is graphic about the pirates' crimes and includes sensational stories about two women pirates, Anne Bonny (1700–c. 1782) and Mary Read (c. 1690–1721), with foldout engravings of them. The book was an immediate success. In the next few years it would go through several editions to which the writer added many more pirate accounts.

The name Captain Charles Johnson has never been found in historical records so there has been great speculation about the identity of the real author of *A General History of Pirates*. In 1932 a respected scholar argued convincingly that Daniel Defoe had written the book, and this theory was so well accepted that for decades libraries cataloged the book under Defoe's name. In the late 1980s, however, two scholars soundly refuted the idea that Defoe authored *A General History of Pirates* and so the real author's identity remains a mystery. The author's sources for the book include newspaper accounts and pirate trial transcripts, but historians contend that his familiarity with pirate terms may mean that he also interviewed pirates or was acquainted with them.

In *A General History of Pirates* readers found what they had long been seeking: a view of the golden-age pirates' personalities and dialogues as well as their most hideous crimes. Although Captain Johnson introduces the subject of pirates with a tone of disapproval, his work shows his fascination with them and admiration for their bravery and cleverness. This is particularly true of his portrait of the frightful, cunning, and

A GENERAL

HISTORY

OF THE *Galton*

Robberies and Murders

Of the moſt notorious

PYRATES,

AND ALSO

Their *Policies, Diſcipline* and *Government*,

From their firſt RISE and SETTLEMENT in the Iſland
of *Providence*. in 1717, to the preſent Year 1724.

WITH

The remarkable ACTIONS and ADVENTURES of the two Female Pyrates, *Mary Read* and *Anne Bonny*.

To which is prefix'd

An ACCOUNT of the famous Captain *Avery* and his Companions; with the Manner of his Death in *England*.

The Whole digeſted into the following CHAPTERS;

Chap. I. Of Captain *Avery*.
  II. The Riſe of Pyrates.
  III. Of Captain *Martel*.
  IV. Of Captain *Bonnet*.
  V. Of Captain *Thatch*.
  VI. Of Captain *Vane*.
  VII. Of Captain *Rackam*.

  VIII. Of Captain *England*.
  IX. Of Captain *Davis*.
  X. Of Captain *Roberts*.
  XI. Of Captain *Worley*.
  XII. Of Captain *Lowther*.
  XIII. Of Captain *Low*.
  XIV. Of Captain *Evans*.

And their ſeveral Crews.

To which is added,

A ſhort ABSTRACT of the Statute and Civil Law, in
Relation to PYRACY.

By Captain CHARLES JOHNSON.

LONDON, Printed for *Ch. Rivington* at the *Bible* and *Crown* in St.
Paul's Church-Yard, J. Lacy at the *Ship* near the *Temple-Gate*, and
J. Stone next the *Crown* Coffee-houſe the back of *Greys-Inn*, 1724.

The title page of A General
History of the Robberies and
Murders of the Most
Notorious Pirates, *published
in 1724 by Captain Charles
Johnson.* © LEBRECHT MUSIC
AND ARTS PHOTO LIBRARY/
ALAMY.

Selected Pirate Fiction

Cooper, James Fenimore. *The Red Rover: A Tale* (1759). Set in Newport, Rhode Island, in 1759, this is a suspenseful mystery about a sea captain who claims to be a pirate and the Royal Navy officer who pursues him.

Defoe, Daniel. *Robinson Crusoe* (1719–20). In this novel a castaway spends twenty-eight years on a remote island in the Caribbean Sea. The book is based on the true story of Alexander Selkirk (1676–1721), a buccaneer who was marooned on an uninhabited island and spent four years there.

Du Maurier, Daphne. *Jamaica Inn* (1936). Set in the English coastal area of Cornwall in the early nineteenth century, this is the story of an orphaned young woman who goes to live with an aunt and slowly discovers that her evil uncle, the landlord of the Jamaica Inn, is the leader of a band of pirates.

Forester, C.S. *The Barbary Pirates* (1953). This is the story of the U.S. naval fight against the Barbary pirates in the Mediterranean Sea.

Goldman, William. *The Princess Bride* (1973). This adventure begins when Buttercup mistakenly learns that her true love Westley has been murdered by the Dread Pirate Roberts.

Meyer, L.A. *Bloody Jack* (2002). When Mary Faber is orphaned by a plague in late–eighteenth-century London, she dresses as a boy, changes her name to Jack, and gets a job on a ship that soon enters into combat with pirates. This is the first in a series of Bloody Jack novels for young adults.

Naifeh, Ted. *Polly and the Pirates* (2002). This is a series of comic strips about Polly, who is abducted from her proper boarding school by a band of pirates who want her to be their captain.

Sabatini, Rafael. *Captain Blood* (1922). This is an action-packed swashbuckler set in the seventeenth century. After physician Peter Blood is convicted of treason in England and sold into slavery in Jamaica, he escapes and becomes a pirate captain.

Stevenson, Robert Louis. *Treasure Island* (1883). After young Jim Hawkins discovers a pirate map for buried treasure, he embarks on a sea voyage. A close association with the ship's cook, Long John Silver, and a pirate mutiny ensue.

Verne, Jules. *The Lighthouse at the End of the World* (1905). Two lighthouse keepers in mid–nineteenth-century South America are killed by pirates, leaving a comrade and a shipwreck survivor to avenge their deaths.

courageous Blackbeard, which, according to many pirate historians, is one of the most enduring portraits of a pirate that has ever been written.

Over the years Captain Johnson's history has proved to be mostly accurate. The basic facts have been verified and appear accurate when compared with other historical evidence. But the overall views of the pirates, the strong and vivid accounts of their words, and the details of their stories seem to many historians to be the fictional work of a great writer as opposed to historical fact. In his book, *Rum, Sodomy, and the Lash: Piracy, Sexuality, and the Masculine Identity*, Hans Turley expresses the problem with *A General History of Pirates*. He writes:

> Its genre ... is [hard] to determine because Johnson embellishes his "history"—the facts that can be found in all the primary pirate sources—with fanciful anecdotes [interesting or amusing stories].... Although the book is a "history"—and has been treated seriously as such by historians through the centuries—I argue that through his use of fact and fiction, Johnson began the process that turned the pirate into the romanticized antihero [a leading character or notable figure who does not have the typical hero traits] twentieth-century readers are familiar with.

David Cordingly, in his introduction to Captain Johnson's book, reaches the same conclusion as Turley. He writes, "It has been said, and there seems no reason to question this, that Captain Johnson created the modern conception of pirates."

Pirate tales in the Romantic era

Nearly a century after the golden age, fascination with piracy rose to new heights during the Romantic era of art and literature, which occurred roughly from 1780 to 1850. The Romantic era is characterized by rebellion against the rational (based on reasoned thinking, as opposed to feelings or passions) philosophy of the era preceding it. Romantic artists and writers favored passion over reason, boldness over restraint, freedom over duty, and imagination over all else. In literature the Romantic hero or heroine is likely to be a loner who has stepped outside of the conventions of his or her society. Pirates, the ultimate outsiders, made ideal subjects for Romantic writers, such as English poet George Gordon, better known as Lord Byron (1788–1824) and Scottish novelist and poet Sir Walter Scott (1771–1832).

Byron's *The Corsair* Byron was an audacious and flamboyant Romantic poet, known during his lifetime as much for his unconventional lifestyle and scandalous love life as for his popular poems. In his Turkish Tales, a series of long poems written between 1813 and 1816, Byron created what has come to be known as the Byronic hero, a lonely, flawed, and defiant but also deep-feeling character whose life is shaped by some terrible wrong he committed in the past. *The Corsair*, the third poem of the series, is a pirate tale.

The hero of *The Corsair* is the fiercely melancholy pirate captain, Conrad, whose one grace is his passionate love for his wife Medora. In the poem, Conrad raids the fortress of his enemy, Seyd [pronounced Seed], the pasha (Turkish ruler). During the raid, he rescues the women of the pasha's harem, which has caught fire, but he is captured in the act. (A harem is the area of a Muslim household historically reserved for wives, concubines, and female relatives.) Gulnare, the pasha's favorite harem slave, gives Conrad a knife to kill her master, but he refuses to commit the murder. Gulnare then kills Seyd in order to save Conrad from a gruesome death by impalement, a process of torture and execution by inserting a long stake through the length of the body and then leaving the person to die a slow and painful death. They escape to Conrad's pirate haven only to discover that Conrad's wife is dead. Guilt ridden and grieving, Conrad disappears forever.

Byron describes the pirate captain as a long-time loner who was rejected as a young man and has remained contemptuous of humankind since. The poem reads:

> Fear'd, shun'd, belied, ere youth had lost her force,
> He hated man too much to feel remorse ...
> He knew himself a villain—but he deem'd
> The rest no better than the thing he seem'd;
> And scorn'd the best as hypocrites who hid
> Those deeds the bolder spirit plainly did.

Byron voices a contention frequently made by historians and other commentators throughout history that, although pirates do immoral and cruel things, people in the conventional world around them commit even worse crimes but hide them behind the law and propriety. Conrad exhibits a haughty contempt for the hypocrisy (pretending to have qualities or beliefs one does not really have) and cowardliness of normal English society. He knows he has done injury to others, but he is proud to live outside the rules of English society. Conrad chooses to live life according to his smoldering passions, if only for a short time.

The English reading public was eager for Byron's pirate-themed poem. On the day *The Corsair* was published in 1814, ten thousand copies were sold, an unheard-of success at that time. The poem went on to inspire the overture (musical introduction) to *Le Corsaire* by composer Hector Berlioz (1803–1869). It was first performed in 1844. The poem was also the basis of the opera *Il Corsaro* (*The Corsair*), by Giuseppe Verdi (1813–1901), first performed in 1848. Within four decades after the poem's publication, five different ballets inspired by the poem were performed in Europe. Byron was a celebrity, and pirates were a sensation in the arts.

Scott's *The Pirate* In 1822 Sir Walter Scott published his novel, *The Pirate*. The novel tells the story of Captain Clement Cleveland, a dashing pirate who is shipwrecked near his home in the northern islands of Scotland. Because he is estranged from his family, Cleveland does not realize he has landed near the home of his reclusive father, a reformed pirate, and that his rescuer from the shipwreck is his half brother. With his pirate crew anchored nearby, he temporarily resides with a wealthy townsman with two beautiful daughters, hiding his pirate identity and courting one of the young women. This results in a rivalry with his half brother.

Scott's novel is based on the life of a pirate named John Gow (c. 1698–1725). Scott drew heavily from Captain Johnson's *A General History of Pirates* for details about Gow's life and exploits. He also drew from Byron; literary critics consider the dashing but apparently amoral Cleveland to be a Byronic hero, or one sharing the characteristics found in Byron's lead characters. To Scott, like Byron, pirates were antiheroes who, though destructive, dared to go where others feared to travel.

Pirate adventure stories

Scottish writer Robert Louis Stevenson (1850–1895) was not as interested in the innermost thoughts of his pirates as he was in creating a good adventure story when he wrote *Treasure Island* (1883). Stevenson wrote the novel, which is considered the most influential pirate fiction of all time, for his twelve-year-old stepson during a vacation. While passing the time, Stevenson drew the boy an imaginary map of an island, marking it with three red crosses to show where buried treasure was hidden. From this map of Treasure Island, a host of characters and a high-seas adventure emerged.

The story's hero, Jim Hawkins, is the son of an English innkeeper. From an old pirate who dies at the inn, Jim acquires a map showing where a pirate named Captain Flint had buried his treasure. He shows the map to two respectable townsmen, Squire Trelawey and Dr. Livesy, and they hatch a plan to sail for the treasure. The squire outfits a sailing ship for their voyage, but he is loose lipped in the process. Soon everyone in the port of Bristol knows about the treasure. For his ship's crew, the squire ends up with a band of pirates, brought into the enterprise by the ship's one-legged cook, Long John Silver. As the voyage begins, Long John Silver and young Jim seem to form a strong attachment. Jim is shocked when he overhears Long John Silver discussing plans for mutiny and murder. (Mutiny is an open rebellion by seamen against their ship's officers.)

Although Stevenson never met a pirate, his Long John Silver character has become the most pervasive image of a pirate in popular culture. Long John Silver is by turns cunning, evil, charming, fierce, and funny. His diction (choice of words and manner of speaking) is that of an old English seaman, yet at times he sounds like a college professor. For example, in one scene, when he and the pirates are resting on the island after a day of fighting against the squire's forces, Long John Silver captures Jim and tries to persuade him to join the pirate band:

> "So," said he, "here's Jim Hawkins, shiver my timbers! Dropped in, like, eh? ... Now, you see, Jim, so be as you ARE here," says he, "I'll give you a piece of my mind. I've always liked you, I have, for a lad of spirit, and the picter of my own self when I was young and handsome. I always wanted you to jine and take your share, and die a gentleman. ... I'm all for argyment; I never seen good come out o' threatening. If you like the service, well, you'll jine; and if you don't, Jim, why, you're free to answer no—free and welcome, shipmate; and if fairer can be said by mortal seaman, shiver my sides!"

The novel, for which Stevenson drew heavily from Captain Johnson's *A General History of Pirates*, is full of the images associated with pirates in popular culture. A good portion, though certainly not all, of the details are historically accurate. The pirate council that debates whether or not it will demote Long John Silver from his position as captain comes from real pirate practices. Long John Silver has a pet parrot named Cap'n Flint, and pirates and other seamen of the time did bring parrots and other exotic animals home with them from their travels. Like Long John Silver, many sailors lost limbs while at sea; a disabled sailor was likely to take the position of ship's cook because he would no longer be able to handle the more physical work. Another historically accurate detail occurs in the story when Jim meets ex-pirate Ben Gunn, who had been marooned on the island several years earlier. Marooning was a punishment real pirates used among themselves, in which the offending pirate was stranded on a deserted island or shore with few provisions.

Other pirate features of the novel came from Stevenson's imagination rather than pirate history. For example, with the exception of William Kidd, golden-age pirates did not bury their treasure. Another fictional element occurs when the pirates sing their sea shanty (a sailor's work song):

> Fifteen men on the dead man's chest—
> Yo-ho-ho, and a bottle of rum!
> Drink and the devil had done for the rest—
> Yo-ho-ho, and a bottle of rum!

Although the sea shanty is almost universally recognized as a pirate song today, Stevenson wrote it for the book. (Dead Man's Chest is an island in the British Virgin Islands that Stevenson had read about.)

The pirates' artists: Howard Pyle and N.C. Wyeth

American illustrator and writer Howard Pyle (1853–1911) created enduring visual images of pirates. Pyle wrote and illustrated books for young readers. In 1900 he founded his own art school, and he is considered one of the founders of American book illustration. During his lifetime, Pyle was fascinated with pirates. He collected pirate stories and drew illustrations to accompany them. Before Pyle created a pirate illustration, he traveled to historic pirate sites and worked with costumes to create the look he sought. In 1921, ten years after his death, his pirate stories and illustrations were compiled and published as *The Book of Pirates*. The pirate adventure stories were not popular, but the vividly detailed illustrations were, and they now appear in many books and Web sites about pirates.

One of Pyle's students, American artist N.C. Wyeth (1882–1945) carried on his mentor's pirate work when he contributed a series of paintings to illustrate a 1911 edition of *Treasure Island*. The illustrations feature dark shadows and rich, colorful backgrounds.

Captain Hook

Scottish writer and dramatist J.M. Barrie (1860–1937) was an avid reader of Stevenson's *Treasure Island*. His Captain Hook, the arch-villain pirate from the 1904 play *Peter Pan, or The Boy Who Wouldn't Grow Up* and his 1911 novel *Peter and Wendy*, is second only to Long John Silver among the popular pirate captains in Western culture.

The story of Peter Pan begins when Peter takes the Darling children to the magical world of Never Land, where they encounter Captain Hook and his crew of pirates. Hook despises Peter, because in an earlier battle, Peter cut off Hook's hand and fed it to a crocodile. Since that time, Hook has worn a hook for an hand. He is constantly followed by the crocodile, which liked the taste of his hand so much, it wants to eat the rest of him. Hook's main goal in life is to capture Peter and force him to walk the plank, a form of punishment in which the victim is blindfolded and forced to walk off the end of a wooden board extended over the side of a ship and into the sea. (Walking the plank, though a common element of the popular culture, seems to be a pirate myth. It did not exist in the golden age of piracy, and it is questionable that it was ever a pirate practice at all.)

This painting by Howard Pyle depicts pirates forcing a captive to walk the plank. HOWARD PYLE/THE BRIDGEMAN ART LIBRARY/GETTY IMAGES.

When Hook's band of pirates enter the play, Barrie notes, "A more villainous-looking brotherhood of men never hung in a row on Execution dock." (Execution Dock is the place in London where pirates were hanged; their bodies were often displayed to discourage others from turning to piracy.) Hook, however, stands apart from his men. He is an educated captain who pays careful attention to his dress. In a whimsical description, Barrie makes fun of Hook, English society, and the overused literary uses of pirates. He writes:

> Cruelest jewel in that dark setting is HOOK himself, cadaverous [thin] and blackavised [dark complexioned], his hair dressed in long curls which look like black candles about to melt, his eyes blue as the forget-me-not [a blue flower] and of a profound insensibility [lack of perception].... He is never more sinister than when he is most polite, and the elegance of his diction, the distinction of his demeanour [the way he behaves], show him one of a different class from his crew, a solitary among uncultured companions. This courtliness impresses even his victims on the high seas, who note that he always says 'Sorry' when prodding them along the plank. A man of indomitable courage, the only thing at which he flinches is the sight of his own blood.... Those, however, who have seen him in the flesh ... agree that the grimmest part of him is his iron claw [hook].

Barrie sets Captain Hook into the mythological world of pirates. He is said to have been Blackbeard's bosun (boatswain; a petty officer on a ship who oversees the work of other seamen) and the only man that Long John Silver ever feared. However, unlike any of his predecessors, Hook is vain, cowardly, and silly.

Rafael Sabatini and the swashbuckler

During the early part of the twentieth century, interest in pirates skyrocketed with the creation of swashbuckler fiction, popular novels or drama featuring daring adventurers. English Italian novelist Rafael Sabatini (1875–1950) made the swashbuckler into a pirate genre with his extremely popular historical adventure novels. His earliest, *Sea Hawk* (1915), is the story of a sixteenth-century English nobleman who is betrayed by his brother and sold into slavery on a Spanish galley, or a long, low ship propelled by oars. When the Barbary corsairs (Muslim pirates and privateers based in northern Africa) free him from Spanish slavery, he converts to Islam, changes his name to Sakr-el-Bahr (which means sea hawk), and wages a war of vengeance against England, particularly those who betrayed him. Sabatini's *Captain Blood: His Odyssey* (1922) is a tale about a doctor, Peter Blood, who has left behind life as a sailor and soldier for a peaceful medical practice. During an uprising in England in the seventeenth century, Blood treats a wounded rebel, and for this he is convicted of treason

Errol Flynn as Captain Blood in the 1935 film. TIME LIFE PICTURES/MANSELL/TIME LIFE PICTURES/GETTY IMAGES.

and sold into slavery in Jamaica. When he escapes with a gang of slaves and steals a Spanish galley, his pirate adventures begin.

Sabatini's novels are still popular among fans of the swashbuckling genre, but he is better known for the films based on his novels. When Warner Bros. released a version of *Captain Blood* in 1935 starring Errol Flynn (1909–1959), both Flynn and the film became overnight sensations. Flynn also starred in the Warner Bros. version of *Sea Hawk* (1940), which changed Sabatini's story of Barbary corsairs drastically to fit Hollywood's rather limited standards of acceptability at the time.

Swashbuckler-pirate films were enormously popular in the first decades of the twentieth century. Among early examples is the acclaimed 1926 silent film *The Black Pirate*, starring Douglas Fairbanks, Jr. (1909–2000), which features one of the greatest swordfight scenes in film history. Fairbanks, like Flynn, went on to swashbuckling fame. Whether played by Flynn, Fairbanks, or other handsome young actors, the pirate heroes of these films were dashing, noble, and courageous, and had social graces unlikely to be found in real pirates. David Cordingly describes the standard swashbuckler-pirate film formula:

> As far as Hollywood was concerned, pirates provided an opportunity for buccaneering heroes to rescue beautiful women from picturesque villains in exotic locations. . . . A common feature of many pirate films, and a number of novels, is the portrayal of the pirate captain as an aristocrat, or as an educated man of some standing in society, who has taken to piracy as the result of some misfortune in his recent past.

Pirates in twenty-first century media

The popularity of swashbucklers subsided at the end of the 1940s, but Hollywood continued to produce a steady stream of pirate films. *Treasure Island* was made for the big screen repeatedly throughout film history. Many critics contend that English actor Robert Newton (1905–1956) in the 1950 Disney version captured the essence of Long John Silver and the American perception of pirates better than any other actor. Newton was born in Dorset, in southwestern England, and critics contend that it was his West Country English accent that formed the basis of the pirate manner of speech in popular culture. After *Treasure Island*, Newton starred in the title role of *Blackbeard, the Pirate* (1952) and went on to star in the television series *The Adventures of Long John Silver* in 1956.

Many of the films of the middle and later twentieth century were remakes of earlier pirate hits. Peter Pan went through many highly acclaimed film versions. The animated Disney film *Peter Pan* (1953), with its magic, flying, and swashbuckling sword fights was a huge hit. *The Pirates of Penzance* was made into a popular movie in 1985 after a successful run as a musical play on Broadway.

By the 1960s and 1970s, however, the theme of piracy had faded in popularity. Attempts to revive the pirate genre resulted in disappointments and utter flops. Films like *Swashbuckler* (1976), *Nate and Hayes* (1983), and *Pirates* (1986) received poor reviews from movie critics and fared poorly at the box office. In 1995 the film *Cutthroat Island*, which features Geena Davis (1956–) as a pirate queen, was such a spectacular dud that its lasting fame is for appearing in the *Guiness Book of World Records* as the worst box office failure of all time. After *Cutthroat Island*, movie critics predicted the end of the pirate movie genre.

Pirates of the Caribbean After a long absence, pirates reappeared in theaters in 2003 in the hugely successful movie, *Pirates of the Caribbean: The Curse of the Black Pearl* produced by Disney. It was followed by *Pirates of the Caribbean: Dead Man's Chest* in 2006, *Pirates of the Caribbean: At World's End* in 2007, and *Pirates of the Caribbean: On Stranger Tides* in 2011. The idea for the films date back to 1967, when Disneyland, an amusement park in Anaheim, California, created its Pirates of the Caribbean ride, a dark, indoor boat ride in which guests float through a pirate adventure including cannon blasts, pillaging pirates, and burning buildings. It is not unusual for Disney to base a ride at Disneyland on a Disney movie, but many commentators found it odd when Disney decided to base a movie on a ride.

The *Pirates of the Caribbean* films are set in the golden age and feature most of the traditional elements of pirate adventure: ships, sword fights, walking the plank, the pirate code (which a pirate captain admits is more "guideline" than law), parrots on shoulders, treasure, the Jolly Roger (pirate flag), and the kidnapping and rescue of a beautiful woman. The film also combines features of earlier pirate movies: the vivid dialogue and clever adventure story of *Treasure Island*, the magic and whimsy of *Peter Pan*, the spoof of *Pirates of Penzance*, and the swashbuckling of *Captain Blood*. To play well for a modern audience, though, there are unusual twists. For example, in the first film of the series, the pirates are trying to give back stolen treasure because its curse has turned them into undead pirates.

The screenwriters for the first film intended for the pirate character of Captain Jack Sparrow to be a supporting character, but actor Johnny Depp stole the show with his portrayal of the eccentric pirate captain. Depp claims to have modeled his character on English rock star Keith Richards (1943–) and cartoon character Pepe Le Pew. Captain Sparrow looks like a typical movie pirate, except for his dark eyeliner, but he walks with a strange, rolling gait; flutters his hands from the wrists, and speaks in a quietly drunken manner. Although he acts incompetent, he generally saves the day using his wits and manages to be utterly charming, though untrustworthy, in the process. Captain Sparrow's eccentricities are refreshing because they draw attention to the favorite clichés of pirate captains, making fun of them while fully engaging in them.

Like all pirate fiction *Pirates of the Caribbean* engages its audience at least partly because so many people find pirate life to be adventurous and exciting. *Pirates of the Caribbean: The Curse of the Black Pearl* begins with

A wax statue of Johnny Depp as Captain Jack Sparrow at Madame Tussauds in London, England. GARETH CATTERMOLE/GETTY IMAGES.

a flashback in which a young version of the female lead, Elizabeth Swann, stands on the deck of a ship, looking dreamily out at the sea and singing a few bars of the theme song to the Disneyland Pirates of the Caribbean ride: "Yo ho (A Pirate's Life for Me)." Like Jim Hawkins of *Treasure Island*, she longs for the adventure, exotic places, and freedom of being a pirate. In an NPR interview, John Baur, the cofounder of International Talk Like a Pirate Day, speculates that people who love pirates are probably longing for their freedom. He says, "That's what appeals to people about pirates. Not the pillaging or plundering or killings. . . . It's the freedom to once in a while say, 'Arrrr! To [heck] with convention! I'm going to misbehave today!'"

For More Information

BOOKS

Barrie, J.M. *Peter Pan, or The Boy Who Would Not Grow Up.* Charles Scribner's Books, 1928, 1956.

Byron, George Gordon. *Byron: Complete Poetical Works.* Edited by Frederick Page. England: Oxford University Press, 1970, p. 281.

Cordingly, David. *Under the Black Flag: The Romance and the Reality of Life Among the Pirates.* New York: Random House, 2006, pp. 171–72.

Defoe, Daniel. *The King of Pirates.* In *Romances and Narratives by Daniel Defoe*, vol. 16. Edited by George A. Aitken. London: J.M. Dent and Company, 1895, p. 3.

Johnson, Captain Charles. *A General History of the Robberies and Murders of the Most Notorious Pirates.* Guilford, CT: The Lyon's Press, 1998, 2002.

Stevenson, Robert Louis. *Treasure Island.* New York: Current Literature Publishing, 1906, pp. 181, 220–21.

Turley, Hans. *Rum, Sodomy, and the Lash: Piracy, Sexuality, and the Masculine Identity.* New York and London: New York University Press, 1999, pp. 3, 64.

Woodard, Colin. *The Republic of Pirates: Being the True and Surprising Story of the Caribbean Pirates and the Man Who Brought Them Down.* New York: Harcourt, 2007, p. 27.

WEB SITES

Baur, John, and Mark Summers. "How It All Started." *Talk Like a Pirate Day.* www.talklikeapirate.com/about.html (accessed on January 3, 2011).

Weeks, Linton. "Why Do Pirates Have Us Hooked?" *NPR.* www.npr.org/templates/story/story.php?storyId=97247166 (accessed on January 3, 2011).

Where to Learn More

Books

Burgess, Douglas R., Jr. *The Pirates' Pact: The Secret Alliances Between History's Most Notorious Buccaneers and Colonial America.* New York: McGraw-Hill, 2009.

Carpenter, John Reeve. *Pirates: Scourge of the Seas.* New York: Sterling, 2006.

Cawthorne, Nigel. *Pirates of the 21st Century: How Modern-day Buccaneers Are Terrorising the World's Oceans.* London: John Blake, 2010.

Clifford, Barry. *Expedition Whydah: The Story of the World's First Excavation of a Pirate Ship.* New York: Cliff Street Books, 1999.

Cordingly, David. *Under the Black Flag: The Romance and the Reality of Life Among the Pirates.* New York: Random House, 2006.

———, ed. *Pirates: Terror on the High Seas from the Caribbean to the South China Sea.* North Dighton, MA: World Publications Group, 2006.

Crowley, Roger. *Empires of the Sea: The Siege of Malta, the Battle of Lepanto, and the Contest for the Center of the World.* New York: Random House, 2008.

Druett, Joan. *She Captains: Heroines and Hellions of the Sea.* New York: Simon and Schuster, 2001.

Forester, C.S. *The Barbary Pirates.* New York: Sterling Point, 2008.

Heller-Roazen, Daniel. *The Enemy of All: Piracy and the Law of Nations.* New York: Zone Books, 2009.

Johnson, Captain Charles. *A General History of the Robberies and Murders of the Most Notorious Pirates.* Guilford, CT: The Lyons Press, 1998, 2002.

Konstam, Angus. *The History of Pirates.* Guilford, CT: The Lyons Press, 2002.

———. *Piracy: The Complete History.* Oxford, England: Osprey, 2008.

Lane, Kris E. *Pillaging the Empire: Piracy in the Americas, 1500–1750.* Armonk, NY: Sharpe, 1998.

Lewis, Jon E., ed. *The Mammoth Book of Pirates: Over 25 True Tales of Devilry and Daring by the Most Infamous Pirates of All Time.* Philadelphia, PA: Running Press, 2006.

Little, Benerson. *The Sea Rover's Practice: Pirate Tactics and Techniques, 1630–1730.* Dulles, VA: Potomac Books, 2007.

Lloyd, Christopher. *English Corsairs on the Barbary Coast.* London: William Collins Sons, 1981.

Matthews, John. *Pirates.* New York: Atheneum, 2006.

Murray, Dian H. *Pirates of the South China Coast, 1790–1810.* California: Stanford University Press, 1987.

Ormerod, Henry A. *Piracy in the Ancient World.* Baltimore: Johns Hopkins University Press, 1996.

Pennell, C.R., ed. *Bandits at Sea.* New York: New York University Press, 2001.

Perry, Dan. *Blackbeard: The Real Pirate of the Caribbean.* New York: Basic Books, 2006.

Rediker, Marcus. *Between the Devil and the Deep Blue Sea: Merchant Seamen, Pirates and the Anglo-American Maritime World, 1700–1750.* Cambridge, UK: Cambridge University Press, 1987.

———. *Villains of All Nations: Atlantic Pirates in the Golden Age.* Boston, MA: Beacon Press, 2004.

Sanders, Richard. *If a Pirate I Must Be . . . The True Story of "Black Bart," King of the Caribbean Pirates.* New York: Skyhorse Publishing, 2009.

Sharp, Anne Wallace. *Daring Pirate Women.* Minneapolis, MN: Lerner, 2002.

Travers, Tim. *Pirates: A History.* Stroud, Gloucestershire, UK: Tempus, 2007.

Wilson, Peter Lamborn. *Pirate Utopias: Moorish Corsairs and European Renegades.* 2nd ed. Rye Brook, NY: Autonomedia, 2003.

Woodard, Colin. *The Republic of Pirates: Being the True and Surprising Story of the Caribbean Pirates and the Man Who Brought Them Down.* New York: Harcourt, 2007.

Wren, Laura Lee. *Pirates and Privateers of the High Seas.* Berkeley Heights, NJ: Enslow, 2003.

Yolen, Jane. *Sea Queens: Women Pirates Around the World.* Watertown, MA: Charlesbridge, 2008.

Zacks, Richard. *The Pirate Coast: Thomas Jefferson, the First Marines, and the Secret Mission of 1805.* New York: Hyperion, 2005.

Periodicals

Antony, Robert. "Piracy in Early Modern China," *IIAS Newsletter,* 36 (March 2005). Also available online at http://www.iias.nl/nl/36/IIAS_NL36_07.pdf (accessed on January 3, 2011).

Baldauf, Scott. "Who Are Somalia's Pirates?" *Christian Science Monitor* (November 20, 2008). Also available online at http://www.csmonitor.com/World/Africa/2008/1120/p25s22-woaf.html (accessed on January 3, 2011).

De Souza, Philip. "Ancient Rome and the Pirates." *History Today* 51, no. 7 (2001).

Gettleman, Jeffrey. "Somalia's Pirates Flourish in a Lawless Nation" *New York Times* (October 31, 2008). Available online at www.nytimes.com/2008/10/31/world/africa/31pirates.html (accessed on January 3, 2011).

Gwin, Peter. "Dangerous Straits." *National Geographic* (October 2007). Also available online at http://ngm.nationalgeographic.com/2007/10/malacca-strait-pirates/pirates-text.html (accessed on January 3, 2011).

Johnson, Keith. "Who's a Pirate? U.S. Court Sees Duel over Definition." *Wall Street Journal* (August 14, 2010). Available online at http://online.wsj.com/article/SB20001424052748703988304575413470900570834.html (accessed on January 3, 2011).

Murray, Dian H. "Pirates of the South China Coast 1790–1810," *Journal of the Economic and Social History of the Orient* 33, no. 2 (1990): 234–6.

Rediker, Marcus. "When Women Pirates Sailed the Seas." *The Wilson Quarterly* 17, no. 4 (Autumn 1993): 102–10.

Tabarrok, Alexander. "The Rise, Fall, and Rise Again of Privateers," *Independent Review* 11, no. 4 (Spring 2007): 565–77.

Web Sites

Adow, Mohammed. "The Pirate Kings of Puntland." *Al Jazeera.net* (June 17, 2009). http://english.aljazeera.net/news/africa/2009/06/2009614125243860630.html (accessed on January 3, 2011).

Davis, Robert. "British Slaves on the Barbary Coast." *BBC British History in Depth.* http://www.bbc.co.uk/history/british/empire_seapower/white_slaves_01.shtml (accessed on January 3, 2011).

Krystek, Lee. "The Golden Age of Piracy." *The Unmuseum.* www.unmuseum.org/pirate.htm (accessed on January 3, 2011).

"Pirates." *National Maritime Museum.* http://www.nmm.ac.uk/explore/sea-and-ships/facts/ships-and-seafarers/pirates (accessed on January 3, 2011).

"Pirates of the Whydah." *National Geographic.* http://www.nationalgeographic.com/whydah/main.html (accessed on January 3, 2011).

Rothwell, Donald R. "Maritime Piracy and International Law." *Crimes of War Project* (February 24, 2009). http://www.crimesofwar.org/onnews/news-piracy.html (accessed on January 3, 2011).

Index

Illustrations are marked by (ill.).